Good Housekeeping

Favourite

One-pot &
Slow-cook

250 Tried, tested, trusted recipes ★ Delicious results

Good Housekeeping

Favourite
One-pot &
Slow-cook

250 Tried, tested, trusted recipes ★ Delicious results

COLLINS & BROWN

First published in the United Kingdom in 2010 by
Collins & Brown
10 Southcombe Street
London
W14 0RA

An imprint of Anova Books Company Ltd

The Good Housekeeping website is
www.allboutyou.com/goodhousekeeping

10 9 8 7 6 5 4 3 2

ISBN 978-1-84340-588-7

A catalogue record for this book is available from
the British Library.

Reproduction by Dot Gradations Ltd UK
Printed by G. Canale&C.S.p.A, Italy

This book can be ordered direct from the publisher at
www.anovabooks.com

Picture Credits:
Martin Brigdale (pages 59, 68, 72, 73, 75, 76, 78, 104, 107, 108,
109, 119, 120, 122, 147, 178, 179, 184, 186, 189, 192, 206,
207, 214, 215, 220, 221, 223, 224, 225, 226, 227, 228, 229,
231, 232 and 235); Neil Barclay (pages 91, 94, 95, 98, 117, 136,
201, 202 and 216); Nicki Dowey (pages 11, 13, 15, 16, 21, 22, 23,
24, 25, 27, 28, 29, 31, 35, 36, 37, 38, 39, 41, 44, 45, 48, 50, 51,
52, 54, 55, 56, 60, 61, 65, 69, 70, 74, 77, 79, 84, 87, 88, 92, 82,
85, 88, 102, 106, 110, 115, 125, 128, 129, 130, 131, 133, 138,
143, 146, 148, 150, 151, 154, 157, 158, 159, 160, 162, 163,
166, 170, 173, 174, 175, 176, 181, 182, 183, 187, 188, 191,
193, 197, 200, 203, 204, 205, 212, 213, 218, 230, 234, 238,
240, 241, 243, 245, 246, 248, 249, 251, 252, 254, 255, 256,
257, 258, 259, 263, 265, 268, 270, 273, 277, 278, 279, 280,
281, 282 and 283); Will Heap (pages 43, 47, 53, 177 and 195);
Craig Robertson (pages 10, 12, 17, 18, 20, 26, 30, 33, 34, 42, 46,
57, 62, 63, 66, 71, 85, 89, 97, 100, 103, 105, 111, 114, 116,
118, 121, 124, 132, 134, 135, 137, 139, 140, 142, 144, 145,
149, 155, 156, 165, 167, 168, 169, 171, 172, 180, 185, 190,
194, 196, 209, 210, 217, 219, 239, 244, 253, 262, 264, 266,
267, 271, 272, 274, 275, 276, 284 and 285); Clive Streeter (page
83); Lucinda Symons (pages 49, 64, 67, 90, 101, 127, 161, 208
and 211)
Home Economists: Joanna Farrow, Emma Jane Frost, Teresa
Goldfinch, Alice Hart, Anna Burges-Lumsden, Lucy McKelvie,
Kim Morphew, Katie Rogers, Bridget Sargeson, Sarah Tildesley,
Jennifer White and Mari Mererid Williams
Stylists: Susannah Blake, Wei Tang, Sarah Tildesley, Helen Trent and

NOTES

★ Both metric and imperial measures are given for the
recipes. Follow either set of measures, not a mixture of
both, as they are not interchangeable.

★ All spoon measures are level.
1 tsp = 5ml spoon; 1 tbsp = 15ml spoon.

★ Ovens and grills must be preheated to the specified
temperature.

★ Medium eggs should be used except where otherwise
specified.

DIETARY GUIDELINES

★ Note that certain recipes contain raw or lightly cooked
eggs. The young, elderly, pregnant women and anyone
with immune-deficiency disease should avoid these
because of the slight risk of salmonella.

★ Note that some recipes contain alcohol. Check the
ingredient list before serving to children.

Contents

Foreword   7

Main Course Soups   8

Fish and Shellfish   40

Chicken   80

Meat and Game   112

Vegetarian and Vegetables   152

Add a Little Extra...   198

For the Slow Cooker   236

Puddings   260

Index   286

Foreword

We live in fast-paced times – with constant technological, ecological and medical advances, relentlessly changing fashion and beauty trends, round-the clock dining and 24-hour shopping, not to mention the endless lists of deadlines and chores that should have been completed yesterday. All in all, there never seems to be enough time in the day to get everything done, so cooking should be quick and give instant gratification. Not so, I say. Sometimes it can be a good thing to step off that treadmill and remember that some of the best things in life are worth waiting for. Whether that be finally meeting the partner of your dreams, wearing the amazing party frock you've spent months saving for, arriving at the airport for that once-in-a-lifetime holiday, or biting into tender lamb shank that's spent half a day sizzling in the oven. For me, it's the anticipation that's half the fun, the crescendo before the climax – and a reliable Good Housekeeping lamb shank recipe helps too!

There are more advantages to slow cooking than anticipation – your oven, hob or slow cooker does the hard work rather than you, and flavours have time to mingle enticingly. The same is true for one-pot cooking, with the added bonus that there's less washing up at the end.

This book is full of our favourite triple-tested one-pot and slow-cook recipes for you to try. So take a step off that treadmill and look forward to the huge sense of satisfaction that comes when that tough cheap cut of meat turns into a meltingly tender centrepiece, just by giving it some of your time.

Enjoy!

Meike.

Meike Beck
Chief Home Economist

Main Course Soups

Simple Vegetable Soup

★

Preparation Time 15 minutes • **Cooking Time** 50 minutes • **Serves 4** • **Per Serving** 96 calories, 6g fat (of which 1g saturates), 8g carbohydrate, 0.2g salt • **Vegetarian** • **Gluten Free** • **Dairy Free** • **Easy**

1 or 2 onions, finely chopped
2 tbsp oil or 1 tbsp oil and 25g (1oz) butter
1 or 2 garlic cloves, crushed (optional)
450g (1lb) chopped mixed vegetables, such as leeks, potatoes, celery, fennel, canned tomatoes and parsnips, chopped finely or cut into larger dice for a chunky soup
1.1 litres (2 pints) stock

1 Fry the onions in the oil or oil and butter until soft and add the garlic, if you like.

2 Add the chopped mixed vegetables and the stock. Bring to the boil, then reduce the heat and simmer for 20–30 minutes until the vegetables are tender.

3 Leave chunky, partially purée or blend until smooth.

Spring Vegetable Broth

Preparation Time 20 minutes • **Cooking Time** 20 minutes • **Serves 4** • **Per Serving** 264 calories, 6g fat
(of which 3g saturates), 35g carbohydrate, 2.4g salt • **Dairy Free** • **Easy**

1 tbsp olive oil
4 shallots, chopped
1 fennel bulb, chopped
1 leek, trimmed and chopped
5 small carrots, chopped
1.1 litres (2 pints) hot chicken stock
2 courgettes, chopped
1 bunch of asparagus, chopped
2 × 400g cans cannellini beans,
    drained and rinsed
50g (2oz) Gruyère or Parmesan
    cheese shavings to serve

1 Heat the oil in a large pan. Add the shallots, fennel, leek and carrots and fry for 5 minutes or until they start to soften.

2 Add the hot stock, cover the pan and bring to the boil. Add the courgettes, asparagus and beans, then reduce the heat and simmer for 5–6 minutes until the vegetables are tender.

3 Ladle into warmed bowls, sprinkle with a little cheese and serve.

★ TRY SOMETHING DIFFERENT
This broth is also good with a tablespoon of pesto (see below) added to each bowl and served with chunks of crusty bread.
Pesto
Put a 20g pack of roughly chopped basil into a food processor. Add 25g (1oz) finely grated Parmesan, 50g (2oz) pinenuts and 4 tbsp extra virgin olive oil and whiz to a rough paste. Alternatively, grind in a pestle and mortar. Season with salt and plenty of ground black pepper.

Summer Vegetable Soup with Herb Pistou

Preparation Time 20 minutes • Cooking Time 1 hour • Serves 6 • Per Serving 163 calories, 7g fat (of which 1g saturates), 17g carbohydrate, 0.1g salt • **Vegetarian • Gluten Free • Dairy Free • Easy**

3 tbsp sunflower oil
1 onion, finely chopped
225g (8oz) waxy potatoes, finely diced
175g (6oz) carrots, finely diced
1 medium turnip, finely diced
4 bay leaves
6 large fresh sage leaves
2 courgettes, about 375g (13oz), finely diced
175g (6oz) green beans, trimmed and halved
125g (4oz) shelled small peas
225g (8oz) tomatoes, seeded and finely diced
1 small broccoli head, broken into florets
salt and ground black pepper
pistou (see Cook's Tip) or ready-made pesto to serve

1 Heat the oil in a large pan over a gentle heat. Add the onion, potatoes, carrots and turnip and cook for 10 minutes. Pour in 1.7 litres (3 pints) cold water, season with salt and pepper, bring to the boil and add the bay and sage leaves. Reduce the heat and simmer for 25 minutes.

2 Add the courgettes, beans, peas and tomatoes. Bring back to the boil and simmer for 10–15 minutes. Add the broccoli 5 minutes before the end of the cooking time.

3 Remove the bay and sage leaves and adjust the seasoning. Pour the soup into warmed bowls and serve immediately; serve the pistou or pesto separately to stir into the hot soup.

 COOK'S TIP
Pistou is a Provençal condiment similar to Italian pesto.
To make your own, using a pestle and mortar or a small bowl and the end of a rolling pin, or a mini processor, pound together ³⁄₄ tsp sea salt and 6 chopped garlic cloves until smooth. Add 15g (¹⁄₂oz) freshly chopped basil and pound to a paste, then mix in 12 tbsp olive oil, a little at a time. Store in a sealed jar in the fridge for up to one week.

Autumn Vegetable Soup

Preparation Time 15 minutes • **Cooking Time** 45 minutes • **Serves 4** • **Per Serving** 326 calories, 17g fat (of which 9g saturates), 29g carbohydrate, 1.1g salt • **Easy**

50g (2oz) butter
1 medium onion, diced
450g (1lb) potatoes, diced
100g (3½oz) diced bacon
1 garlic clove, chopped
100g (3½oz) white of leek, chopped
2 Cox's Orange Pippin apples, unpeeled, cored and chopped
2 tsp dried thyme
1 tsp dill seeds (optional)
600ml (1 pint) dry cider
900ml (1½ pints) hot vegetable stock
125g (4oz) Savoy cabbage leaves, shredded
salt and ground black pepper

1 Melt the butter in a large pan, then add the onion, potatoes, bacon, garlic, leek, apples, thyme and dill seeds, if using. Season to taste with salt and pepper, stir, then cover the pan and cook gently for 15 minutes.

2 Add the cider and bring to the boil, then reduce the heat and simmer for 5 minutes. Add the hot stock and simmer for about 15 minutes or until the potatoes are soft.

3 Pour half the soup into a blender or liquidiser and whiz until smooth, then add to the remaining soup in the pan. Reheat gently, add the shredded cabbage and simmer for a further 3 minutes. Ladle into warmed bowls and serve.

Quick Winter Minestrone

Preparation Time 10 minutes • **Cooking Time** 45 minutes • **Serves 4** • **Per Serving** 334 calories, 11g fat (of which 3g saturates), 47g carbohydrate, 1.5g salt • **Dairy Free** • **Easy**

2 tbsp olive oil
1 small onion, finely chopped
1 carrot, chopped
1 celery stick, chopped
1 garlic clove, crushed
2 tbsp freshly chopped thyme
1 litre (1¾ pints) vegetable stock
400g can chopped tomatoes
400g can borlotti beans, drained
   and rinsed
125g (4oz) minestrone pasta
175g (6oz) Savoy cabbage,
   shredded
salt and ground black pepper
fresh ready-made pesto (see
   page 11), toasted ciabatta and
   extra virgin olive oil to serve

1 Heat the oil in a large pan and add the onion, carrot and celery. Cook for 8–10 minutes until softened, then add the garlic and thyme. Fry for another 2–3 minutes.

2 Add the stock, tomatoes and half the borlotti beans and bring to the boil. Mash the remaining beans and stir into the soup, then reduce the heat and simmer for 30 minutes, adding the minestrone pasta and cabbage for the last 10 minutes of cooking time.

3 Check the seasoning and correct, if necessary. Ladle into warmed bowls and serve with a dollop of fresh pesto on top and slices of toasted ciabatta drizzled with extra virgin olive oil on the side.

Fish and Vegetable Soup

★

Preparation Time 15 minutes • **Cooking Time** about 25 minutes • **Serves 4** • **Per Serving** 250 calories, 2.1g fat (of which trace saturates), 28.2g carbohydrate, 0.2g salt • **Gluten Free** • **Dairy Free** • **Easy**

1 tbsp olive oil
4 × 125g (4oz) white fish fillets,
    with skin on, such as pollack
1 mint sprig
2 shallots, finely sliced
1 small garlic clove, sliced
50ml (2fl oz) dry white wine
250ml (9fl oz) hot vegetable stock
125g (4oz) each asparagus and
    carrots, chopped
500g (1lb 2oz) new potatoes,
    chopped
100g (3½oz) frozen peas
zest and juice of 1 lemon
salt and ground black pepper

1 Put the oil into a wide shallow sauté pan over a medium heat. Season the fish and cook, skin side down, until golden. Remove from the pan and set aside. Chop the mint leaves and finely chop the stalk.

2 In the same pan, gently fry the shallots and garlic for 2–3 minutes until softened. Add the wine and boil to reduce by half. Stir in the hot stock, vegetables, lemon zest and juice and mint and season. Cover the pan and cook over a medium heat for 10 minutes or until the vegetables are tender.

3 Return the fish to the pan, cover and cook for 5 minutes. Divide among four wide shallow bowls and serve immediately.

★ COOK'S TIPS
● *Pollack is the cheaper, more eco-friendly alternative to cod.*
● *British asparagus is in season in late spring, so this is the one time of year when it's a good price. Make the most of it in this healthy broth.*

Seafood Gumbo

Preparation Time 10 minutes • **Cooking Time** 30 minutes • **Serves 4** • **Per Serving** 559 calories, 23g fat (of which 3g saturates), 58g carbohydrate, 1.2g salt • **Easy**

125g (4oz) butter
50g (2oz) plain flour
1–2 tbsp Cajun spice mix
1 onion, chopped
1 green pepper, seeded and
    chopped
5 spring onions, sliced
1 tbsp freshly chopped flat-leafed
    parsley
1 garlic clove, crushed
1 beef tomato, chopped
125g (4oz) garlic sausage, finely
    sliced
75g (3oz) American easy-cook rice
1.1 litres (2 pints) vegetable stock
450g (1lb) okra, sliced
1 bay leaf
1 fresh thyme sprig
2 tsp salt
¼ tsp cayenne pepper
juice of ½ lemon
4 cloves
500g (1lb 2oz) frozen mixed
    seafood (containing mussels,
    squid and prawns), thawed and
    drained
ground black pepper

1 Heat the butter in a 2.5 litre (4¼–4½ pint) heavy-based pan over a low heat. Add the flour and Cajun spice and cook, stirring, for 1–2 minutes until golden brown. Add the onion, green pepper, spring onions, parsley and garlic. Cook for 5 minutes.

2 Add the tomato, garlic sausage and rice to the pan and stir well to coat. Add the stock, okra, bay leaf, thyme, salt, cayenne pepper, lemon juice and cloves. Season with black pepper. Bring to the boil, then reduce the heat and simmer, covered, for 12 minutes or until the rice is tender.

3 Add the seafood and cook for 2 minutes to heat through. Serve the gumbo in deep bowls.

★ COOK'S TIP
Gumbo is a traditional stew from the southern states of the USA, containing meat, vegetables and shellfish and thickened with okra.

Fast Fish Soup

Preparation Time 10 minutes • **Cooking Time** about 15 minutes • **Serves 4** • **Per Serving** 269 calories, 10g fat (of which 2g saturates), 6g carbohydrate, 0.4g salt • **Gluten Free** • **Dairy Free** • **Easy**

1 leek, trimmed and finely chopped
4 fat garlic cloves, crushed
3 celery sticks, finely chopped
1 small fennel bulb, finely chopped
1 red chilli, seeded and finely
    chopped (see Cook's Tip)
3 tbsp olive oil
50ml (2fl oz) dry white wine
about 750g (1lb 11oz) mixed fish
    and shellfish, such as haddock
    and monkfish fillets, peeled and
    deveined raw prawns, and fresh
    mussels, scrubbed and cleaned
    (see page 57)
4 tomatoes, chopped
20g (¾ oz) freshly chopped thyme
salt and ground black pepper

1 Put the leek into a large pan and add the garlic, celery, fennel, chilli and oil. Cook over a medium heat for 5 minutes or until the vegetables are soft and beginning to colour.

2 Stir in 1.1 litres (2 pints) boiling water and the wine. Bring to the boil, then reduce the heat, cover the pan and simmer for 5 minutes.

3 Cut the white fish into large chunks. Add to the soup with the tomatoes and thyme. Continue to simmer gently until the fish has just turned opaque. Add the prawns, simmer for 1 minute, then add the mussels, if you're using them.

4 As soon as all the mussels have opened (discard any that do not), season the soup with salt and pepper. Ladle into warmed bowls and serve immediately.

★ TRY SOMETHING DIFFERENT
To give the soup more of a kick, stir in 2 tbsp Pernod instead of the wine. Garlic croûtes are traditionally served with fish soup; they can be made while the soup is simmering. Toast small slices of baguette, spread with garlic mayonnaise and sprinkle with grated cheese. Float in the hot soup just before serving.

★ COOK'S TIP
Chillies vary enormously in strength, from quite mild to blisteringly hot, depending on the type of chilli and its ripeness. Taste a small piece first to check that it's not too hot for you. When handling chillies, be extremely careful not to touch or rub your eyes with your fingers, as it will make them sting. Wash knives immediately after chopping chillies. As a precaution, use rubber gloves when preparing them if you like.

Smoked Cod and Sweetcorn Chowder

★

Preparation Time 5 minutes • **Cooking Time** 20 minutes • **Serves 6** • **Per Serving** 517 calories, 28g fat (of which 15g saturates), 35g carbohydrate, 4.7g salt • **Easy**

130g pack cubed pancetta
50g (2oz) butter
3 leeks, about 450g (1lb), trimmed and thinly sliced
25g (1oz) plain flour
600ml (1 pint) semi-skimmed or full-fat milk
700g (1½lb) undyed smoked cod loin or haddock, skinned and cut into 2cm (¾in) cubes
326g can sweetcorn in water, drained
450g (1lb) small new potatoes, sliced

150ml (¼ pint) double cream
½ tsp paprika
salt and ground black pepper
2 tbsp freshly chopped flat-leafed parsley to garnish

1 Fry the pancetta in a large pan over a gentle heat until the fat runs out. Add the butter to the pan to melt, then add the leeks and cook until softened.

2 Stir in the flour and cook for a few seconds, then pour in the milk and 300ml (½ pint) cold water. Add the fish to the pan with the sweetcorn and potatoes. Bring to the boil, then reduce the heat and simmer for 10–15 minutes until the potatoes are cooked.

3 Stir in the cream, season with salt and pepper and the paprika and cook for 2–3 minutes to warm through. Ladle into warmed shallow bowls and sprinkle each one with a little chopped parsley. Serve immediately.

Spinach and Rice Soup

Preparation Time 10 minutes • **Cooking Time** 25–30 minutes • **Serves 4** • **Per Serving** 335 calories, 20g fat (of which 4g saturates), 29g carbohydrate, 0.7g salt • **Vegetarian** • **Gluten Free** • **Easy**

4 tbsp extra virgin olive oil, plus
    extra to serve
1 onion, finely chopped
2 garlic cloves, crushed
2 tsp freshly chopped thyme or a
    large pinch of dried thyme
2 tsp freshly chopped rosemary or
    a large pinch of dried rosemary
zest of ½ lemon
2 tsp ground coriander
¼ tsp cayenne pepper
125g (4oz) arborio rice
1.1 litres (2 pints) vegetable stock
225g (8oz) fresh or frozen and
    thawed spinach, shredded
4 tbsp fresh ready-made pesto (see
    page 11)
salt and ground black pepper
freshly grated Parmesan to serve

1 Heat half the oil in a pan. Add the onion, garlic, herbs, lemon zest and spices, then fry gently for 5 minutes.

2 Add the remaining oil with the rice and cook, stirring, for 1 minute. Add the stock and bring to the boil, then reduce the heat and simmer gently for 20 minutes or until the rice is tender.

3 Stir the spinach into the soup with the pesto. Cook for 2 minutes, then season to taste with salt and pepper.

4 Ladle into warmed bowls and serve drizzled with a little oil and topped with Parmesan.

Spicy Bean and Courgette Soup

Preparation Time 10 minutes • **Cooking Time** 30 minutes • **Serves 4** • **Per Serving** 289 calories, 8g fat (of which 1g saturates), 43g carbohydrate, 1.5g salt • **Vegetarian** • **Dairy Free** • **Easy**

2 tbsp olive oil
175g (6oz) onions, finely chopped
2 garlic cloves, crushed
2 tsp ground coriander
1 tbsp paprika
1 tsp mild curry powder
450g (1lb) courgettes, trimmed,
   halved and sliced
225g (8oz) potatoes, diced
400g can red kidney beans, drained
   and rinsed
425g can flageolet beans, drained
   and rinsed
1.5 litres (2½ pints) vegetable stock

salt and ground black pepper
crusty bread to serve

1 Heat the oil in a pan. Add the onions and garlic and sauté for 2 minutes. Add the spices and cook, stirring, for 1 minute. Mix in the courgettes and potatoes and cook for 1–2 minutes.

2 Add the remaining ingredients and bring to the boil, then reduce the heat, cover the pan and simmer for 25 minutes, stirring occasionally, or until the potatoes are tender. Adjust the seasoning if necessary.

3 Ladle into warmed bowls and serve with crusty bread.

 COOK'S TIP
Courgettes are baby marrows. Look for small firm vegetables. They lose their flavour as they grow larger.

Autumn Barley Soup

Preparation Time 10 minutes • **Cooking Time** 1 hour 5 minutes • **Serves 4** • **Per Serving** 86 calories, trace fat (of which 0.2g saturates), 17g carbohydrate, 0.1g salt • **Vegetarian** • **Dairy Free** • **Easy**

25g (1oz) pot barley, washed and
   drained
1 litre (1¾ pints) vegetable stock
2 large carrots, diced
1 turnip, diced
2 leeks, trimmed and sliced
2 celery sticks, diced
1 small onion, finely chopped
1 bouquet garni (see Cook's Tip)
2 tbsp freshly chopped parsley
salt and ground black pepper

1 Put the barley and stock into a pan and bring to the boil. Reduce the heat and simmer for 45 minutes or until the barley is tender.

2 Add the vegetables to the pan with the bouquet garni and season to taste with black pepper. Bring to the boil, then reduce the heat and simmer for about 20 minutes or until the vegetables are tender.

3 Discard the bouquet garni. Add the parsley to the soup, season to taste with salt and pepper and stir well, then ladle into warmed bowls and serve immediately.

★ COOK'S TIP
To make a bouquet garni, tie together a sprig each of thyme and parsley with a bay leaf and a piece of celery.

Spicy Lamb Soup

Preparation Time 15 minutes • **Cooking Time** about 1 hour • **Serves 4** • **Per serving** 367 calories, 17g fat (of which 6g saturates), 31g carbohydrate, 0.6g salt • **Gluten Free** • **Dairy Free** • **Easy**

1 tbsp olive oil
350g (12oz) lamb mince
1 medium onion, finely chopped
227g can tomatoes
3 tsp harissa paste
1.5 litres (2½ pints) hot lamb stock
100g (3½oz) couscous
410g can chickpeas, drained and
   rinsed
salt and ground black pepper
1 tbsp each freshly chopped flat-
   leafed parsley and mint to
   garnish
flatbread and lemon wedges
   (optional) to serve

1 Heat half the oil in a large pan and brown the mince in batches. Set aside.

2 Add the remaining oil and gently fry the onion for 10 minutes or until softened. Add the tomatoes and harissa and simmer, covered, for 30 minutes.

3 Add the hot stock and couscous and simmer for 10 minutes. Stir in the chickpeas and heat through for 2–3 minutes. Add the herbs and check the seasoning. Serve immediately with warmed flatbread, and lemon wedges, if you like, to squeeze into the soup.

★GET AHEAD
To prepare ahead *Complete the recipe to the end of step 1. Cool, cover and chill for up to three days.*
To use *Complete the recipe.*

Full-of-goodness Soup

★

Preparation Time 10 minutes • **Cooking Time** 6–8 minutes • **Serves 4** • **Per Serving** 107 calories, 4g fat (of which trace saturates), 9g carbohydrate, 1g salt • **Vegetarian** • **Dairy Free** • **Easy**

1–2 tbsp medium curry paste
200ml (7fl oz) reduced-fat coconut milk
600ml (1 pint) hot vegetable stock
200g (7oz) smoked tofu, cubed
2 pak choi, chopped
a handful of sugarsnap peas
4 spring onions, chopped
lime wedges to serve

1 Heat the curry paste in a pan for 1–2 minutes. Add the coconut milk and hot stock and bring to the boil.

2 Add the smoked tofu, pak choi, sugarsnap peas and spring onions, reduce the heat and simmer for 1–2 minutes.

3 Ladle into warmed bowls and serve with a wedge of lime to squeeze in.

★ TRY SOMETHING DIFFERENT
Replace the smoked tofu with shredded leftover roast chicken and simmer for 2–3 minutes.

Mushroom, Spinach and Miso Soup

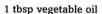

Preparation Time 5 minutes • **Cooking Time** 25 minutes • **Serves 6** • **Per Serving** 55 calories, 2g fat (of which trace saturates), 6g carbohydrate, 1.3g salt • **Gluten Free** • **Dairy Free** • **Easy**

1 tbsp vegetable oil

1 onion, finely sliced

125g (4oz) shiitake mushrooms, finely sliced

225g (8oz) baby spinach leaves

1.1 litres (2 pints) fresh hot fish stock

4 tbsp mugi miso (see Cook's Tip)

1 Heat the oil in a large pan over a low heat, add the onion and cook gently for 15 minutes or until soft.

2 Add the mushrooms and cook for 5 minutes, then stir in the spinach and hot stock. Heat for 3 minutes, then stir in the miso – don't boil, as miso is a live culture. Ladle the soup into warmed bowls and serve hot.

★ COOK'S TIP

Miso (fermented barley and soya beans) is a living food in the same way that yogurt is and contains bacteria and enzymes that are destroyed by boiling. Miso is best added as a flavouring at the end of cooking. It's available from Asian shops and larger supermarkets.

Pasta and Chickpea Soup with Pesto

Preparation Time 25 minutes • **Cooking Time** about 1 hour • **Serves 6** • **Per Serving** 211 calories, 8g fat (of which 1g saturates), 26g carbohydrate, 0.3g salt • **Easy**

3 tbsp olive oil
1 onion, chopped
2 garlic cloves, finely chopped
1 small leek, trimmed and sliced
1 tsp freshly chopped rosemary
400g can chickpeas
1.1 litres (2 pints) vegetable stock
4 ripe tomatoes, skinned and
    chopped
1 courgette, diced
125g (4oz) shelled peas
125g (4oz) French beans, halved
125g (4oz) shelled broad beans
50g (2oz) dried pastina (small soup
    pasta)
2 tbsp freshly chopped parsley
salt and ground black pepper
fresh ready-made pesto (see
    page 11) and freshly grated
    pecorino or Parmesan to serve

1 Heat the oil in a large pan, add the onion, garlic, leek and rosemary and fry gently for 5–6 minutes or until softened but not coloured. Add the chickpeas with their liquid, the stock and tomatoes. Bring to the boil, then reduce the heat, cover the pan and simmer for 40 minutes.

2 Add the courgette, peas, French beans and broad beans. Return to the boil, then reduce the heat and simmer for 10 minutes. Add the pasta and parsley and simmer for 6–8 minutes until al dente. Season to taste with salt and pepper.

3 Ladle into warmed bowls and serve topped with a spoonful of pesto and a sprinkling of cheese.

Green Lentil and Coconut Soup

★

Preparation Time 20 minutes • **Cooking Time** 40 minutes • **Serves 4** • **Per Serving** 442 calories, 22g fat
(of which 10g saturates), 48g carbohydrate, 0.3g salt • **Vegetarian** • **Dairy Free** • **Easy**

225g (8oz) whole green lentils
4 tbsp sunflower oil
350g (12oz) floury potatoes, diced
1 large onion, chopped
2 garlic cloves, crushed
¼ tsp ground turmeric
2 tsp ground cumin
50g (2oz) creamed coconut
750ml (1¼ pints) vegetable stock
300ml (½ pint) coconut milk
finely grated zest of 1 lemon
salt and ground black pepper
toasted fresh coconut and
　coriander sprigs (optional) to
　garnish

1 Put the lentils into a sieve and wash thoroughly under cold running water. Drain well.

2 Heat the oil in a large pan. Add the potatoes and fry gently for 5 minutes or until beginning to colour. Remove with a slotted spoon and drain on kitchen paper.

3 Add the onion to the pan and fry gently for 10 minutes or until soft. Add the garlic, turmeric and cumin and fry for 2–3 minutes. Add the coconut, stock, coconut milk

and lentils and bring to the boil, then reduce the heat, cover the pan and simmer gently for 20 minutes or until the lentils are just tender.

4 Add the potatoes and lemon zest and season to taste with salt and pepper. Cook gently for a further 5 minutes or until the potatoes are tender. Ladle into warmed bowls, garnish with toasted coconut and the coriander sprigs, if you like, and serve hot.

Pepper and Lentil Soup

Preparation Time 15 minutes • **Cooking Time** 45 minutes • **Serves 6** • **Per Serving** 165 calories, 3g fat (of which 1g saturates), 27g carbohydrate, 0.5g salt • **Vegetarian** • **Dairy Free** • **Easy**

1 tbsp oil
1 medium onion, finely chopped
1 celery stick, chopped
1 leek, trimmed and chopped
1 carrot, chopped
2 red peppers, seeded and diced
225g (8oz) red lentils
400g can chopped tomatoes
1 litre (1¾ pints) hot light
   vegetable stock
25g pack flat-leafed parsley,
   chopped
salt and ground black pepper
toast to serve

1 Heat the oil in a pan. Add the onion, celery, leek and carrot and cook for 10–15 minutes until soft.

2 Add the red peppers and cook for 5 minutes. Stir in the red lentils, add the tomatoes and hot stock and season to taste with salt and pepper.

3 Cover the pan and bring to the boil, then reduce the heat and cook, uncovered, for 25 minutes or until the lentils are soft and the vegetables are tender.

4 Stir in the parsley. Ladle into warmed bowls and serve with toast.

Roasted Tomato and Pepper Soup

★

Preparation Time 20 minutes • **Cooking Time** about 1 hour • **Serves 6** • **Per Serving** 239 calories, 16g fat (of which 6g saturates), 15g carbohydrate, 0.4g salt • **Gluten Free** • **Easy**

1.4kg (3lb) full-flavoured tomatoes, preferably vine-ripened
2 red peppers, seeded and chopped
4 garlic cloves, crushed
3 small onions, thinly sliced
20g (¾oz) fresh thyme sprigs
4 tbsp olive oil
4 tbsp Worcestershire sauce
4 tbsp vodka
salt and ground black pepper
6 tbsp double cream to serve

1 Preheat the oven to 200°C (180°C fan oven) mark 6. Put the tomatoes into a large roasting tin with the red peppers, garlic and onions. Scatter 6 thyme sprigs over the top, drizzle with the oil and roast in the oven for 25 minutes. Turn the vegetables over and roast for a further 30–40 minutes until tender and slightly charred.

2 Put one-third of the vegetables into a blender or food processor with 300ml (½ pint) boiled water. Add the Worcestershire sauce and vodka and season with salt and pepper. Whiz until smooth, then pass through a sieve into a pan.

3 Whiz the remaining vegetables with 450ml (¾ pint) boiled water, then sieve and add to the pan.

4 To serve, warm the soup thoroughly, stirring occasionally. Pour into warmed bowls, add 1 tbsp double cream to each bowl, then drag a cocktail stick through the cream to swirl. Scatter a few fresh thyme leaves over the top and serve immediately.

Parsnip Soup with Chorizo

Preparation Time 20 minutes • **Cooking Time** 1 hour • **Serves 8** • **Per Serving** 278 calories, 20g fat (of which 9g saturates), 18g carbohydrate, 0.7g salt • **Gluten Free** • **Easy**

40g (1½oz) butter
1 onion, roughly chopped
225g (8oz) floury potatoes, such as
   King Edward, chopped
400g (14oz) parsnips, chopped
4 tsp paprika, plus extra to dust
1.1 litres (2 pints) vegetable stock
450ml (¾ pint) milk
4 tbsp double cream
75g (3oz) sliced chorizo sausage,
   cut into fine strips
salt and ground black pepper
parsnip crisps and freshly grated
   Parmesan to serve

1 Melt the butter in a large heavy-based pan over a gentle heat. Add the onion and cook for 5 minutes or until soft. Add the potatoes, parsnips and paprika. Mix well and cook gently, stirring occasionally, for 15 minutes or until the vegetables begin to soften.

2 Add the stock, milk and cream and season with salt and pepper. Bring to the boil, then reduce the heat and simmer for about 25 minutes or until the vegetables are very soft. Add 50g (2oz) of the chorizo. Allow the soup to cool a little, then whiz in a blender or food processor until smooth. The soup can be thinned with additional stock or milk, if you like. Check the seasoning and put back in the pan.

3 To serve, reheat the soup. Serve in warmed bowls and top each with parsnip crisps. Sprinkle with the remaining chorizo and a little Parmesan, and dust with paprika.

★ FREEZING TIP
To freeze Complete the recipe to the end of step 2, then cool, pack and freeze for up to one month.
To use Thaw the soup overnight at cool room temperature, then complete the recipe.

Spiced Beef and Noodle Soup

.... ★

Preparation Time 20 minutes • **Cooking Time** 15 minutes • **Serves 4** • **Per Serving** 215 calories, 13g fat
(of which 3g saturates), 11g carbohydrate, 1.2g salt • **Dairy Free** • **Easy**

2 tbsp sunflower oil
225g (8oz) fillet steak, cut into thin
 strips
1.1 litres (2 pints) beef stock
2–3 tbsp Thai fish sauce (nam pla)
1 large red chilli, seeded and finely
 sliced (see page 19)
1 lemongrass stalk, trimmed and
 thinly sliced
2.5cm (1in) piece fresh root ginger,
 peeled and finely shredded
6 spring onions, halved lengthways
 and cut into 2.5cm (1in) lengths
1 garlic clove, crushed
¼ tsp caster sugar
15g (½ oz) dried porcini or shiitake
 mushrooms, broken into pieces
 and soaked in 150ml (¼ pint)
 boiling water for 15 minutes
50g (2oz) medium egg noodles
125g (4oz) spinach leaves, roughly
 chopped
4 tbsp freshly chopped coriander
salt and ground black pepper

1 Heat the oil in a large pan, then brown the meat in two batches and put to one side.

2 Pour the stock into the pan with 2 tbsp of the fish sauce, the chilli, lemongrass, ginger, spring onions, garlic and sugar. Add the mushrooms and their soaking liquid. Bring the mixture to the boil.

3 Break up the noodles slightly and add them to the pan, then stir gently until they begin to separate. Reduce the heat and simmer the soup, stirring occasionally, for 4–5 minutes until the noodles are just tender.

4 Stir in the spinach, coriander and reserved beef. Season with salt and pepper, add the remaining fish sauce to taste, then serve the soup in warmed bowls.

Thai Chicken Broth

★

Preparation Time 20 minutes • **Cooking Time** 20–25 minutes • **Serves 4** • **Per Serving** 198 calories, 5g fat
(of which 1g saturates), 13g carbohydrate, 1.1g salt • **Dairy Free** • **Easy**

1 tbsp olive oil

4 boneless, skinless chicken thighs, around 300g (11oz), shredded

3 garlic cloves, roughly chopped

2 red chillies, seeded and finely diced (see page 19)

1 lemongrass stalk, trimmed and finely sliced

5cm (2in) piece fresh root ginger, peeled and finely chopped

150ml (¼ pint) white wine

1 litre (1¾ pints) chicken stock

8 fresh coriander sprigs

50g (2oz) rice noodles

125g (4oz) green beans, trimmed and halved

125g (4oz) bean sprouts

4 spring onions, finely sliced

2 tbsp Thai fish sauce (nam pla)

juice of ½ lime

salt and ground black pepper

1 Heat the oil in a large pan over a medium heat. Add the chicken, garlic, chillies, lemongrass and ginger and cook for 3–5 minutes until the chicken is opaque.

2 Add the wine and bring to the boil, then reduce the heat and simmer until reduced by half. Add the stock and bring to the boil, then reduce the heat and simmer for 5 minutes or until the chicken is cooked through.

3 Pick the leaves off the coriander and put them to one side. Finely chop the coriander stalks. Add the noodles to the pan and cook for 1 minute, then add the beans and coriander stalks. Cook for 3 minutes.

4 Add the bean sprouts and spring onions (reserving a few of each to garnish) along with the fish sauce and lime juice. Bring to the boil and taste for seasoning. Ladle the noodles and broth into four warmed bowls, making sure that each serving has some chicken and bean sprouts. Garnish with the coriander leaves, spring onions and bean sprouts and serve.

Hearty Chicken Soup with Dumplings

★

Preparation Time 20 minutes • **Cooking Time** 40 minutes • **Serves 4** • **Per Serving** 335 calories, 15g fat (of which 5g saturates), 31g carbohydrate, 0.3g salt • **Easy**

2 tbsp olive oil
2 celery sticks, roughly chopped
150g (5oz) carrots, roughly chopped
150g (5oz) waxy salad potatoes, thinly sliced
275g (10oz) chicken breast, thinly sliced
2 litres (3½ pints) hot chicken stock
75g (3oz) frozen peas
salt and ground black pepper
a handful of chives, roughly chopped, to garnish (optional)

FOR THE DUMPLINGS
100g (3½oz) plain flour
½ tsp baking powder
½ tsp salt
1 medium egg, well beaten
25g (1oz) butter, melted
a splash of milk

1 Heat the oil in a large pan, then add the celery, carrots and potatoes. Cook for 5 minutes or until the vegetables are beginning to caramelise around the edges. Add the chicken and fry for 3 minutes or until just starting to turn golden. Pour in the hot stock and simmer for 15 minutes, skimming the surface occasionally to remove any scum.

2 To make the dumplings, sift the flour, baking powder and salt into a bowl, then season with black pepper. Combine the egg, melted butter and milk in a separate bowl, then stir quickly into the flour to make a stiff batter.

3 Drop half-teaspoonfuls of the dumpling mixture into the soup, then cover and simmer for a further 15 minutes.

4 Stir in the peas and heat through. Check the seasoning, sprinkle with pepper and serve garnished with chives, if you like.

Chicken and Bean Soup

Preparation Time 10 minutes • **Cooking Time** 15 minutes • **Serves 4** • **Per Serving** 150 calories, 6g fat
(of which 1g saturates), 15g carbohydrate, 0.8g salt • **Vegetarian** • **Gluten Free** • **Dairy Free** • **Easy**

1 tbsp olive oil
1 onion, finely chopped
4 celery sticks, chopped
1 red chilli, seeded and roughly
  chopped (see page 19)
2 boneless, skinless chicken
  breasts, cut into strips
1 litre (1¾ pints) hot chicken or
  vegetable stock
100g (3½oz) bulgur wheat
2 × 400g cans cannellini beans,
  drained
400g can chopped tomatoes

25g (1oz) flat-leafed parsley,
  roughly chopped
wholegrain bread and hummus to
  serve

1 Heat the oil in a large heavy-based pan. Add the onion, celery and chilli and cook over a low heat for 10 minutes or until softened. Add the chicken and stir-fry for 3–4 minutes until golden.

2 Add the hot stock to the pan and bring to a simmer. Stir in the bulgur wheat and simmer for 15 minutes. Stir in the cannellini beans and tomatoes and return to a simmer. Sprinkle the chopped parsley over and ladle into warmed bowls. Serve with wholegrain bread and hummus.

Turkey and Chestnut Soup

Preparation Time 5 minutes • **Cooking Time** 45 minutes • **Serves 4** • **Per Serving** 330 calories, 10g fat (of which 5g saturates), 52g carbohydrate, 0.2g salt • **Gluten Free** • **Easy**

25g (1oz) butter or margarine
1 large onion, chopped
225g (8oz) Brussels sprouts
900ml (1½ pints) turkey stock
   made from leftover carcass and
   any leftover turkey meat
400g can whole chestnuts, drained
2 tsp freshly chopped thyme or
   1 tsp dried thyme
salt and ground black pepper
stock or milk to finish
thyme sprigs to garnish

1 Melt the fat in a large heavy-based pan, add the onion and fry gently for 5 minutes or until it has softened.

2 Trim the sprouts and cut a cross in the base of each one. Add to the onion, cover the pan with a lid and cook gently for 5 minutes, shaking the pan frequently.

3 Pour in the stock and bring to the boil, then add the remaining ingredients, with salt and pepper to taste. Reduce the heat, cover the pan and simmer for 30 minutes or until the vegetables are tender.

4 Leave the soup to cool a little, then whiz in batches in a blender or food processor until smooth. Return to the rinsed-out pan and reheat gently, then thin down with either stock or milk, according to taste.

5 Taste and adjust the seasoning. To serve, ladle into warmed bowls and garnish with sprigs of thyme.

★ COOK'S TIP
Serve for an informal family lunch with hot garlic bread, wholemeal toast, cheese on toast or hot sausage rolls.

Pork and Chilli Noodle Soup

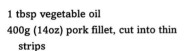

Preparation Time 10 minutes • **Cooking Time** 10 minutes • **Serves 4** • **Per Serving** 359 calories, 11g fat (of which 3g saturates), 39g carbohydrate, 0.7g salt • **Dairy Free** • **Easy**

1 tbsp vegetable oil

400g (14oz) pork fillet, cut into thin strips

¼ red chilli, finely chopped (see page 19)

2.5cm (1in) piece fresh root ginger, peeled and cut in slivers

½ tsp smoked paprika

1 red pepper, seeded and thinly sliced

400ml can coconut milk

700ml (1 pint 3½fl oz) hot chicken stock

175g (6oz) medium egg noodles

50g (2oz) spinach

a large handful of fresh coriander, roughly chopped

1 Heat the oil in a pan and fry the meat in two batches until golden. Add the chilli, ginger, paprika and sliced pepper and cook for a further minute.

2 Add the coconut milk and hot stock and simmer for 5 minutes. Stir in the noodles and cook for 4 minutes.

3 Divide among four warmed bowls, scatter the spinach and coriander on top and serve.

Hot and Sour Soup

★

Preparation Time 20 minutes • **Cooking Time** 30–35 minutes • **Serves 4** • **Per Serving** 255 calories, 10g fat (of which 1g saturates), 19g carbohydrate, 0.7g salt • **Dairy Free** • **Easy**

1 tbsp vegetable oil

2 turkey breasts, about 300g (11oz), or the same quantity of tofu, cut into strips

5cm (2in) piece fresh root ginger, peeled and grated

4 spring onions, finely sliced

1–2 tbsp Thai red curry paste

75g (3oz) long-grain wild rice

1.1 litres (2 pints) hot weak chicken or vegetable stock or boiling water

200g (7oz) mangetouts, sliced

juice of 1 lime

4 tbsp roughly chopped fresh coriander to garnish

1 Heat the oil in a deep pan. Add the turkey or tofu and cook over a medium heat for 5 minutes or until browned. Add the ginger and spring onions and cook for a further 2–3 minutes. Stir in the curry paste and cook for 1–2 minutes to warm the spices.

2 Add the rice and stir to coat in the curry paste. Pour the hot stock or boiling water into the pan, stir once and bring to the boil. Reduce the heat, cover the pan and simmer for 20 minutes.

3 Add the mangetouts and cook for a further 5 minutes or until the rice is cooked. Just before serving, squeeze in the lime juice and stir to mix.

4 To serve, ladle into warmed bowls and sprinkle with the coriander.

Fish and Shelfish

Prawn and Vegetable Pilau

Preparation Time 10 minutes • **Cooking Time** 15–20 minutes • **Serves 4** • **Per Serving** 360 calories, 5g fat (of which 1g saturates), 61g carbohydrate, 1.8g salt • **Dairy Free** • **Easy**

250g (9oz) long-grain rice
1 broccoli head, broken into florets
150g (5oz) baby sweetcorn, halved
200g (7oz) sugarsnap peas
1 red pepper, sliced into thin strips
400g (14oz) cooked and peeled king prawns

FOR THE DRESSING
1 tbsp sesame oil
5cm (2in) piece fresh root ginger, peeled and grated
juice of 1 lime
1–2 tbsp light soy sauce

1 Put the rice into a large wide pan – it needs to be really big, as you're cooking the rice and steaming the vegetables on top, then tossing it all together. Add 600ml (1 pint) boiling water. Cover the pan and bring to the boil, then reduce the heat to low and cook the rice according to the pack instructions.

2 About 10 minutes before the end of the rice cooking time, add the broccoli, corn, sugarsnaps and red pepper. Stir well, then cover the pan and cook until the vegetables and rice are just tender.

3 Meanwhile, put the prawns into a bowl. Add the sesame oil, ginger, lime juice and soy sauce. Mix the prawns and dressing into the cooked vegetables and rice and toss through well. Serve immediately.

★ COOK'S TIP
The word 'pilau', or 'pilaf', comes from the Persian pilaw. *The dish originated in the East and consists of rice flavoured with spices, to which vegetables, poultry, meat, fish or shellfish are added.*

Coconut Fish Pilau

Preparation Time 15 minutes • **Cooking Time** 30 minutes • **Serves 4** • **Per Serving** 398 calories, 7g fat (of which 1g saturates), 53g carbohydrate, 0.4g salt • **Gluten Free** • **Dairy Free** • **Easy**

2 tsp olive oil
1 shallot, chopped
1 tbsp Thai green curry paste
225g (8oz) brown basmati rice
600ml (1 pint) hot fish or vegetable
   stock
150ml (¼ pint) reduced-fat coconut
   milk
350g (12oz) skinless white fish fillet,
   such as coley (saithe) or pollack,
   cut into bite-size pieces
350g (12oz) sugarsnap peas
125g (4oz) cooked and peeled
   prawns
25g (1oz) flaked almonds, toasted
a squeeze of lemon juice
salt and ground black pepper
2 tbsp freshly chopped coriander
   to garnish

1 Heat the oil in a frying pan, add the shallot and 1 tbsp water and fry for 4–5 minutes until golden. Stir in the curry paste and cook for 1–2 minutes.

2 Add the rice, hot stock and coconut milk and bring to the boil. Reduce the heat, cover the pan and simmer for 15–20 minutes until all the liquid has been absorbed.

3 Add the fish and cook for 3–5 minutes. Add the sugarsnap peas, prawns, almonds and lemon juice and stir over the heat for 3–4 minutes until heated through. Check the seasoning and serve immediately, garnished with coriander.

★ TRY SOMETHING DIFFERENT
There are plenty of alternatives to cod: try coley (saithe), sea bass or pollack.

Salmon and Bulgur Wheat Pilau

★

Preparation Time 5 minutes • **Cooking Time** 20 minutes • **Serves 4** • **Per Serving** 323 calories, 11g fat (of which 2g saturates), 30g carbohydrate, 1.5g salt • **Dairy Free** • **Easy**

1 tbsp olive oil
1 onion, chopped
175g (6oz) bulgur wheat
450ml (¾ pint) vegetable stock
400g can pink salmon, drained and flaked
125g (4oz) spinach, roughly chopped
225g (8oz) frozen peas
zest and juice of 1 lemon
salt and ground black pepper

1 Heat the oil in a large pan, add the onion and cook until softened. Stir in the bulgur wheat to coat in the oil, then stir in the stock and bring to the boil. Cover the pan, reduce the heat and simmer for 10–15 minutes until the stock has been fully absorbed.

2 Stir in the salmon, spinach, peas and lemon juice and cook until the spinach has wilted and the salmon and peas are heated through. Season and sprinkle with lemon zest before serving.

★ TRY SOMETHING DIFFERENT
Instead of salmon, use 200g (7oz) cooked peeled prawns and 200g (7oz) cherry tomatoes.

Salmon and Coriander Kedgeree

Preparation Time 5 minutes • **Cooking Time** 20 minutes • **Serves 4** • **Per Serving** 368 calories, 7g fat (of which 1g saturates), 50g carbohydrate, 3.8g salt • **Gluten Free** • **Dairy Free** • **Easy**

1 tbsp olive oil

4 shallots, chopped

225g (8oz) basmati rice

450ml (¾ pint) hot fish stock

100g (3½oz) frozen peas

300g (11oz) hot-smoked salmon flakes

a handful of freshly chopped coriander

salt and ground black pepper

lime wedges to serve

1 Heat the oil in a large pan over a low heat and fry the shallots for 5 minutes or until soft. Add the rice and stir to mix everything together. Pour in the hot stock. Cover the pan and cook for 10 minutes over a low heat or until the rice is almost cooked and most of the liquid has been absorbed.

2 Add the peas and salmon and cook, uncovered, for 2–3 minutes until the peas are tender. Season with salt and pepper, scatter the chopped coriander over and serve with lime wedges to squeeze on.

★ COOK'S TIP
Basmati rice is prized for its delicate fragrant flavour. Its long grains are firm and separate when cooked, not sticky, making it perfect for this tasty kedgeree.

Salmon Kedgeree

★

Preparation Time 15 minutes, plus soaking • **Cooking Time** 55 minutes • **Serves 4** • **Per Serving** 490 calories, 15g fat (of which 2g saturates), 62g carbohydrate, 0.1g salt • **Gluten Free** • **Easy**

50g (2oz) butter
700g (1½lb) onions, sliced
2 tsp garam masala
1 garlic clove, crushed
75g (3oz) split green lentils, soaked
    in 300ml (½ pint) boiling water
    for 15 minutes, then drained
750ml (1¼ pints) hot vegetable
    stock
225g (8oz) basmati rice
1 green chilli, seeded and finely
    chopped (see page 19)
350g (12oz) salmon fillet
salt and ground black pepper

1 Melt the butter in a flameproof casserole over a medium heat. Add the onions and cook for 5 minutes or until soft. Remove a third of the onions and put to one side. Increase the heat and cook the remaining onions for 10 minutes to caramelise. Remove and put to one side.

2 Put the first batch of onions back into the casserole, add the garam masala and garlic and cook, stirring, for 1 minute. Add the drained lentils and hot stock, cover the pan and cook for 15 minutes. Add the rice and chilli and season with salt and

pepper. Bring to the boil, then reduce the heat, cover the pan and simmer for 5 minutes.

3 Put the salmon fillet on top of the rice, cover and continue to cook gently for 15 minutes or until the rice is cooked, the stock absorbed and the salmon opaque.

4 Lift off the salmon and divide into flakes. Put it back into the casserole and fork through the rice. Garnish with the reserved caramelised onion and serve.

Fish with Cherry Tomatoes

Preparation Time 15 minutes • **Cooking Time** 20–25 minutes • **Serves 4** • **Per Serving** 168 calories, 7g fat (of which 1g saturates), 8g carbohydrate, 0.2g salt • **Gluten Free** • **Dairy Free** • **Easy**

4 × 100g (3½oz) cod steaks or
    tilapia fillets
1 tbsp gluten-free flour
2 tbsp olive oil
1 small onion, sliced
1 large red chilli, seeded and
    chopped (see page 19)
1 garlic clove, crushed
250g (9oz) cherry tomatoes, halved
4 spring onions, chopped
2 tbsp freshly chopped coriander
salt and ground black pepper

1 Season the fish with salt and pepper, then lightly dust with the flour. Heat 1 tbsp oil in a large frying pan, add the onion and fry for 5–10 minutes until golden.

2 Pour the remaining oil into the pan. Add the fish and fry for 3 minutes on each side. Add the chilli, garlic, cherry tomatoes, spring onions and coriander and season with salt and pepper. Cover the pan and continue to cook for 5–10 minutes until everything is heated through. Serve immediately.

Gurnard with a Summer Vegetable Broth

Preparation Time 20 minutes • **Cooking Time** about 20 minutes • **Serves 6** • **Per Serving** 483 calories, 26g fat (of which 13g saturates), 38g carbohydrate, 1.6g salt • **Easy**

3–4 tbsp plain flour
zest of 1 lemon
6 × 200g (7oz) gurnard fillets
25g (1oz) butter
1 tsp oil
salt and ground black pepper

FOR THE VEGETABLE BROTH
a handful each peas in their pods,
    runner beans and baby leeks
1 tomato, seeded and chopped
18 cherry tomatoes
2 shallots, finely chopped
1 thyme sprig
1 bay leaf

450ml (¾ pint) light vegetable
    stock
leaves picked from 8 tarragon
    sprigs

1 Start the vegetable broth: pod the peas and put into a large bowl. Thickly slice the runner beans and leeks. Add both to the bowl with the chopped tomato and cherry tomatoes.

2 Put the flour on to a large plate. Add the lemon zest and season with salt and pepper. Toss the fish in the mixture and set aside.

3 Heat the butter and oil in a large sauté pan for 1–2 minutes. Add the fish and fry in batches, skin side down, until crisp. Set aside.

4 Add the shallots to the pan and cook for 3–4 minutes until just golden. Add the thyme, bay leaf and stock and bring to the boil, then reduce the heat and simmer for 3–4 minutes.

5 Add the mixed vegetables. Roughly chop the tarragon leaves, add to the mixture and stir well, then cover and cook for 5 minutes until the vegetables are tender. Add the fish and cook gently for 3–4 minutes to heat through, then serve.

Lime and Chilli Swordfish

Preparation Time 10 minutes, plus marinating • **Cooking Time** 5 minutes • **Serves 4** • **Per Serving** 216 calories, 10g fat (of which 2g saturates), 0g carbohydrate, 0.6g salt • **Gluten Free** • **Dairy Free** • **Easy**

1 tsp dried chilli flakes
4 tbsp olive oil
grated zest and juice of 1 lime, plus
   1 whole lime, sliced, to serve
1 garlic clove, crushed
4 × 175g (6oz) swordfish steaks
salt and ground black pepper
mixed salad to serve

1 Put the chilli flakes into a large shallow bowl. Add the oil, lime zest and juice and garlic and mix everything together. Add the swordfish steaks to the marinade and toss several times to coat completely. Leave to marinate for 30 minutes.

2 Preheat the barbecue or preheat a griddle pan until hot.

3 Lift the swordfish out of the marinade and season well with salt and pepper, then cook the steaks for 2 minutes on each side. Top with slices of lime and continue to cook for 1 minute or until the fish is opaque right through. Serve immediately, with a mixed salad.

Roasted Salmon

★

Preparation Time 20 minutes, plus cooling and chilling • **Cooking Time** about 30 minutes • **Serves 20** •
Per Serving 347 calories, 25g fat (of which 9g saturates), 3g carbohydrate, 0.2g salt • **Gluten Free** • **Easy**

3 lemons, 2 sliced and the juice of
  ½, plus extra lemon slices to
  garnish
2 salmon sides, filleted, each 1.4kg
  (3lb), with skin on, boned and
  trimmed
2 tbsp dry white wine
salt and ground black pepper
cucumber slices and 2 large
  bunches of watercress to garnish

FOR THE DRESSING
500g carton crème fraîche
500g carton natural yogurt
2 tbsp horseradish sauce

3 tbsp freshly chopped tarragon
4 tbsp capers, roughly chopped,
  plus extra to garnish
¼ cucumber, halved lengthways,
  seeded and finely chopped, to
  garnish

1 Preheat the oven to 190°C (170°C
fan oven) mark 5. Take two pieces of
foil, each large enough to wrap one
side of salmon, and put a piece of
greaseproof paper on top. Divide
the lemon slices between each piece
of greaseproof paper and lay the

salmon on top, skin side up. Season
with salt and pepper, then pour the
lemon juice and wine over.

2 Score the skin of each salmon
fillet at 4cm (1½in) intervals to mark
10 portions. Scrunch the foil around
each fillet, keeping it loose so that
the fish doesn't stick. Cook for
25 minutes or until the flesh is just
opaque. Unwrap the foil and cook
for a further 5 minutes until the skin
is crisp. Leave the fish to cool quickly
in a cold place. Re-wrap and chill.

3 Put all the dressing ingredients,
except the garnishes, into a bowl
and season with salt and pepper.
Mix well, then cover and chill.

4 Serve the salmon on a platter
garnished with lemon, cucumber
and watercress. Garnish the
dressing with capers and chopped
cucumber.

★ COOK'S TIPS
● *There'll be a lot of hot liquid in the
parcel of salmon, so ask someone to
help you lift it out of the oven.*
● *To check the fish is cooked, ease a
knife into one of the slashes in the skin.
The flesh should look opaque and the
knife should come out hot.*
● *If you want to prepare this in
advance, complete the recipe to the end
of step 3, then keep the salmon wrapped
and chilled for up to one day.*

Salmon with a Spicy Yogurt Crust

Preparation Time 10 minutes • **Cooking Time** 10 minutes • **Serves 4** • **Per Serving** 250 calories, 14g fat (of which 3g saturates), 3g carbohydrate, 0.2g salt • **Gluten Free** • **Easy**

3 tbsp freshly chopped coriander
1 garlic clove, crushed
2.5cm (1in) piece fresh root ginger, peeled and grated
½ tsp each ground cumin and coriander
¼ tsp cayenne pepper
150g (5oz) natural yogurt
4 × 125g (4oz) salmon fillets
salt
lime wedges and herb salad to serve

1 Preheat the grill. Mix together the chopped coriander, garlic, ginger, cumin, ground coriander, cayenne, yogurt and a pinch of salt. Add the salmon and turn to coat.

2 Grill the fish for 7–10 minutes or until cooked through. Serve with lime wedges to squeeze over the fish and a herb salad.

⭐ TRY SOMETHING DIFFERENT
Use another fish instead of salmon: try trout or plump mackerel fillets.

Tuna Melt Pizza

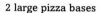

Preparation Time 5 minutes • **Cooking Time** 10–12 minutes • **Serves 4** • **Per Serving** 688 calories, 26g fat (of which 9g saturates), 72g carbohydrate, 3.5g salt • **Easy**

2 large pizza bases
4 tbsp sun-dried tomato pesto
2 × 185g cans tuna, drained
50g can anchovies, drained and chopped
125g (4oz) mature Cheddar cheese, grated
rocket to serve

1 Preheat the oven to 220°C (200°C fan oven) mark 7. Spread each pizza base with 2 tbsp sun-dried tomato pesto. Top each with half the tuna, half the anchovies and half the grated cheese.

2 Put on to a baking sheet and cook in the oven for 10–12 minutes until the cheese has melted. Sprinkle with rocket to serve.

★ TRY SOMETHING DIFFERENT

Mozzarella and Tomato
Spread the pizza bases with 4 tbsp pesto and top with 125g (4oz) chopped sunblush tomatoes and 2 x 125g (4oz) sliced mozzarella balls. Cook, then serve topped with a handful of baby spinach leaves.

Ham and Pineapple
Spread the pizza bases with 4 tbsp tomato pasta sauce. Top with a 225g can drained unsweetened pineapple chunks, 125g (4oz) diced ham and 125g (4oz) grated Gruyère.

Crusted Trout

★

Preparation Time 10 minutes • **Cooking Time** 10–13 minutes • **Serves 4** • **Per Serving** 259 calories, 15g fat (of which 3g saturates), 1g carbohydrate, 0.8g salt • **Gluten Free** • **Dairy Free** • **Easy**

1 tbsp sesame oil
1 tbsp soy sauce
juice of 1 lime
4 × 150g (5oz) trout fillets
2 tbsp sesame seeds
lime wedges, herb salad and fennel
   to serve

1 Preheat the grill. Put the sesame oil into a bowl. Add the soy sauce and lime juice and whisk together.

2 Put the trout fillets on a baking sheet, pour the sesame mixture over them and grill for 8–10 minutes. Sprinkle with the sesame seeds and grill for a further 2–3 minutes until the seeds are golden. Serve with lime wedges, a herb salad and some finely sliced fennel.

★ COOK'S TIP
Sesame seeds are deliciously nutty and highly nutritious. They are a valuable source of protein, good omega fats and vitamin E. Lightly toasted sesame seeds, crushed with a little salt and stirred into 1–2 tbsp of olive oil, make an excellent dressing for cooked green beans, broccoli and carrots.

Grilled Sardines with Harissa

Preparation Time 2 minutes • **Cooking Time** 10–20 minutes • **Serves 2** • **Per Serving** 292 calories, 21g fat (of which 4g saturates), 2g carbohydrate, 0.3g salt • **Gluten Free** • **Dairy Free** • **Easy**

1 garlic clove, crushed
2 tbsp olive oil
1–2 tsp harissa paste
4 whole sardines
salt and ground black pepper
tomato salad, watercress and lime
** wedges to serve**

1 Preheat the grill to high. Put the garlic into a bowl. Add the oil and harissa, season to taste with salt and pepper and mix together.

2 Slash the sardines a couple of times on each side, then brush the harissa and oil mixture all over. Grill for 5–10 minutes on each side until cooked through.

3 Serve with tomato salad and watercress, and lime wedges to squeeze over the sardines.

Sardines on Toast

Preparation Time 5 minutes • **Cooking Time** 8–10 minutes • **Serves 4** • **Per Serving** 240 calories, 9g fat (of which 2g saturates), 25g carbohydrate, 1.6g salt • **Gluten Free** • **Dairy Free** • **Easy**

4 thick slices wholemeal bread
2 large tomatoes, sliced
2 × 120g cans sardines in olive oil,
    drained
juice of ½ lemon
a small handful of parsley, chopped

1 Preheat the grill. Toast the slices of bread on both sides.

2 Divide the tomato slices and the sardines among the toast slices, squeeze the lemon juice over them, then put back under the grill for 2–3 minutes to heat through. Scatter the parsley over the sardines and serve immediately.

★ COOK'S TIP
Oily fish such as sardines are one of the best sources of essential heart-protecting omega-3 oils. Eat them at least once a week. Fresh Cornish sardines, when they are available, are a treat and are cheap. Look out for them at your fishmonger or on the fresh fish counter at the supermarket.

Peppered Mackerel

Preparation Time 10 minutes • **Cooking Time** 15 minutes • **Serves 4** • **Per Serving** 764 calories, 63g fat (of which 22g saturates), 1g carbohydrate, 0.4g salt • **Gluten Free** • **Easy**

4 tsp whole mixed peppercorns
4 fresh mackerel, gutted, about
    250g (9oz) each
1 tbsp sunflower oil
200ml (7fl oz) crème fraîche
lemon wedges to garnish
asparagus and sugarsnap peas
    to serve

1 Lightly crush 2 tsp of the peppercorns using a pestle and mortar. Sprinkle one side of each mackerel with half the crushed peppercorns.

2 Heat the oil in a frying pan over a medium-high heat. Add the fish, peppered side down, and cook for 5–7 minutes. Sprinkle the mackerel with the remaining crushed peppercorns, turn the fish over and continue to fry for 5–7 minutes until cooked (see Cook's Tips). Remove and keep warm.

3 Wipe out the pan, add the crème fraîche and bring to the boil. Stir in the remaining whole peppercorns. (If the sauce becomes too thick, add some boiling water.)

4 To serve, spoon the sauce over the mackerel, garnish with lemon wedges and serve with asparagus and sugarsnap peas.

★ COOK'S TIPS
● *If the mackerel are large, make three shallow slashes on either side of the fish.*
● *To test whether the fish is cooked, prise the flesh from the backbone with a knife; it should be opaque and come away easily.*

Moules Marinière

Preparation Time 15 minutes • Cooking Time 20 minutes • Serves 4 • Per Serving 266 calories, 13g fat (of which 7g saturates), 2g carbohydrate, 0.9g salt • **Gluten Free** • **Easy**

2kg (4½lb) fresh mussels,
    scrubbed, rinsed and beards
    removed (see Cook's Tip)
25g (1oz) butter
4 shallots, finely chopped
2 garlic cloves, crushed
200ml (7fl oz) dry white wine
2 tbsp freshly chopped flat-leafed
    parsley
100ml (3½fl oz) single cream
salt and ground black pepper
crusty bread to serve

1 Tap the mussels on the worksurface and discard any that do not close or have broken shells. Heat the butter in a large non-stick lidded frying pan and sauté the shallots over a medium-high heat for about 10 minutes or until soft.

2 Add the garlic, wine and half the parsley to the pan and bring to the boil. Tip in the mussels and reduce the heat a little. Cover and cook for about 5 minutes or until all the shells have opened; discard any mussels that don't open.

3 Lift out the mussels with a slotted spoon and put into serving bowls, then cover with foil to keep warm. Add the cream to the stock, season with salt and pepper and cook for 1–2 minutes to heat through.

4 Pour a little sauce over the mussels and sprinkle with the rest of the parsley. Serve immediately with crusty bread.

 COOK'S TIP
To prepare mussels, scrape off the fibres attached to the shells (beards). If the mussels are very clean, give them a quick rinse under the cold tap. If they are very sandy, scrub them with a stiff brush. If the shells have sizeable barnacles on them, it's best (though not essential) to remove them. Tap them sharply with a metal spoon or the back of a washing-up brush, then scrape off. Discard any open mussels that don't shut when tapped sharply; this means they are dead and could be dangerous to eat.

Thai Coconut Mussels

Preparation Time 15 minutes • **Cooking Time** about 12 minutes • **Serves 4** • **Per Serving** 210 calories, 7g fat (of which 1g saturates), 13g carbohydrate, 1.6g salt • **Gluten Free** • **Dairy Free** • **Easy**

1 tbsp vegetable oil

2 shallots, finely chopped

2–3 tbsp Thai green curry paste

400ml can coconut milk

2kg (4½lb) mussels, scrubbed, rinsed and beards removed (see page 57)

a small handful of coriander, chopped, plus extra sprigs to garnish

1 Heat the oil in a large deep pan. Add the shallots and curry paste and fry gently for 5 minutes, stirring regularly, until the shallots are starting to soften. Stir in the coconut milk, cover with a tight-fitting lid and bring to the boil.

2 Add the mussels to the pan, cover, shake the pan well and cook over a medium heat for 4–5 minutes. Give the pan another good shake. Check the mussels and discard any that are still closed. Stir in the chopped coriander and serve immediately, garnished with coriander sprigs.

★ TRY SOMETHING DIFFERENT
Instead of mussels you could use 500g (1lb 2oz) large raw peeled prawns: simmer for 5 minutes until the prawns are cooked and pink.

Mussel and Potato Stew

★

Preparation Time 15 minutes • **Cooking Time** 15 minutes • **Serves 4** • **Per Serving** 470 calories, 23g fat (of which 11g saturates), 42g carbohydrate, 2.8g salt • **Gluten Free** • **Easy**

25g (1oz) butter
200g (7oz) rindless back bacon rashers, cut into strips
700g (1½lb) white potatoes, cut into large chunks
200g can sweetcorn, drained
1kg (2¼lb) mussels, scrubbed, rinsed and beards removed (see page 57)
150ml (¼ pint) single cream
1 tbsp freshly chopped flat-leafed parsley
salt and ground black pepper

1 Melt the butter in a large pan, add the bacon and cook, stirring, until the strips separate. Add the potatoes and 150ml (¼ pint) water and season lightly with salt and pepper. Cover with a tight-fitting lid and cook for 10 minutes or until the potatoes are almost tender.

2 Add the sweetcorn and mussels to the pan, cover and bring to the boil, then reduce the heat and simmer for 2–3 minutes until the mussels open; discard any mussels that don't open. Add the cream and chopped parsley and serve immediately.

Spanish Fish Stew

★

Preparation Time 20 minutes • **Cooking Time** 1 hour 10 minutes • **Serves 4** • **Per Serving** 463 calories, 22g fat
(of which 6g saturates), 32g carbohydrate, 1.8g salt • **Gluten Free** • **Dairy Free** • **Easy**

350g (12oz) small salad potatoes,
   halved
175g (6oz) chorizo sausage, skinned
   and roughly chopped
350g jar roasted peppers in olive
   oil, drained and chopped, oil
   reserved
1 garlic clove, crushed
2 small red onions, cut into thick
   wedges
175ml (6fl oz) dry white wine
300g (11oz) passata
25g (1oz) pitted black olives
450g (1lb) chunky white fish, such
   as cod and haddock, cut into
   large cubes
salt and ground black pepper
freshly chopped flat-leafed parsley
   to garnish

1 Preheat the oven to 170°C (150°C fan oven) mark 3. Put the potatoes, chorizo, roasted peppers, garlic, onions, wine and passata into a large flameproof casserole with 2 tbsp of the oil from the peppers. Season with salt and pepper.

2 Bring to the boil over a medium heat, then cover with a tight-fitting lid and cook in the oven for 45 minutes.

3 Add the olives and fish and put back in the oven for 15 minutes or until the fish is opaque and completely cooked through. Spoon into warmed bowls and serve garnished with chopped parsley.

★ COOK'S TIP
Passata is a useful storecupboard ingredient from the Italian kitchen, which can be used in sauces and stews. It is made from ripe tomatoes that have been puréed and sieved to make a very smooth sauce.

Spicy Monkfish Stew

Preparation Time 10 minutes • **Cooking Time** 35 minutes • **Serves 6** • **Per Serving** 142 calories, 3g fat (of which 1g saturates), 16g carbohydrate, 0.2g salt • **Dairy Free** • **Easy**

1 tbsp olive oil

1 onion, finely sliced

1 tbsp tom yum paste (see Cook's Tip)

450g (1lb) potatoes, cut into 2cm (³⁄₄in) chunks

400g can chopped tomatoes in rich tomato juice

600ml (1 pint) hot fish stock

450g (1lb) monkfish, cut into 2cm (³⁄₄in) chunks

200g (7oz) ready-to-eat baby spinach

salt and ground black pepper

1 Heat the oil in a pan over a medium heat and fry the onion for 5 minutes until golden.

2 Add the tom yum paste and potatoes and stir-fry for 1 minute. Add the tomatoes and hot stock, season well with salt and pepper and cover. Bring to the boil, then reduce the heat and simmer, partially covered, for 15 minutes or until the potatoes are just tender.

3 Add the monkfish to the pan and continue to simmer for 5–10

minutes until the fish is cooked. Add the baby spinach leaves and stir through until wilted.

4 Spoon the fish stew into warmed bowls and serve immediately.

★ COOK'S TIP
Tom yum paste is a hot and spicy Thai mixture used in soups and stews. It is available from large supermarkets and Asian food shops.

Easy Fish Stew

Preparation Time 15 minutes • **Cooking Time** about 30 minutes • **Serves 4** • **Per Serving** 347 calories, 7g fat (of which 1g saturates), 30g carbohydrate, 0.5g salt • **Gluten Free** • **Easy**

2 tbsp olive oil
1 onion, chopped
1 leek, trimmed and chopped
2 tsp smoked paprika
2 tbsp tomato purée
450g (1lb) haddock or cod, roughly chopped
125g (4oz) basmati rice
175ml (6fl oz) dry white wine
450ml (¾ pint) hot fish stock
200g (7oz) cooked and peeled king prawns
a large handful of baby spinach leaves
crusty bread to serve

1 Heat the oil in a large pan. Add the onion and leek and fry for 8–10 minutes until they start to soften. Add the smoked paprika and tomato purée and cook for 1–2 minutes.

2 Add the fish, rice, wine and hot stock. Bring to the boil, then reduce the heat, cover the pan and simmer for 10 minutes or until the fish is cooked through and the rice is tender.

3 Add the prawns and cook for 1 minute or until heated through. Stir in the spinach until wilted, then serve with chunks of bread.

Smoked Haddock and Potato Pie

Preparation Time 15 minutes • **Cooking Time** 1¼ hours–1 hour 25 minutes • **Serves 4** • **Per Serving** 380 calories, 20g fat (of which 11g saturates), 37g carbohydrate, 1.5g salt • **Gluten Free** • **Easy**

142ml carton double cream
150ml (¼ pint) fish stock
3 medium baking potatoes, thinly sliced
300g (11oz) skinless smoked haddock fillets, roughly chopped
20g pack fresh chives, chopped
1 large onion, finely chopped
salt and ground black pepper
lemon slice to garnish
green salad to serve

1 Preheat the oven to 200°C (180°C fan oven) mark 6. Pour the cream into a large bowl. Add the fish stock and stir well to combine.

2 Add the potatoes, haddock, chives and onion and season with salt and pepper. Toss everything together to coat. Spoon the mixture into a shallow 2.4 litre (4¼ pint) ovenproof dish.

3 Cover the dish with foil, put it on a baking tray and cook for 45 minutes. Remove the foil and cook for 30–40 minutes until bubbling and the top is golden.

4 To check that the potatoes are cooked, insert a skewer or small knife – it should push in easily. If you like, you can put the dish under a hot grill to make the top layer crisp. Leave to cool slightly, then serve with a green salad.

 COOK'S TIP

For the lightest texture, make sure you use floury baking potatoes, as salad potatoes are too waxy.

Baked Salmon with Jersey Royals and Watercress Mayonnaise

Preparation Time 15 minutes • **Cooking Time** 50 minutes • **Serves 6** • **Per Serving** 560 calories, 41g fat (of which 7g saturates), 15g carbohydrate, 0.8g salt • **Gluten Free** • **Easy**

1 tsp fennel seeds (optional)
1 tsp rock salt
2 tbsp olive oil
450g (1lb) Jersey Royal potatoes, sliced thickly
6 skinless salmon fillets
6 slices prosciutto
150g (5oz) good-quality mayonnaise
75g (3oz) plain yogurt
juice of ½ lemon
40g (1½oz) watercress, finely chopped
1 tbsp capers, roughly chopped
300g (11oz) cherry tomatoes on the vine, cut into bunches
salt and ground black pepper
lemon wedges to serve

1 Preheat the oven to 200°C (180°C fan oven) mark 6. Crush the fennel seeds, if using, and the salt in a pestle and mortar. Put into a bowl with half the oil, then add the potatoes and toss. Layer the potatoes in a large roasting dish and cover with foil. Cook in the oven for 20 minutes.

2 Check the fish for stray bones, then season with salt and pepper. Wrap a slice of prosciutto around the middle of each fillet, making sure the seam is underneath.

3 Mix the mayonnaise with the yogurt and lemon juice. Stir in the watercress and capers and check the seasoning.

4 Remove the foil from the potatoes and continue cooking for 10 minutes or until they are almost tender. Arrange the tomatoes and fish on top of the potatoes, then sprinkle the fish with the remaining oil. Cook for 15–20 minutes.

5 Serve with the lemon mayonnaise and lemon wedges.

Navarin of Cod

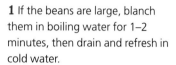

Preparation Time 15 minutes • **Cooking Time** 25 minutes • **Serves 6** • **Per Serving** 346 calories, 13g fat (of which 5g saturates), 16g carbohydrate, 0.4g salt • **Easy**

175g (6oz) podded broad beans
25g (1oz) butter
2 tbsp sunflower oil
1 onion, sliced
225g (8oz) baby carrots, trimmed and halved
225g (8oz) courgettes, cut into 2cm (¾in) chunks
1 garlic clove, crushed
1.1kg (2½lb) thick cod fillet or other white fish, such as pollack, skinned
4 tbsp plain flour
150ml (¼ pint) dry white wine
300ml (½ pint) fish stock

1 tbsp lemon juice
3 tbsp double cream
2 tbsp freshly chopped flat-leafed parsley
salt and ground black pepper
baby new potatoes to serve (optional)

1 If the beans are large, blanch them in boiling water for 1–2 minutes, then drain and refresh in cold water.

2 Heat half the butter and half the oil in a large sauté pan. Add the onion, carrots, courgettes and garlic and cook gently until softened and just beginning to brown. Remove from the pan and put to one side.

3 Season the fish with salt and pepper, then dust lightly with the flour. Heat the remaining butter and oil in the pan, add the fish and brown on all sides. Remove from the pan and put to one side.

4 Add the wine to the pan, scraping up any sediment from the bottom. Simmer for 1–2 minutes, then put the carrot mixture and fish back into the pan. Add the beans and stock. Bring to a simmer, then cover the pan and simmer gently for about 10 minutes or until the fish is opaque and flakes easily. Stir in the lemon juice, cream and parsley. Divide among six warmed bowls and serve with baby new potatoes, if you like.

Quick Crab Cakes

★

Preparation Time 15 minutes • **Cooking Time** 6 minutes • **Serves 4** • **Per Serving** 124 calories, 4g fat (of which 1g saturates), 12g carbohydrate, 0.9g salt • **Gluten Free** • **Dairy Free** • **Easy**

200g (7oz) fresh crabmeat
2 spring onions, finely chopped
2 red chillies, seeded and finely chopped (see page 19)
finely grated zest of 1 lime
4 tbsp freshly chopped coriander
about 40g (1½oz) stoneground wholemeal breadcrumbs
1 tbsp groundnut oil
1 tbsp plain flour
1 red chilli, thinly sliced, to garnish
1 lime, cut into wedges, and salad leaves to serve

1 Put the crabmeat into a bowl, then add the spring onions, chillies, lime zest and coriander and stir to mix. Add enough breadcrumbs to hold the mixture together, then form into four small patties.

2 Heat ½ tbsp oil in a pan. Dredge the patties with flour and fry on one side for 3 minutes. Add the rest of the oil, turn the patties over and fry for a further 2–3 minutes. Garnish the crab cakes with thinly sliced red chilli and serve with lime wedges to squeeze over them, and salad leaves.

Quick Pad Thai

Preparation Time 12 minutes, plus soaking • **Cooking Time** 8 minutes • **Serves 4** • **Per Serving** 451 calories, 13g fat (of which 3g saturates), 56g carbohydrate, 2.6g salt • **Dairy Free** • **Easy**

250g (9oz) wide ribbon rice noodles

3 tbsp satay and sweet chilli pesto (see Cook's Tips)

125g (4oz) mangetouts, thinly sliced

125g (4oz) sugarsnap peas, thinly sliced

3 medium eggs, beaten

3 tbsp chilli soy sauce, plus extra to serve (see Cook's Tips)

250g (9oz) cooked peeled tiger prawns

25g (1oz) dry-roasted peanuts, roughly crushed

lime wedges to serve (optional)

1 Put the noodles into a heatproof bowl, cover with boiling water and soak for 4 minutes or until softened. Drain, rinse under cold water and set aside.

2 Heat a wok or large frying pan until hot, add the chilli pesto and stir-fry for 1 minute. Add the mangetouts and sugarsnap peas and cook for a further 2 minutes. Tip into a bowl. Put the pan back on the heat, add the eggs and cook, stirring, for 1 minute.

3 Add the soy sauce, prawns and noodles to the pan. Toss well and cook for 3 minutes or until piping hot. Return the vegetables to the pan, cook for a further 1 minute or until heated through, then sprinkle with the peanuts. Serve with extra soy sauce and lime wedges to squeeze over, if you like.

★ COOK'S TIPS

● *If you can't find satay and sweet chilli pesto, substitute 2 tbsp peanut butter and 1 tbsp sweet chilli sauce.*

● *Chilli soy sauce can be replaced with 2 tbsp light soy sauce and $\frac{1}{2}$ red chilli, finely chopped (see page 19).*

Thai Fish in a Bag

★

Preparation Time 10 minutes • **Cooking Time** about 20 minutes • **Serves 4** • **Per Serving** 484 calories, 36g fat (of which 18g saturates), 9g carbohydrate, 0.4g salt • **Gluten Free** • **Dairy Free** • **Easy**

½ tbsp Thai red curry paste
2.5cm (1in) piece fresh root ginger, peeled and grated
100ml (3½fl oz) hot fish stock
200ml (7fl oz) coconut cream
4 × 125g (4oz) skinless salmon fillets, defrosted if frozen
1 yellow pepper, seeded and finely sliced
2 medium carrots, cut into thin strips
150g (5oz) broccoli, cut into small florets
a handful of coriander and lime wedges to serve

1 Preheat the oven to 200°C (180°C fan oven) mark 6. Fry the curry paste and ginger in a pan for 1 minute. Add the hot stock and coconut cream and mix well. Pour into a jug and cool slightly.

2 Cut out four 35.5cm (14in) squares of baking parchment and snip four 30.5cm (12in) lengths of string. Cut each salmon fillet into four pieces. Put a square of baking parchment over a small bowl and push down gently. Fill with a quarter each of the peppers, carrots and broccoli and top with four salmon pieces. Pour a quarter of the reserved liquid into each of the parcels.

3 Tie the parcel tightly using the string, leaving about 2.5cm (1in) space above the level of the salmon. Repeat with the other three parcels. Put into a roasting dish and cook in the oven for 15–20 minutes.

4 To serve, lift each parcel into a bowl, leaving them tied, so that everyone can unwrap them at the table. Serve with coriander and lime wedges.

Salmon with Black Bean Sauce

★

Preparation Time 15 minutes • **Cooking Time** about 15 minutes • **Serves 2** • **Per Serving** 265 calories, 17g fat (of which 3g saturates), 9g carbohydrate, 0.9g salt • **Gluten Free** • **Dairy Free** • **Easy**

1 tbsp sunflower oil

2 × 150g (5oz) salmon fillets, with skin on

2.5cm (1in) piece fresh root ginger, peeled and chopped into shards

2 spring onions, sliced into thick pieces

150g (5oz) chestnut mushrooms, sliced

2 heads pak choi, roughly chopped

4 tbsp black bean sauce

1 Heat half the oil in a wok or non-stick pan. Fry the salmon, skin side down, over a medium heat for 5 minutes. Turn and cook on the other side for 1 minute. Set aside on a plate – the salmon will continue to cook.

2 Heat the remaining oil in the same pan. Add the ginger, spring onions and mushrooms. Cook for 2–3 minutes over a medium heat until the mushrooms and spring onions begin to colour.

3 Add the pak choi, black bean sauce and 2 tbsp water to the wok and stir-fry for 2–3 minutes until the pak choi is cooked. Divide between two warmed plates and top with the salmon to serve.

Prawns in Yellow Bean Sauce

⭐

Preparation Time 10 minutes, plus standing • **Cooking Time** 5 minutes • **Serves 4** • **Per Serving** 394 calories, 10g fat (of which 2g saturates), 59g carbohydrate, 0.9g salt • **Dairy Free** • **Easy**

250g pack medium egg noodles
1 tbsp stir-fry oil or sesame oil
1 garlic clove, sliced
1 tsp freshly grated ginger
1 bunch of spring onions, each
    stem cut into four lengthways
250g (9oz) frozen raw peeled tiger
    prawns, thawed
200g (7oz) pak choi, leaves
    separated and the white base cut
    into thick slices
160g jar Chinese yellow bean
    stir-fry sauce

1 Put the noodles into a bowl, pour 2 litres (3½ pints) boiling water over them and leave to soak for 4 minutes. Drain and set aside.

2 Heat the oil in a wok over a medium heat. Add the garlic and ginger and stir-fry for 30 seconds. Add the spring onions and prawns and cook for 2 minutes.

3 Add the chopped white part of the pak choi and the yellow bean sauce. Fill the empty sauce jar with boiling water and pour this into the wok too.

4 Add the noodles to the pan and continue to cook for 1 minute, tossing every now and then to heat through. Finally, stir in the green pak choi leaves and serve immediately.

⭐ TRY SOMETHING DIFFERENT
Instead of prawns, use skinless chicken breast, cut into thin strips.

Prawns and Cucumber in a Spicy Sauce

Preparation Time 20 minutes, plus standing • **Cooking Time** 30 minutes • **Serves 4** • **Per Serving** 273 calories, 13g fat (of which 7g saturates), 27g carbohydrate, 2.5g salt • **Easy**

2 medium cucumbers, halved
  lengthways, seeded and cut into
  2.5cm (1in) chunks
50g (2oz) butter
2 onions, sliced
2 garlic cloves, finely chopped
4 tsp plain flour
2 tsp ground turmeric
1 tsp ground cinnamon
2 tsp sugar
½ tsp ground cloves
750ml (1¼ pints) coconut milk
300ml (½ pint) fish stock
15g (½oz) fresh root ginger, peeled
  and thinly sliced

3–4 green chillies, thinly sliced (see
  page 19)
450g (1lb) raw tiger prawns, peeled
  and deveined (see page 73)
grated zest and juice of 1 lime
2 tbsp freshly chopped coriander
salt

1 Put the cucumber into a colander set over a bowl and sprinkle with salt. Leave for 30 minutes, to allow the salt to extract the excess juices.

2 Melt the butter in a pan, add the onions and garlic and cook for about 5 minutes or until softened. Add the flour, turmeric, cinnamon, 1 tsp salt, the sugar and cloves and cook, stirring, for 2 minutes. Add the coconut milk and stock, bring to the boil, then reduce the heat, cover the pan and simmer for 5 minutes.

3 Meanwhile, rinse the cucumber thoroughly under cold running water to remove the salt. Add the cucumber, ginger and chillies to the sauce and cook for a further 10 minutes.

4 Add the prawns to the sauce and cook for a further 5–6 minutes until they turn pink.

5 Just before serving, stir in the lime juice and chopped coriander and sprinkle with lime zest.

★ COOK'S TIP
If raw prawns are difficult to find, use cooked ones instead. Add them to the sauce and heat through for 2–3 minutes – no longer or they will become rubbery.

Prawns with Okra

★

Preparation Time 25 minutes • **Cooking Time** 10 minutes • **Serves 4** • **Per Serving** 215 calories, 12g fat (of which 2g saturates), 5g carbohydrate, 0.5g salt • **Gluten Free** • **Dairy Free** • **Easy**

3 tbsp ghee or vegetable oil

2 red onions, thinly sliced

700g (1½lb) large raw prawns, peeled and deveined (see Cook's Tips)

450g (1lb) fresh small okra, trimmed (see Cook's Tips)

2 small green chillies, sliced (see page 19)

1 garlic clove (optional), sliced

2 tsp ground cumin

1 tbsp mustard seeds

3 medium ripe juicy tomatoes, cut into small wedges

squeeze of lemon juice to taste

2 tsp garam masala

3 tbsp coarsely grated fresh coconut or desiccated coconut, toasted

salt and ground black pepper

1 Heat the ghee or oil in a wok or large heavy-based frying pan. Add the onions and cook over a high heat until browned. Add the prawns, okra, chillies, garlic, if using, ground cumin and mustard seeds. Cook over a high heat, shaking the pan constantly, for 5 minutes or until the prawns are bright pink and the okra is softened but not soggy.

2 Add the tomato wedges and salt and pepper to taste. Cook for 1–2 minutes until heated through; the tomatoes should retain their shape. Add a little lemon juice to taste.

3 Tip the mixture into a serving dish and sprinkle with the garam masala and coconut. Serve immediately.

 ★ COOK'S TIPS

● *When trimming okra, snip only a tiny piece from each end. Avoid cutting into the flesh or the okra will become sticky and soggy during cooking.*

● *To devein prawns, pull off the head and discard (or put to one side and use later for making stock). Using pointed scissors, cut through the soft shell on the belly side. Prise off the shell, leaving the tail attached. (The shell can also be used later for making stock.) Using a small sharp knife, make a shallow cut along the back of the prawn. Using the point of the knife, remove and discard the black vein (the intestinal tract) that runs along the back of the prawn.*

Thai Noodles with Prawns

Preparation Time 10 minutes • **Cooking Time** 5 minutes • **Serves 4** • **Per Serving** 343 calories, 11g fat
(of which 2g saturates), 40g carbohydrate, 1g salt • **Dairy Free** • **Easy**

4–6 tsp Thai red curry paste
175g (6oz) medium egg noodles
  (wholewheat if possible)
2 small red onions, chopped
1 lemongrass stalk, trimmed and
  sliced
1 fresh red bird's-eye chilli, seeded
  and finely chopped (see page 19)
300ml (½ pint) reduced-fat coconut
  milk
400g (14oz) raw tiger prawns,
  peeled and deveined (see
  page 73)

4 tbsp freshly chopped coriander,
  plus extra freshly torn coriander
  to garnish
salt and ground black pepper

1 Put 2 litres (3½ pints) boiling
water into a large pan. Add the
curry paste, noodles, onions,
lemongrass, chilli and coconut milk.
Bring to the boil, then add the
prawns and chopped coriander.

2 Reduce the heat and simmer for
2–3 minutes until the prawns turn
pink. Season with salt and pepper.
Divide the noodles among four large
bowls and sprinkle with the torn
coriander.

★ COOK'S TIP
Don't overcook this dish or the noodles
will be soggy and the prawns tough.

Five-minute Stir-fry

Preparation Time 2 minutes • Cooking Time 5 minutes • Serves 2 • Per Serving 170 calories, 7g fat (of which 1g saturates), 11g carbohydrate, 1.6g salt • **Gluten Free** • **Dairy Free** • **Easy**

1 tbsp sesame oil
175g (6oz) raw peeled tiger prawns, deveined (see page 73)
50ml (2fl oz) ready-made sweet chilli and ginger sauce
225g (8oz) ready-prepared mixed stir-fry vegetables, such as sliced courgettes, broccoli and green beans

1 Heat the oil in a large wok or frying pan, add the prawns and sweet chilli and ginger sauce and stir-fry for 2 minutes.

2 Add the mixed vegetables and stir-fry for a further 2–3 minutes until the prawns are cooked and the vegetables are heated through. Serve immediately.

★ TRY SOMETHING DIFFERENT
Instead of prawns, try chicken cut into strips; stir-fry for 5 minutes in step 1.

Scallops with Ginger

★

Preparation Time 15 minutes • **Cooking Time** 3 minutes • **Serves 4** • **Per Serving** 197 calories, 7g fat (of which 1g saturates), 6g carbohydrate, 2g salt • **Dairy Free** • **Easy**

2 tbsp vegetable oil

500g (1lb 2oz) shelled large scallops, cut into 5mm (¼in) slices

4 celery sticks, sliced diagonally

1 bunch of spring onions, sliced diagonally

25g (1oz) piece fresh root ginger, peeled and sliced

2 large garlic cloves, sliced

¼ tsp chilli powder

2 tbsp lemon juice

2 tbsp light soy sauce

3 tbsp freshly chopped coriander

salt and ground black pepper

1 Heat the oil in a wok or large frying pan. Add the scallops, celery, spring onions, ginger, garlic and chilli powder and stir-fry over a high heat for 2 minutes or until the vegetables are just tender.

2 Pour in the lemon juice and soy sauce, allow to bubble up, then stir in about 2 tbsp chopped coriander and season with salt and pepper. Serve immediately, sprinkled with the remaining coriander.

Stir-fried Prawns with Cabbage

Preparation Time 30 minutes • **Cooking Time** 5–7 minutes • **Serves 4** • **Per Serving** 193 calories, 8g fat (of which 1g saturates), 7g carbohydrate, 1.4g salt • **Gluten Free** • **Dairy Free** • **Easy**

2 tbsp vegetable oil
2 garlic cloves, thinly sliced
1 lemongrass stalk, trimmed, halved and bruised
2 kaffir lime leaves, finely torn
1 small red onion, thinly sliced
1 hot red chilli, seeded and sliced (see page 19)
4cm (1½in) piece fresh root ginger, peeled and cut into long thin shreds
1 tbsp coriander seeds, lightly crushed
450g (1lb) large raw peeled prawns, deveined (see page 73)
175g (6oz) mangetouts, halved
225g (8oz) pak choi or Chinese mustard cabbage (see Cook's Tip), torn into bite-size pieces
2 tbsp Thai fish sauce
juice of 1 lime, or to taste

1 Heat the oil in a wok or large frying pan. Add the garlic, lemongrass, lime leaves, onion, chilli, ginger and coriander seeds and stir-fry for 2 minutes.

2 Add the prawns, mangetouts and pak choi or cabbage and stir-fry until the vegetables are cooked but still crisp and the prawns are pink and opaque, about 2–3 minutes.

3 Add the fish sauce and lime juice and cook for 1 minute or until heated through. Remove the lemongrass and discard; serve immediately.

★ COOK'S TIP
Chinese mustard cabbage, otherwise called mustard greens, is a green or red Oriental leaf that has a mild mustard flavour.

Thai Red Seafood Curry

.... ★

Preparation Time 15 minutes • **Cooking Time** 8–10 minutes • **Serves 4** • **Per Serving** 252 calories, 8g fat (of which 1g saturates), 9g carbohydrate, 2.2g salt • **Gluten Free** • **Dairy Free** • **Easy**

1 tbsp vegetable oil
3 tbsp Thai red curry paste
450g (1lb) monkfish tail, boned to make 350g (12oz) fillet, sliced into rounds
350g (12oz) large raw peeled prawns, deveined (see page 73)
400ml can half-fat coconut milk
200ml (7fl oz) fish stock
juice of 1 lime
1–2 tbsp Thai fish sauce
125g (4oz) mangetouts
3 tbsp fresh coriander, roughly torn
salt and ground black pepper
1 red chilli, seeded and finely sliced, to garnish

1 Heat the oil in a wok or large non-stick frying pan. Add the curry paste and cook for 1–2 minutes.

2 Add the monkfish and prawns and stir well to coat in the curry paste. Add the coconut milk, stock, lime juice and fish sauce, stir all the ingredients together and bring just to the boil.

3 Add the mangetouts, reduce the heat and simmer for 5 minutes or until the mangetouts and fish are tender. Stir in the coriander and check the seasoning, adding salt and pepper to taste. Garnish with the chilli and serve immediately.

★ COOK'S TIP
If you can't find half-fat coconut milk, use half a can of full-fat coconut milk and make up the difference with water or stock. Freeze the remaining milk for up to one month.

Chinese-style Fish

★

Preparation Time 5 minutes • **Cooking Time** 10 minutes • **Serves 4** • **Per Serving** 150 calories, 3g fat
(of which 1g saturates), 10g carbohydrate, 0.7g salt • **Gluten Free** • **Dairy Free** • **Easy**

2 tsp sunflower oil
1 small onion, finely chopped
1 green chilli, seeded and finely
   chopped (see page 19)
2 courgettes, thinly sliced
125g (4oz) frozen peas (defrosted)
350g (12oz) skinless haddock fillet,
   cut into bite-size pieces
2 tsp lemon juice
4 tbsp hoisin sauce
lime wedges to serve

1 Heat the oil in a large non-stick frying pan. Add the onion, chilli, courgettes and peas. Stir over a high heat for 5 minutes or until the onion and courgettes begin to soften.

2 Add the fish to the pan with the lemon juice, hoisin sauce and 150ml (¼ pint) water. Bring to the boil, then reduce the heat and simmer, uncovered, for 2–3 minutes until the fish is cooked through. Serve with lime wedges.

★ TRY SOMETHING DIFFERENT
There are plenty of alternatives to haddock: try sea bass, sea bream or gurnard.

Chicken

One-pot Chicken

★

Preparation Time 20 minutes • **Cooking Time** 1 hour 40 minutes • **Serves 6** • **Per Serving** 474 calories, 33g fat (of which 9g saturates), 6g carbohydrate, 0.6g salt • **Dairy Free** • **Easy**

2 tbsp olive oil
1 large onion, cut into wedges
2 rindless streaky bacon rashers, chopped
1 chicken, about 1.6kg (3½lb)
6 carrots
2 small turnips, cut into wedges
1 garlic clove, crushed
bouquet garni (1 bay leaf, a few fresh parsley and thyme sprigs)
600ml (1 pint) hot chicken stock
100ml (3½fl oz) dry white wine
12 button mushrooms
3 tbsp freshly chopped flat-leafed parsley
salt and ground black pepper
mashed potatoes to serve (optional)

1 Heat the oil in a non-stick flameproof casserole, then add the onion and bacon and fry for 5 minutes or until golden. Remove and set aside.

2 Add the whole chicken to the casserole and fry for 10 minutes, turning carefully to brown all over. Remove and set aside.

3 Preheat the oven to 200°C (180°C fan oven) mark 6. Add the carrots, turnips and garlic to the casserole. Fry for 5 minutes, then add the bacon and onion. Put the chicken back into the casserole, add the bouquet garni, hot stock and wine and season with salt and pepper. Bring to a simmer, then cover the pan and cook in the oven for 30 minutes.

4 Remove the casserole from the oven and add the mushrooms. Baste the chicken, then re-cover and cook for a further 50 minutes.

5 Lift out the chicken, then stir the parsley into the cooking liquid. Carve the chicken and serve with the vegetables and cooking liquid, and mashed potatoes, if you like.

★ TRY SOMETHING DIFFERENT
Use chicken pieces such as drumsticks or thighs, reducing the cooking time in step 4 to 20 minutes.

One-pan Chicken with Tomatoes

Preparation Time 5 minutes • **Cooking Time** 20–25 minutes • **Serves 4** • **Per Serving** 238 calories, 4g fat (of which 1g saturates), 20g carbohydrate, 1g salt • **Gluten Free** • **Dairy Free** • **Easy**

4 chicken thighs
1 red onion, sliced
400g can chopped tomatoes with
    herbs
400g can mixed beans, drained and
    rinsed
2 tsp balsamic vinegar
freshly chopped flat-leafed parsley
    to garnish

1 Heat a non-stick pan and fry the chicken thighs, skin side down, until golden. Turn over and fry for 5 minutes.

2 Add the onion and fry for 5 minutes. Add the tomatoes, mixed beans and vinegar, cover the pan and simmer for 10–12 minutes until piping hot. Garnish with parsley and serve immediately.

★ TRY SOMETHING DIFFERENT
Use flageolet beans or other canned beans instead of mixed beans, and garnish with fresh basil or oregano.

Lemon Chicken

★

Preparation Time 2 minutes • **Cooking Time** 6–8 minutes • **Serves 4** • **Per Serving** 231 calories, 7g fat (of which 1g saturates), 13g carbohydrate, 0.2g salt • **Gluten Free** • **Dairy Free** • **Easy**

4 small boneless, skinless chicken breasts, about 125g (4oz) each, cut into chunky strips
juice of 2 lemons
2 tbsp olive oil
4–6 tbsp demerara sugar
salt
green salad to serve

1 Put the chicken into a large bowl and season with salt. Add the lemon juice and oil and stir to mix.

2 Preheat the grill to medium. Spread out the chicken on a large baking sheet and sprinkle with 2–3 tbsp demerara sugar. Grill for 3–4 minutes until caramelised, then turn the chicken over, sprinkle with the remaining sugar and grill until the chicken is cooked through and golden.

3 Divide the chicken among four plates and serve with a green salad.

Chicken with Green Olives and Lemons

Preparation Time 15 minutes • Cooking Time about 1 hour 20 minutes • Serves 6 • Per Serving 347 calories, 22g fat (of which 5g saturates), 7g carbohydrate, 0.9g salt • **Dairy Free** • **Easy**

½ tsp each ground turmeric, ginger and coriander

1½ tbsp plain flour

6 chicken legs, with skin on

2 tbsp olive oil

1 medium onion, roughly chopped

1 garlic clove, thinly sliced

100ml (3½fl oz) manzanilla or fino sherry

900ml (1½ pints) hot chicken stock

3 preserved lemons

75g (3oz) green olives, sliced

juice of ½ lemon

salt and ground black pepper

1 Put the spices and flour into a polythene bag and season. Add the chicken and shake until covered with the flour mixture. Shake off the excess and set aside any leftover flour.

2 Heat 1 tbsp oil in a large flameproof casserole over a medium heat. Fry the chicken in batches until golden. Avoid overcrowding the pan, as it will lower the temperature and the chicken won't brown. Remove the chicken and set aside.

3 Put the remaining oil into the same pan and cook the onion over a low heat for 10 minutes. Add the garlic and cook for 1 minute. Turn up the heat to medium and add the leftover flour. Cook for 1 minute, stirring to soak up the oil. Scrape up any browned bits from the base of the pan – these will add flavour. Gradually stir in the sherry (it will bubble and thicken), followed by the hot stock.

4 Halve the lemons, scrape out the pulp and discard. Add the peel to the pan along with the chicken. Cover the pan and simmer over a low heat for 30 minutes. Stir in the olives and cook for 15 minutes or until the chicken is done – the juices should run clear when you pierce the flesh with a knife.

5 Remove the chicken, olives, onions and lemons with a slotted spoon (don't worry if you leave some onion behind) and keep them warm. Turn up the heat and boil the sauce rapidly until it reduces by about one-third and turns syrupy. Taste and add more seasoning if it needs it, along with the lemon juice.

6 Return the chicken, olives, onion and lemons to the casserole and serve from the dish.

 COOK'S TIP

If you have leftover preserved lemons, the next time you roast a whole chicken pop a couple inside the bird along with a few thyme sprigs.

Tarragon Chicken with Fennel

Preparation Time 10 minutes • **Cooking Time** 45–55 minutes • **Serves 4** • **Per Serving** 334 calories, 26g fat (of which 15g saturates), 3g carbohydrate, 0.5g salt • **Easy**

1 tbsp olive oil

4 chicken thighs

1 onion, finely chopped

1 fennel bulb, finely chopped

juice of ½ lemon

200ml (7fl oz) hot chicken stock

200ml (7fl oz) crème fraîche

a small bunch of tarragon, roughly chopped

salt and ground black pepper

1 Preheat the oven to 200°C (180°C fan oven) mark 6. Heat the oil in a large flameproof casserole over a medium to high heat. Add the chicken thighs and fry for 5 minutes or until browned, then remove and put them to one side to keep warm.

2 Add the onion to the pan and fry for 5 minutes, then add the fennel and cook for 5–10 minutes until softened.

3 Add the lemon juice to the pan, followed by the hot stock. Bring to a simmer and cook until the sauce is reduced by half.

4 Stir in the crème fraîche and put the chicken back into the pan. Stir once to mix, then cover and cook in the oven for 25–30 minutes. Stir the tarragon into the sauce, season with salt and pepper and serve.

Chicken and Vegetable Hotpot

★

Preparation Time 5 minutes • **Cooking Time** 30 minutes • **Serves 4** • **Per Serving** 338 calories, 14g fat
(of which 3g saturates), 14g carbohydrate, 1.2g salt • **Dairy Free** • **Easy**

**4 chicken breasts, with skin on,
    about 125g (4oz) each
2 large parsnips, chopped
2 large carrots, chopped
300ml (½ pint) ready-made gravy
125g (4oz) cabbage, shredded
ground black pepper**

1 Heat a non-stick frying pan or flameproof casserole until hot. Add the chicken breasts, skin side down, and cook for 5–6 minutes. Turn them over, add the parsnips and carrots and cook for a further 7–8 minutes.

2 Pour the gravy over the chicken and vegetables, then cover the pan and cook gently for 10 minutes.

3 Season with pepper and stir in the cabbage, then cover and continue to cook for 4–5 minutes until the chicken is cooked through, the cabbage has wilted and the vegetables are tender. Serve hot.

Oven-baked Chicken with Garlic Potatoes

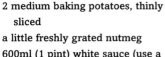

Preparation Time 10 minutes • **Cooking Time** 1½ hours • **Serves 6** • **Per Serving** 376 calories, 16g fat (of which 5g saturates), 32g carbohydrate, 1.2g salt • **Easy**

2 medium baking potatoes, thinly
   sliced
a little freshly grated nutmeg
600ml (1 pint) white sauce (use a
   ready-made sauce or make your
   own, see Cook's Tip)
½ × 390g can fried onions
250g (9oz) frozen peas
450g (1lb) cooked chicken,
   shredded
20g pack garlic butter, sliced
a little butter to grease
salt and ground black pepper
Granary bread to serve (optional)

1 Preheat the oven to 180°C (160°C fan oven) mark 4. Layer half the potatoes over the base of a 2.4 litre (4¼ pint) shallow ovenproof dish and season with the nutmeg, salt and pepper. Pour the white sauce over and shake the dish, so that the sauce settles through the gaps in the potatoes.

2 Spread half the onions on top, then scatter on half the peas. Arrange the shredded chicken on top, then add the remaining peas and onions. Finish with the remaining potatoes, arranged in an even layer, and dot with garlic butter. Season with salt and pepper.

3 Cover tightly with buttered foil and cook for 1 hour. Turn up the heat to 200°C (180°C fan oven) mark 6, remove the foil and continue to cook for 20–30 minutes until the potatoes are golden and tender. Serve with Granary bread, if you like, to mop up the juices.

⭐ COOK'S TIP
White Sauce
To make 600ml (1 pint) white sauce, melt 25g (1oz) butter in a pan, then stir in 25g (1oz) plain flour. Cook, stirring constantly, for 1 minute. Remove from the heat and gradually pour in 600ml (1 pint) milk, beating after each addition. Return to the heat and cook, stirring, until the sauce has thickened and is velvety and smooth. Season with salt, black pepper and freshly grated nutmeg.

Herb Chicken with Roasted Vegetables

★

Preparation Time 15 minutes, plus marinating • **Cooking Time** 40 minutes • **Serves 4** • **Per Serving** 453 calories, 29g fat (of which 7g saturates), 10g carbohydrate, 0.3g salt • **Gluten Free** • **Dairy Free** • **Easy**

2 garlic cloves
25g (1oz) fresh basil
25g (1oz) fresh mint
8 fresh lemon thyme sprigs
4 tbsp olive oil
4 whole chicken legs (drumsticks and thighs)
1 small aubergine, chopped
200g (7oz) baby plum tomatoes
2 red peppers, seeded and chopped
2 courgettes, sliced
juice of 1 lemon
salt and ground black pepper
green salad to serve

1 Put the garlic, two-thirds of the basil and mint and the leaves from 4 lemon thyme sprigs into a food processor and whiz, adding half the oil gradually until the mixture forms a thick paste. (Alternatively, use a mortar and pestle.)

2 Rub the paste over the chicken legs, then put into a bowl. Cover, then chill and leave to marinate for at least 30 minutes.

3 Preheat the oven to 200°C (180°C fan oven) mark 6. Put the aubergine, plum tomatoes, red peppers and courgettes into a large roasting tin with the remaining oil and season with salt and pepper. Toss to coat. Add the chicken and roast for 30–40 minutes until the vegetables are tender and the chicken cooked through.

4 Squeeze the lemon juice over and stir in the remaining herbs. Serve immediately with a crisp green salad.

Chicken Tarragon Burgers

Preparation Time 30 minutes, plus chilling • **Cooking Time** 12 minutes • **Serves 2** • **Per Serving** 205 calories, 4g fat (of which 1g saturates), 12g carbohydrate, 0.4g salt • **Dairy Free** • **Easy**

225g (8oz) minced chicken
2 shallots, finely chopped
1 tbsp freshly chopped tarragon
25g (1oz) fresh breadcrumbs
1 large egg yolk
vegetable oil to grease
salt and ground black pepper
toasted burger buns, mayonnaise or
   Greek yogurt, salad leaves and
   tomato salad to serve

1 Put the chicken into a bowl with the shallots, tarragon, breadcrumbs and egg yolk. Mix well, then beat in about 75ml (2½fl oz) cold water and season with salt and pepper.

2 Lightly oil a foil-lined baking sheet. Divide the chicken mixture into two or four portions (depending on how large you want the burgers) and put on the foil. Using the back of a wet spoon, flatten each portion to a thickness of 2.5cm (1in). Cover and chill for 30 minutes.

3 Preheat the barbecue or grill. If cooking on the barbecue, lift the burgers straight on to the grill rack; if cooking under the grill, slide the baking sheet under the grill. Cook the burgers for 5–6 minutes on each side until cooked through, then serve in a toasted burger bun with a dollop of mayonnaise or Greek yogurt, a few salad leaves and tomato salad.

★ TRY SOMETHING DIFFERENT
Pork and Apricot Burgers
Replace the chicken with minced pork, use freshly chopped sage instead of tarragon, and add 100g (3½oz) chopped ready-to-eat dried apricots to the mixture before shaping.

Turkey and Bean Stew

Preparation Time 15 minutes • **Cooking Time** 30 minutes • **Serves 4** • **Per Serving** 218 calories, 6g fat (of which 2g saturates), 21g carbohydrate, 1.3g salt • **Gluten Free** • **Easy**

1 tbsp olive oil
1 medium onion, finely chopped
2 celery sticks, chopped
2 medium carrots, sliced
900ml (1½ pints) hot chicken stock
200g (7oz) turkey strips
2 rosemary sprigs – one whole and
    the leaves of one finely chopped
1 bay leaf
400g can butter beans, drained and
    rinsed
¼ savoy cabbage, finely shredded
salt and ground black pepper
25g (1oz) Parmesan shavings,
    to garnish

1 Heat the oil in a large pan. Gently fry the onion, celery and carrots for 10 minutes until softened. Pour in the hot stock, then add the turkey, whole rosemary sprig and bay leaf. Season, then bring to the boil. Reduce the heat and simmer for 15 minutes.

2 Mash half the butter beans with a fork. Stir the mashed and whole butter beans and the cabbage into the pan and simmer for 3 minutes. Check the seasoning; remove the bay leaf and rosemary.

3 Divide among four warmed bowls and garnish with rosemary leaves and the Parmesan.

★ COOK'S TIP
The healthiest and cheapest way of bulking up a dish is to add beans. Stars of the pulse world, butter beans are rich in fibre, which keeps you feeling fuller for longer.

Jambalaya

Preparation Time 15 minutes • **Cooking Time** about 50 minutes, plus standing • **Serves 4** • **Per Serving** 558 calories, 25g fat (of which 6g saturates), 49g carbohydrate, 0g salt • **Gluten Free** • **Dairy Free** • **Easy**

2 tbsp olive oil
300g (11oz) boneless, skinless
    chicken thighs, cut into chunks
75g (3oz) French sausage, such as
    saucisse sèche, chopped
2 celery sticks, chopped
1 large onion, finely chopped
225g (8oz) long-grain rice
1 tbsp tomato purée
2 tsp Cajun spice mix
500ml (18fl oz) hot chicken stock
1 bay leaf
4 large tomatoes, roughly chopped
200g (7oz) raw tiger prawns, peeled
    and deveined (see page 73)

1 Heat 1 tbsp oil in a large pan and fry the chicken and sausage over a medium heat until browned. Remove with a slotted spoon and set aside.

2 Add the remaining oil to the pan with the celery and onion. Fry gently for 15 minutes or until the vegetables are softened but not coloured. Tip in the rice and stir for 1 minute to coat in the oil. Add the tomato purée and spice mix and cook for another 2 minutes.

3 Pour in the hot stock and return the browned chicken and sausage to the pan with the bay leaf and tomatoes. Simmer for 20–25 minutes until the stock has been fully absorbed and the rice is cooked.

4 Stir in the prawns and cover the pan. Leave to stand for 10 minutes or until the prawns have turned pink. Serve immediately.

Classic Paella

Preparation Time 15 minutes, plus infusing • **Cooking Time** 50 minutes • **Serves 6** • **Per Serving** 554 calories, 16g fat (of which 3g saturates), 58g carbohydrate, 0.5g salt • **Dairy Free** • **A Little Effort**

1 litre (1¾ pints) chicken stock
½ tsp saffron threads
6 boneless, skinless chicken thighs
5 tbsp extra virgin olive oil
1 large onion, chopped
4 large garlic cloves, crushed
1 tsp paprika
2 red peppers, seeded and sliced
400g can chopped tomatoes
350g (12oz) long-grain rice
200ml (7fl oz) dry sherry
500g (1lb 2oz) cooked mussels
200g (7oz) cooked tiger prawns
juice of ½ lemon
salt and ground black pepper
lemon wedges and fresh flat-leafed
  parsley to serve

1 Heat the stock, then add the saffron and leave to infuse for 30 minutes. Meanwhile, cut each chicken thigh into three pieces.

2 Heat half the oil in a large frying pan and, working in batches, fry the chicken for 3–5 minutes until pale golden brown. Set the chicken aside.

3 Reduce the heat slightly and add the remaining oil. Fry the onion for 5 minutes or until soft. Add the garlic and paprika and stir for 1 minute. Add the chicken, red peppers and tomatoes.

4 Stir in the rice, then add one-third of the stock and bring to the boil. Season with salt and pepper.

5 Reduce the heat to a simmer. Cook, uncovered, stirring continuously, until most of the liquid is absorbed.

6 Add the remaining stock a little at a time, letting it become absorbed into the rice before adding more – this should take about 25 minutes. Add the sherry and continue cooking for another 2 minutes – the rice should be quite wet, as it will continue to absorb liquid.

7 Add the mussels and prawns to the pan, including all their juices, with the lemon juice. Stir them in and cook for 5 minutes to heat through. Adjust the seasoning, then garnish with lemon wedges and fresh parsley and serve.

Spiced Chicken Pilau

Preparation Time 15 minutes • **Cooking Time** 35–40 minutes • **Serves 4** • **Per Serving** 649 calories, 18g fat (of which 2g saturates), 87g carbohydrate, 2.8g salt • **Dairy Free** • **Easy**

50g (2oz) pinenuts
2 tbsp olive oil
2 onions, sliced
2 garlic cloves, crushed
2 tbsp medium curry powder
6 boneless, skinless chicken thighs or 450g (1lb) skinless cooked chicken, cut into strips
350g (12oz) American easy-cook rice
2 tsp salt
a pinch of saffron threads
50g (2oz) sultanas
225g (8oz) ripe tomatoes, roughly chopped

1 Spread the pinenuts over a baking sheet and toast under a hot grill until golden brown, turning them frequently. Put to one side.

2 Heat the oil in a large heavy-based pan over a medium heat. Add the onions and garlic and cook for 5 minutes or until soft. Remove half the onion mixture and put to one side.

3 Add the curry powder and cook for 1 minute, then add the chicken and stir. Cook for 10 minutes if the meat is raw, or for 4 minutes if you're using cooked chicken, stirring from time to time until browned.

4 Add the rice to the pan and stir to coat in the oil, then add 900ml (1½ pints) boiling water, the salt and saffron. Cover the pan and bring to the boil, then reduce the heat to low and cook for 20 minutes or until the rice is tender and most of the liquid has been absorbed. Stir in the reserved onion mixture and the sultanas, tomatoes and pinenuts. Cook for a further 5 minutes to warm through, then serve.

 COOK'S TIP
This is a good way to use leftover roast turkey.

Saffron Paella

★

Preparation Time 5 minutes, plus infusing • **Cooking Time** 20 minutes • **Serves 6** • **Per Serving** 609 calories, 22g fat (of which 6g saturates), 59g carbohydrate, 1.5g salt • **Dairy Free** • **Easy**

½ tsp saffron threads
900ml–1.1 litres (1½–2 pints) hot chicken stock
5 tbsp olive oil
2 × 70g packs sliced chorizo sausage
6 boneless, skinless chicken thighs, each cut into three pieces
1 large onion, chopped
4 large garlic cloves, crushed
1 tsp paprika
2 red peppers, seeded and sliced
400g can chopped tomatoes in tomato juice
350g (12oz) long-grain rice
200ml (7fl oz) dry sherry
500g pack ready-cooked mussels
200g (7oz) cooked tiger prawns, drained
juice of ½ lemon
salt and ground black pepper
fresh flat-leafed parsley sprigs to garnish (optional)
lemon wedges to serve

1 Add the saffron to the hot stock and leave to infuse for 30 minutes. Meanwhile, heat half the oil in a large heavy-based frying pan. Add half the chorizo and fry for 3–4 minutes until crisp. Remove with a slotted spoon and drain on kitchen paper. Repeat with the remaining chorizo; put to one side.

2 Heat 1 tbsp oil in the pan, add half the chicken and cook for 3–5 minutes until pale golden brown. Remove from the pan and put to one side. Cook the remaining chicken and put to one side.

3 Reduce the heat slightly, heat the remaining oil and add the onion. Cook for 5 minutes or until soft. Add the garlic and paprika and cook for 1 minute. Put the chicken back into the pan, then add the peppers and the tomatoes.

4 Stir the rice into the pan, then add one-third of the stock and bring to the boil. Season with salt and pepper, reduce the heat and simmer, uncovered, stirring continuously until most of the liquid has been absorbed.

5 Add the remaining stock, a little at a time, allowing the liquid to become absorbed after each addition (this should take about 25 minutes). Add the sherry and cook for a further 2 minutes.

6 Add the mussels and their juices to the pan with the prawns, lemon juice and reserved chorizo. Cook for 5 minutes to heat through. Adjust the seasoning, then garnish with the parsley, if you like, and serve with lemon wedges.

Moroccan Chicken with Chickpeas

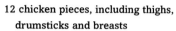

Preparation Time 10 minutes • **Cooking Time** 50 minutes • **Serves 6** • **Per Serving** 440 calories, 18g fat (of which 6g saturates), 33g carbohydrate, 1g salt • **Easy**

12 chicken pieces, including thighs, drumsticks and breasts
25g (1oz) butter
1 large onion, sliced
2 garlic cloves, crushed
2 tbsp harissa paste
a generous pinch of saffron threads
1 tsp salt
1 cinnamon stick
600ml (1 pint) chicken stock
75g (3oz) raisins
2 × 400g cans chickpeas, drained and rinsed
ground black pepper
plain naan or pitta bread to serve

1 Heat a large wide non-stick pan. Add the chicken pieces and fry until well browned all over. Add the butter and, when melted, add the onion and garlic. Cook, stirring, for 5 minutes.

2 Add the harissa, saffron, salt and cinnamon stick, then season well with pepper. Pour in the stock and bring to the boil. Reduce the heat, cover the pan and simmer gently for 25–30 minutes.

3 Add the raisins and chickpeas and bring to the boil, then reduce the heat and simmer uncovered for 5–10 minutes.

4 Serve with warm flatbread such as plain naan or pitta.

★ FREEZING TIP
To freeze *Freeze leftover portions separately. Complete the recipe, then cool quickly. Put into a sealable container and freeze for up to three months.*
To use *Thaw overnight in the fridge. Put into a pan, cover and bring to the boil. Reduce the heat to low, then reheat for 40 minutes or until the chicken is hot right through.*

Fiery Mango Chicken

Preparation Time 15 minutes, plus marinating • Cooking Time 10 minutes • Serves 4 • Per Serving 220 calories, 8g fat (of which 2g saturates), 7g carbohydrate, 0.3g salt • **Gluten Free** • **Easy**

4 tbsp hot mango chutney (or ordinary mango chutney, plus ½ tsp Tabasco)
grated zest and juice of 1 lime
4 tbsp natural yogurt
2 tbsp freshly chopped coriander
1 small green chilli (optional), seeded and finely chopped (see page 19)
4 chicken breasts, with skin on
1 large ripe mango, peeled and stoned
oil to brush
salt and ground black pepper
fresh coriander sprigs and lime wedges to garnish

1 Mix together the chutney, lime zest and juice, yogurt, chopped coriander and, if you like it spicy, the finely chopped chilli.

2 Put the chicken breasts, skin side down, on the worksurface, cover with clingfilm and lightly beat with a rolling pin. Slice each into three pieces and put into the yogurt mixture; stir to coat. Cover and chill for at least 30 minutes or overnight.

3 Preheat the barbecue or grill. Slice the mango into four thick pieces. Brush lightly with oil and season well with salt and pepper. Barbecue or grill for about 2 minutes on each side – the fruit should be lightly charred but still firm. Put to one side.

4 Barbecue or grill the chicken for 3–5 minutes on each side until golden. Serve with the grilled mango, garnished with coriander sprigs and lime wedges.

Spanish Chicken Parcels

Preparation Time 15 minutes • **Cooking Time** about 30 minutes • **Serves 6** • **Per Serving** 444 calories, 29g fat (of which 9g saturates), 4g carbohydrate, 3.1g salt • **Gluten Free** • **Dairy Free** • **Easy**

12 boneless, skinless chicken thighs, about 900g (2lb)
180g jar pimientos or roasted red peppers, drained
12 thin slices chorizo sausage
2 tbsp olive oil
1 onion, finely chopped
4 garlic cloves, crushed
225g can chopped tomatoes
4 tbsp dry sherry
18 queen green olives (see Cook's Tip)
salt and ground black pepper
crusty bread to serve

1 Put the chicken thighs on a board, season well with salt and pepper and put a piece of pimiento or roasted pepper inside each one. Wrap a slice of chorizo around the outside and secure with two cocktail sticks. Set aside.

2 Heat the oil in a pan over a medium heat and fry the onion for 10 minutes. Add the garlic and cook for 1 minute. Put the chicken parcels, chorizo side down, into the pan and brown them all over for 10–15 minutes.

3 Add the tomatoes and sherry to the pan and bring to the boil. Simmer for 5 minutes or until the juices run clear when the chicken is pierced with a skewer. Add the olives and warm through. Remove the cocktail sticks and serve with crusty bread.

★ COOK'S TIP
Queen green olives are large, meaty olives with a mild flavour. Remember to tell people the olives still have stones.

Spiced One-pot Chicken

★

Preparation Time 10 minutes, plus marinating • **Cooking Time** 1 hour 10 minutes • **Serves 6** • **Per Serving** 604 calories, 36g fat (of which 10g saturates), 20g carbohydrate, 0.5g salt • **Gluten Free** • **Dairy Free** • **Easy**

3 tbsp Thai red curry paste
150ml (¼ pint) orange juice
2 garlic cloves, crushed
6 chicken pieces, 2.3kg (5lb) total weight, with bone in
700g (1½lb) squash or pumpkin, peeled and cut into 5cm (2in) cubes
5 red onions, quartered
2 tbsp capers, drained and chopped
salt and ground black pepper

1 Combine the curry paste, orange juice and garlic in a bowl. Put the chicken pieces in the marinade and leave to marinate for 15 minutes.

2 Preheat the oven to 220°C (200°C fan oven) mark 7. Put the vegetables into a large roasting tin, then remove the chicken from the marinade and arrange on top of the vegetables. Pour the marinade over and season with salt and pepper. Mix everything together to cover with the marinade, then scatter with the capers.

3 Cook for 1 hour 10 minutes, turning from time to time, or until the chicken is cooked through and the skin is golden.

★ GET AHEAD

To prepare ahead *Complete the recipe to the end of step 2. Cover and chill for up to one day.*
To use *Complete the recipe, but cook for a further 5–10 minutes.*

Sticky Chicken Thighs

Preparation Time 5 minutes • **Cooking Time** 20 minutes • **Serves 4** • **Per Serving** 218 calories, 12g fat (of which 3g saturates), 5g carbohydrate, 0.4g salt • **Gluten Free** • **Dairy Free** • **Easy**

1 garlic clove, crushed
1 tbsp clear honey
1 tbsp Thai sweet chilli sauce
4 chicken thighs
rice (optional) and green salad
    to serve

1 Preheat the oven to 200°C (180°C fan oven) mark 6. Put the garlic into a bowl with the honey and chilli sauce and stir to mix. Add the chicken thighs and toss to coat.

2 Put into a roasting tin and roast for 15–20 minutes until the chicken is golden and cooked through. Serve with rice, if you like, and a crisp green salad.

⭐ TRY SOMETHING DIFFERENT
Try this with sausages instead of the chicken.
Italian Marinade
Mix 1 crushed garlic clove with 4 tbsp olive oil, the juice of 1 lemon and 1 tsp dried oregano. If you like, leave to marinate for 1–2 hours before cooking.
Oriental Marinade
Mix together 2 tbsp soy sauce, 1 tsp demerara sugar, 2 tbsp dry sherry or apple juice, 1 tsp finely chopped fresh root ginger and 1 crushed garlic clove.
Honey and Mustard Marinade
Mix together 2 tbsp grain mustard, 3 tbsp clear honey and the grated zest and juice of 1 lemon.

Caribbean Chicken

Preparation Time 40 minutes, plus marinating • Cooking Time 45–50 minutes • Serves 5 • Per Serving 617 calories, 39g fat (of which 12g saturates), 25g carbohydrate, 2.1g salt • Easy

10 chicken pieces, such as thighs, drumsticks, wings or breasts, skinned
1 tsp salt
1 tbsp ground coriander
2 tsp ground cumin
1 tbsp paprika
a pinch of ground nutmeg
1 fresh Scotch bonnet or other hot red chilli, seeded and chopped (see page 19)
1 onion, chopped
5 fresh thyme sprigs
4 garlic cloves, crushed
2 tbsp dark soy sauce
juice of 1 lemon
2 tbsp vegetable oil
2 tbsp light muscovado sugar
350g (12oz) American easy-cook rice
3 tbsp dark rum (optional)
25g (1oz) butter
2 × 300g cans black-eye beans, drained
ground black pepper
a few fresh thyme sprigs to garnish

1 Pierce the chicken pieces with a knife, put into a container and sprinkle with ½ tsp salt, some pepper, the coriander, cumin, paprika and nutmeg. Add the chilli, onion, thyme leaves and garlic. Pour the soy sauce and lemon juice over and stir to combine. Cover and chill for at least 4 hours.

2 Heat a 3.4 litre (6 pint) heavy-based pan over a medium heat for 2 minutes. Add the oil and sugar and cook for 3 minutes or until it turns a golden caramel colour. (Don't overcook it as the mixture will blacken and taste burnt – watch it closely.) Remove the chicken from the marinade. Add to the caramel mixture. Cover and cook over a medium heat for 5 minutes. Turn the chicken and cook, covered, for another 5 minutes or until evenly browned. Add the onion mixture and any marinade juices. Turn again, then re-cover and cook for 10 minutes.

3 Add the rice and stir to combine with the chicken, then pour in 900ml (1½ pints) cold water. Add the rum, if using, the butter and the remaining ½ tsp salt. Cover and simmer over a gentle heat, without lifting the lid, for 20 minutes or until the rice is tender and most of the liquid has been absorbed.

4 Add the black-eye beans to the pan and mix well. Cover the pan and cook for 3–5 minutes until the beans are warmed through and all the liquid has been absorbed, taking care that the rice doesn't stick to the bottom of the pan. Garnish with the thyme sprigs and serve hot.

Hot Jungle Curry

Preparation Time 10 minutes • **Cooking Time** 18–20 minutes • **Serves 4** • **Per Serving** 160 calories, 5g fat (of which 1g saturates), 5g carbohydrate, 1.1g salt • **Gluten Free** • **Dairy Free** • **Easy**

1 tbsp vegetable oil

350g (12oz) boneless, skinless chicken breasts, cut into 5cm (2in) strips

2 tbsp Thai red curry paste

2.5cm (1in) piece fresh root ginger, peeled and thinly sliced

125g (4oz) aubergine, cut into bite-size pieces

125g (4oz) baby sweetcorn, halved lengthways

75g (3oz) green beans, trimmed

75g (3oz) button or brown-cap mushrooms, halved if large

2–3 kaffir lime leaves (optional)

450ml (¾ pint) chicken stock

2 tbsp Thai fish sauce

grated zest of ½ lime, plus extra to garnish

1 tsp tomato purée

1 tbsp soft brown sugar

1 Heat the oil in a wok or large frying pan. Add the chicken and cook, stirring, for 5 minutes or until the chicken turns golden brown.

2 Add the curry paste and cook for a further 1 minute. Add the ginger, aubergine, sweetcorn, beans, mushrooms and lime leaves, if using, and stir until coated in the curry paste. Add all the remaining ingredients and bring to the boil. Simmer gently for 10–12 minutes or until the chicken and vegetables are just tender. Serve immediately, sprinkled with lime zest.

★ TRY SOMETHING DIFFERENT
Add a drained 225g can of bamboo shoots with the other vegetables in step 2, if you like.

Chicken, Bean and Spinach Curry

Preparation Time 10 minutes • **Cooking Time** about 20 minutes • **Serves 4** • **Per Serving** 358 calories, 11g fat (of which 2g saturates), 38g carbohydrate, 2.9g salt • **Gluten Free** • **Easy**

1 tbsp sunflower oil
350g (12oz) boneless, skinless
  chicken breasts, cut into strips
1 garlic clove, crushed
300–350g tub or jar curry sauce
400g can aduki beans, drained and
  rinsed
175g (6oz) ready-to-eat dried
  apricots
150g (5oz) natural bio yogurt, plus
  extra to serve
125g (4oz) baby spinach leaves
naan bread to serve

1 Heat the oil in a large pan over a medium heat and fry the chicken strips with the garlic until golden. Add the curry sauce, beans and apricots, then cover the pan and simmer gently for 15 minutes or until the chicken is tender.

2 Over a low heat, stir in the yogurt, keeping the curry hot without boiling it, then stir in the spinach until it just begins to wilt. Add a spoonful of yogurt and serve with naan bread.

⭐ TRY SOMETHING DIFFERENT
Instead of chicken, use pork escalopes, cut into thin strips.

Chicken Curry

Preparation Time 20–25 minutes • Cooking Time about 50 minutes • Serves 4 • Per Serving 342 calories, 10g fat (of which 2g saturates), 25g carbohydrate, 0.5g salt • **Gluten Free** • **Dairy Free** • **Easy**

1 tbsp oil
4 chicken legs, skinned
1 onion, finely chopped
2 tbsp mild or medium curry paste
2 leeks, trimmed and sliced
200g can chopped tomatoes
1 small cauliflower, broken into
   florets
250g (9oz) small new potatoes
600ml (1 pint) hot chicken stock
150g (5oz) each spinach and
   frozen peas
naan bread or rice (optional)
   to serve

1 Heat the oil in a large non-stick casserole dish and brown the chicken all over. After 5 minutes, add the onion to the pan and cook for 5–10 minutes until golden.

2 Add the curry paste and cook for 1 minute, then add the leeks, tomatoes, cauliflower, potatoes and hot stock. Bring to the boil, then reduce the heat, cover the pan and simmer for 20–30 minutes until the chicken is cooked and the potatoes are tender.

3 Add the spinach and peas and cook for 5 minutes or until heated through. Serve with naan bread, or rice, if you like.

Thai Red Turkey Curry

Preparation Time 20 minutes • **Cooking Time** 18–25 minutes • **Serves 6** • **Per Serving** 248 calories, 8g fat
(of which 1g saturates), 16g carbohydrate, 1.2g salt • **Gluten Free** • **Dairy Free** • **Easy**

3 tbsp vegetable oil
450g (1lb) onions, finely chopped
200g (7oz) green beans, trimmed
125g (4oz) baby sweetcorn, cut on
   the diagonal
2 red peppers, seeded and cut into
   thick strips
1 tbsp Thai red curry paste, or to
   taste
1 red chilli, seeded and finely
   chopped (see page 19)
1 lemongrass stalk, trimmed and
   very finely chopped
4 kaffir lime leaves, bruised
2 tbsp fresh root ginger, peeled and
   finely chopped
1 garlic clove, crushed
400ml can coconut milk
600ml (1 pint) chicken or turkey
   stock
450g (1lb) cooked turkey, cut into
   strips
150g (5oz) bean sprouts
fresh basil leaves to garnish

1 Heat the oil in a wok or large frying pan, add the onions and cook for 4–5 minutes or until soft.

2 Add the beans, baby corn and peppers to the pan and stir-fry for 3–4 minutes. Add the curry paste, chilli, lemongrass, kaffir lime leaves, ginger and garlic and cook for a further 2 minutes, stirring. Remove from the pan and set aside.

3 Add the coconut milk and stock to the pan, bring to the boil and bubble vigorously for 5–10 minutes until reduced by one-quarter. Return the vegetables to the pan with the turkey and bean sprouts. Bring to the boil, then reduce the heat and simmer for 1–2 minutes until heated through. Serve immediately, garnished with basil leaves.

★ COOK'S TIP
This is a great way to use leftover turkey.

Chicken with Oyster Sauce

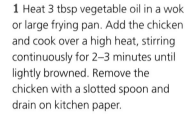

Preparation Time 10 minutes • **Cooking Time** about 18 minutes • **Serves 4** • **Per Serving** 344 calories, 23g fat (of which 3g saturates), 7g carbohydrate, 1.1g salt • **Dairy Free** • **Easy**

6 tbsp vegetable oil

450g (1lb) boneless, skinless chicken breasts, cut into bite-size pieces

3 tbsp oyster sauce

1 tbsp dark soy sauce

100ml (3½fl oz) chicken stock

2 tsp lemon juice

1 garlic clove, thinly sliced

6–8 large flat mushrooms, about 250g (9oz) total weight, sliced

125g (4oz) mangetouts

1 tsp cornflour mixed with 1 tbsp water

1 tbsp toasted sesame oil

salt and ground black pepper

rice to serve (optional)

1 Heat 3 tbsp vegetable oil in a wok or large frying pan. Add the chicken and cook over a high heat, stirring continuously for 2–3 minutes until lightly browned. Remove the chicken with a slotted spoon and drain on kitchen paper.

2 In a bowl, mix the oyster sauce with the soy sauce, stock and lemon juice. Add the chicken and mix thoroughly.

3 Heat the remaining vegetable oil in the pan over a high heat and stir-fry the garlic for about 30 seconds. Add the mushrooms and cook for 1 minute. Add the chicken mixture, cover and simmer for 8 minutes.

4 Stir in the mangetouts and cook for a further 2–3 minutes. Remove the pan from the heat and stir in the cornflour mixture. Put the pan back on the heat, add the sesame oil and stir until the sauce has thickened. Season with salt and pepper and serve immediately with rice, if you like.

Thai Green Curry

★

Preparation Time 10 minutes • **Cooking Time** 15 minutes • **Serves 6** • **Per Serving** 132 calories, 2g fat (of which 0g saturates), 4g carbohydrate, 1.4g salt • **Dairy Free** • **Easy**

2 tsp vegetable oil
1 green chilli, seeded and finely
   chopped (see page 19)
4cm (1½in) piece fresh root ginger,
   peeled and finely grated
1 lemongrass stalk, trimmed and
   cut into three
225g (8oz) brown-cap or oyster
   mushrooms
1 tbsp Thai green curry paste
300ml (½ pint) coconut milk
150ml (¼ pint) chicken stock
1 tbsp Thai fish sauce
1 tsp light soy sauce
350g (12oz) boneless, skinless
   chicken breasts, cut into bite-size
   pieces
350g (12oz) cooked peeled large
   prawns
fresh coriander sprigs to garnish

1 Heat the oil in a wok or large frying pan, add the chilli, ginger, lemongrass and mushrooms and stir-fry for about 3 minutes or until the mushrooms begin to turn golden. Add the curry paste and fry for a further 1 minute.

2 Pour in the coconut milk, stock, fish sauce and soy sauce and bring to the boil. Stir in the chicken, then reduce the heat and simmer for about 8 minutes or until the chicken is cooked. Add the prawns and cook for a further 1 minute. Garnish with coriander sprigs and serve immediately.

Turkey and Broccoli Stir-fry

Preparation Time 15 minutes • **Cooking Time** 8–12 minutes • **Serves 4** • **Per Serving** 254 calories, 8g fat (of which 1g saturates), 8g carbohydrate, 1.3g salt • **Dairy Free** • **Easy**

2 tbsp vegetable or sunflower oil

500g (1lb 2oz) turkey fillet, cut into strips

2 garlic cloves, crushed

2.5cm (1in) piece fresh root ginger, peeled and grated

1 broccoli head, cut into florets

8 spring onions, finely chopped

150g (5oz) button mushrooms, halved

100g (3½oz) bean sprouts

3 tbsp oyster sauce

1 tbsp light soy sauce

125ml (4fl oz) hot chicken stock

juice of ½ lemon

1 Heat 1 tbsp oil in a wok or large non-stick frying pan, add the turkey strips and stir-fry for 4–5 minutes until golden and cooked through. Remove from the pan and set aside.

2 Heat the remaining oil in the same pan over a medium heat, add the garlic and ginger and cook for 30 seconds, stirring all the time so that they don't burn. Add the broccoli, onions and mushrooms, increase the heat and cook for 2–3 minutes until the vegetables start to brown but are still crisp.

3 Return the turkey to the pan and add the bean sprouts, oyster and soy sauces, hot stock and lemon juice. Cook for 1–2 minutes, stirring well, until everything is heated through.

★ TRY SOMETHING DIFFERENT
Use pork fillet instead of turkey, cutting the fillet into thin slices.

Throw-it-all-together Chicken Salad

Preparation Time 10 minutes • **Serves 4** • **Per Serving** 215 calories, 9g fat (of which 2g saturates), 9g carbohydrate, 0.6g salt • **Gluten Free** • **Dairy Free** • **Easy**

4 chargrilled chicken breasts, about 125g (4oz) each, torn into strips
2 carrots, cut into strips
½ cucumber, halved lengthways, seeded and cut into ribbons
a handful of fresh coriander leaves, roughly chopped
½ head of Chinese leaves, shredded
4 handfuls of watercress
4 spring onions, shredded

FOR THE DRESSING
5 tbsp peanut butter
2 tbsp sweet chilli sauce
juice of 1 lime
salt and ground black pepper

1 Put the chicken strips and all the salad ingredients into a large salad bowl.

2 To make the dressing, put the peanut butter, chilli sauce and lime juice into a small bowl and mix well. Season with salt and pepper. If the dressing is too thick to pour, add 2–3 tbsp cold water, a tablespoon at a time, to thin it – use just enough water to make the dressing the correct consistency.

3 Drizzle the dressing over the salad, toss gently together and serve.

⭐ COOK'S TIPS
● *Use leftover roast chicken or beef, or cooked ham for this recipe.*
● *Use washed and prepared salad instead of Chinese leaves and watercress.*

Meat and Game ★

Beef Casserole with Black Olives

Preparation Time 20 minutes • **Cooking Time** 2 hours 10 minutes • **Serves 6** • **Per Serving** 704 calories, 45g fat (of which 13g saturates), 9g carbohydrate, 3.3g salt • **Dairy Free** • **Easy**

6 tbsp oil

1.1kg (2½lb) stewing steak, cut into 4cm (1½in) cubes

350g (12oz) unsmoked streaky bacon rashers, rind removed and sliced into thin strips

450g (1lb) onions, roughly chopped

3 large garlic cloves

2 tbsp tomato purée

125ml (4fl oz) brandy

1 tbsp plain flour

150ml (¼ pint) red wine

300ml (½ pint) beef stock

1 bouquet garni

225g (8oz) flat mushrooms, quartered if large

125g (4oz) black olives

fresh flat-leafed parsley sprigs to garnish (optional)

1 Heat 3 tbsp oil in a large flameproof casserole over a high heat. Brown the steak in batches until dark chestnut brown; remove and keep warm. Add the bacon and fry until golden brown, then put to one side with the beef.

2 Add the remaining oil and cook the onions over a medium heat for 10–15 minutes until golden. Add the garlic, fry for 30 seconds, then add the tomato purée and cook, stirring, for 1–2 minutes. Add the brandy.

3 Preheat the oven to 170°C (150°C fan oven) mark 3. Bring the casserole to the boil and bubble to reduce by half, then add the flour and mix until smooth. Pour in the wine, bring back to the boil and bubble for 1 minute. Put the steak and bacon back into the casserole, then add enough stock to barely cover the meat. Add the bouquet garni. Bring to the boil, then cover, put into the oven and cook for 1¼–1½ hours until the steak is tender. Add the mushrooms and cook for a further 4–5 minutes.

4 Just before serving, remove the bouquet garni and stir in the black olives. Serve hot, garnished with parsley, if you like.

★ FREEZING TIP

To freeze *Complete the recipe to the end of step 3. Cool quickly and put into a freezerproof container. Seal and freeze for up to one month.*

To use *Thaw overnight at cool room temperature. Preheat the oven to 180°C (160°C fan oven) mark 4. Bring slowly to the boil on the hob, then cover and reheat in the oven for 20–25 minutes. Complete the recipe.*

Braised Beef with Pancetta and Mushrooms

Preparation Time 20 minutes • **Cooking Time** about 3½ hours • **Serves 4** • **Per Serving** 541 calories, 25g fat (of which 9g saturates), 30g carbohydrate, 1.6g salt • **Dairy Free** • **Easy**

175g (6oz) smoked pancetta or
   smoked streaky bacon, cubed
2 leeks, trimmed and thickly sliced
1 tbsp olive oil
450g (1lb) braising steak, cut into
   5cm (2in) pieces
1 large onion, finely chopped
2 carrots, thickly sliced
2 parsnips, thickly sliced
1 tbsp plain flour
300ml (½ pint) red wine
1–2 tbsp redcurrant jelly
125g (4oz) chestnut mushrooms,
   halved
ground black pepper
freshly chopped flat-leafed parsley
   to garnish

1 Preheat the oven to 170°C (150°C fan oven) mark 3. Fry the pancetta or bacon in a shallow flameproof casserole for 2–3 minutes until golden. Add the leeks and cook for a further 2 minutes or until they are just beginning to colour. Remove with a slotted spoon and set aside.

2 Heat the oil in the casserole. Fry the beef in batches for 2–3 minutes until golden brown on all sides. Remove and set aside. Add the onion and fry over a gentle heat for 5 minutes or until golden. Stir in the carrots and parsnips and fry for 1–2 minutes.

3 Put the beef back into the casserole and stir in the flour to soak up the juices. Gradually add the wine and 300ml (½ pint) water, then stir in the redcurrant jelly. Season with pepper and bring to the boil. Cover with a tight-fitting lid and cook in the oven for 2 hours.

4 Stir in the leeks, pancetta and mushrooms, cover and cook for a further 1 hour or until everything is tender. Serve hot, sprinkled with chopped parsley.

 FREEZING TIP

To freeze Complete the recipe to the end of step 4, without the garnish. Put into a freezerproof container, cool and freeze for up to three months.

To use Thaw overnight at cool room temperature. Preheat the oven to 180°C (160°C fan oven) mark 4. Bring to the boil on the hob, cover tightly and reheat in the oven for about 30 minutes or until piping hot.

Beef Jambalaya

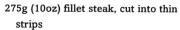

Preparation Time 10 minutes • **Cooking Time** 40 minutes • **Serves 4** • **Per Serving** 554 calories, 30g fat (of which 9g saturates), 40g carbohydrate, 1.8g salt • **Gluten Free** • **Dairy Free** • **Easy**

275g (10oz) fillet steak, cut into thin strips
4 tsp mild chilli powder
1 tsp ground black pepper
about 5 tbsp oil
150g (5oz) chorizo sausage, sliced and cut into strips, or 125g (4oz) cubed
2 celery sticks, cut into 5cm (2in) strips
2 red peppers, seeded and cut into 5cm (2in) strips
150g (5oz) onions, roughly chopped
2 garlic cloves, crushed
275g (10oz) long-grain white rice
1 tbsp tomato purée

1 tbsp ground ginger
2 tsp Cajun spice mix
900ml (1½ pints) beef stock
8 large cooked prawns, peeled and deveined (see page 73)
salt
mixed salad to serve

1 Put the steak into a plastic bag with 1 tsp chilli powder and the black pepper, seal and shake to mix.

2 Heat 1 tbsp oil in a large heavy-based frying pan and cook the chorizo until golden. Add the celery and red peppers to the pan and cook for 3–4 minutes until just beginning to soften and brown. Remove from the pan and put to one side. Add 2 tbsp oil to the pan and fry the steak in batches; put to one side and keep warm.

3 Add a little more oil to the pan, if needed, and cook the onion until transparent. Add the garlic, rice, tomato purée, remaining chilli powder, ground ginger and Cajun spice mix, then cook for 2 minutes or until the rice turns translucent. Stir in the stock, season with salt and bring to the boil. Reduce the heat, cover the pan and simmer for about 20 minutes, stirring occasionally, or until the rice is tender and most of the liquid has been absorbed (add a little more water during cooking if needed).

4 Add the reserved steak, chorizo, red peppers and celery and the prawns. Heat gently, stirring, until piping hot. Adjust the seasoning and serve with a mixed salad.

★ COOK'S TIP
Jambalaya is a rice-based dish from Louisiana that traditionally contains spicy sausage, chicken, ham or prawns and lots of chilli pepper.

Chunky One-pot Bolognese

Preparation Time 15 minutes • **Cooking Time** about 1 hour • **Serves 6** • **Per Serving** 506 calories, 31g fat (of which 11g saturates), 40g carbohydrate, 1.5g salt • **Dairy Free** • **Easy**

3 tbsp olive oil
2 large red onions, finely diced
a few fresh rosemary sprigs
1 large aubergine, finely diced
8 plump coarse sausages
350ml (12fl oz) full-bodied red wine
700g (1½lb) passata
4 tbsp sun-dried tomato paste
300ml (½ pint) hot vegetable stock
175g (6oz) small dried pasta, such as orecchiette
salt and ground black pepper

1 Heat 2 tbsp oil in a large shallow non-stick pan. Add the onions and rosemary and cook over a gentle heat for 10 minutes or until soft and golden.

2 Add the aubergine and remaining oil and cook over a medium heat for 8–10 minutes until soft and golden.

3 Meanwhile, pull the skin off the sausages and divide each into four rough chunks. Tip the aubergine mixture on to a plate and add the sausage chunks to the hot pan. You won't need any extra oil.

4 Stir the sausage pieces over a high heat for 6–8 minutes until golden and beginning to turn crisp at the edges. Pour in the wine and allow to bubble for 6–8 minutes until only a little liquid remains. Put the aubergine mixture back into the pan, along with the passata, tomato paste and hot stock.

5 Stir the pasta into the liquid, cover, then simmer for 20 minutes or until the pasta is cooked. Taste and season with salt and pepper if necessary.

★ FREEZING TIP

To freeze *Freeze leftover portions separately. Complete the recipe to the end of step 4. Add the pasta and cook for 10 minutes – it will continue to cook right through when you reheat the Bolognese. Cool, put into a freezerproof container and freeze for up to three months.*
To use *Thaw overnight at cool room temperature, put into a pan and add 150ml (¼ pint) water. Bring to the boil, then simmer gently for 10 minutes or until the sauce is hot and the pasta is cooked.*

One-pot Spicy Beef

Preparation Time 10 minutes • **Cooking Time** about 40 minutes • **Serves 4** • **Per Serving** 380 calories, 13g fat (of which 8g saturates), 36g carbohydrate, 1.8g salt • **Gluten Free** • **Dairy Free** • **Easy**

2 tsp sunflower oil
1 large onion, roughly chopped
1 garlic clove, finely chopped
1 small red chilli, finely chopped
   (see page 19)
2 red peppers, seeded and roughly
   chopped
2 celery sticks, diced
400g (14oz) lean beef mince
400g can chopped tomatoes
2 × 400g cans mixed beans, drained
   and rinsed
1–2 tsp Tabasco sauce
salsa to serve (see Cook's Tip)

1 Heat the oil in a large frying pan. Add the onion to the pan with 2 tbsp water and cook for 10 minutes or until softened. Add the garlic and chilli and cook for 1–2 minutes until golden, then add the red peppers and celery and cook for 5 minutes.

2 Add the beef to the pan and brown all over. Add the tomatoes, beans and Tabasco, then simmer for 20 minutes. Serve with the salsa.

★ COOK'S TIP
Salsa
Put ½ ripe avocado, peeled and roughly chopped, 4 roughly chopped tomatoes, 1 tsp olive oil and the juice of ½ lime into a bowl and stir well. Serve at once.

Beef with Mushrooms and Oyster Sauce

Preparation Time 15 minutes, plus soaking and marinating • **Cooking Time** about 15 minutes • **Serves 2** •
Per Serving 390 calories, 22g fat (of which 6g saturates), 19g carbohydrate, 0.9g salt • **Dairy Free** • **Easy**

175–225g (6–8oz) rump steak, cut
   into thin strips
2 tbsp oyster sauce
2 tbsp dry sherry
25g (1oz) dried black or shiitake
   mushrooms, soaked in boiling
   water for 30 minutes
2 tbsp vegetable oil
1 small onion, thinly sliced
1 garlic clove, crushed
2.5cm (1in) piece fresh root ginger,
   peeled and cut into thin strips
2 carrots, cut into matchsticks
2 tsp cornflour
salt and ground black pepper

1 Put the steak, oyster sauce and sherry into a bowl and add salt and pepper to taste. Stir well to mix, then cover, chill and leave to marinate for 30 minutes. Drain the mushrooms and reserve the soaking liquid. Squeeze the mushrooms dry; discard any hard stalks.

2 Heat the oil in a wok or large frying pan. Add the onion and garlic and stir-fry gently for about 5 minutes or until soft but not coloured. Add the mushrooms, ginger and carrots to the pan and stir-fry over a medium heat for about 6 minutes or until slightly softened. Remove the vegetables with a slotted spoon and set aside.

3 Add the beef and marinade to the pan and stir-fry for 2–3 minutes until the beef is tender. Mix the cornflour in a cup with 4 tbsp of the soaking water from the mushrooms. Pour the mixture into the pan, put the vegetables back in and stir-fry until the sauce is thickened. Taste and adjust the seasoning with salt and pepper, if necessary. Serve immediately.

Szechuan Beef

★

Preparation Time 15 minutes, plus marinating • **Cooking Time** 5–10 minutes • **Serves 4** • **Per Serving** 298 calories, 14g fat (of which 4g saturates), 15g carbohydrate, 0.6g salt • **Dairy Free** • **Easy**

350g (12oz) beef skirt or rump
   steak, cut into thin strips
5 tbsp hoisin sauce
4 tbsp dry sherry
2 tbsp vegetable oil
2 red or green chillies, finely
   chopped (see page 19)
1 large onion, thinly sliced
2 garlic cloves, crushed
2 red peppers, seeded and cut into
   diamond shapes
2.5cm (1in) piece fresh root ginger,
   peeled and grated
225g can bamboo shoots, drained
   and sliced
1 tbsp sesame oil

1 Put the beef into a bowl, add the hoisin sauce and sherry and stir to coat. Cover and leave to marinate for 30 minutes.

2 Heat the vegetable oil in a wok or large frying pan until smoking hot. Add the chillies, onion and garlic and stir-fry over a medium heat for 3–4 minutes until softened. Remove with a slotted spoon and set aside. Add the red peppers, increase the heat and stir-fry for a few seconds. Remove and set aside.

3 Add the steak and marinade to the pan in batches. Stir-fry each batch over a high heat for about 1 minute, removing with a slotted spoon.

4 Return the vegetables to the pan. Add the ginger and bamboo shoots, then the beef, and stir-fry for a further 1 minute or until heated through. Transfer to a warmed serving dish, sprinkle the sesame oil over the top and serve immediately.

Peppered Winter Stew

Preparation Time 20 minutes • **Cooking Time** 2¾ hours • **Serves 6** • **Per Serving** 540 calories, 24g fat (of which 7g saturates), 24g carbohydrate, 1.5g salt • **Dairy Free** • **Easy**

25g (1oz) plain flour
900g (2lb) stewing venison, beef or
    lamb, cut into 4cm (1½in) cubes
5 tbsp oil
225g (8oz) button onions or
    shallots, peeled with root end
    intact
225g (8oz) onion, finely chopped
4 garlic cloves, crushed
2 tbsp tomato purée
125ml (4fl oz) red wine vinegar
75cl bottle red wine
2 tbsp redcurrant jelly
1 small bunch of fresh thyme, plus
    extra sprigs to garnish (optional)
4 bay leaves
6 cloves
900g (2lb) mixed root vegetables,
    such as carrots, parsnips, turnips
    and celeriac, cut into 4cm (1½in)
    chunks; carrots cut a little
    smaller
600–900ml (1–1½ pints) beef stock
salt and ground black pepper

1 Preheat the oven to 180°C (160°C fan oven) mark 4. Put the flour into a plastic bag, season with salt and pepper, then toss the meat in it.

2 Heat 3 tbsp oil in a large flameproof casserole over a medium heat and brown the meat well in small batches. Remove and put to one side.

3 Heat the remaining oil and fry the button onions or shallots for 5 minutes or until golden. Add the chopped onion and the garlic and cook, stirring, until soft and golden.

Add the tomato purée and cook for a further 2 minutes, then add the vinegar and wine and bring to the boil. Bubble for 10 minutes.

4 Add the redcurrant jelly, thyme, bay leaves, 1 tbsp coarsely ground black pepper, the cloves and meat to the pan, with the vegetables and enough stock to barely cover the meat and vegetables. Bring to the boil, then reduce the heat, cover the pan and cook in the oven for 1¾–2¼ hours until the meat is very tender. Serve hot, garnished with thyme sprigs, if you like.

⭐ FREEZING TIP
To freeze *Complete the recipe to the end of step 4, without the garnish. Cool quickly and put in a freezerproof container. Seal and freeze for up to one month.*
To use *Thaw overnight at cool room temperature. Preheat the oven to 180°C (160°C fan oven) mark 4. Put into a flameproof casserole and add an extra 150ml (¼ pint) beef stock. Bring to the boil. Cover and reheat for 30 minutes.*

Marinated Beef and Vegetable Stir-fry

Preparation Time 15 minutes, plus chilling • **Cooking Time** about 10 minutes • **Serves 4** • **Per Serving** 543 calories, 15g fat (of which 4g saturates), 74g carbohydrate, 1.8g salt • **Dairy Free** • **Easy**

2 rump steaks, about 175g (6oz) each, trimmed
1 tsp vegetable oil
300g pack straight-to-wok noodles
1 red pepper, seeded and thinly sliced
300g (11oz) cabbage, shredded
2 carrots, cut into matchsticks
150g (5oz) shiitake mushrooms, sliced
300g (11oz) bean sprouts

FOR THE SAUCE
1 red chilli, finely chopped (see page 19)
1 garlic clove, finely chopped
2 tbsp soy sauce
2 tbsp sweet chilli sauce
juice of 1 lime

1 First, make the sauce. Put all the sauce ingredients into a large shallow bowl and mix well. Add the steaks and turn to coat. Cover and chill in the fridge for up to 24 hours, if you like.

2 Heat the oil in a wok or large frying pan over a high heat. Remove the steaks from the sauce, setting aside the sauce, and cook them for 1–2 minutes on each side. Remove from the pan and set aside.

3 Add the noodles, red pepper, cabbage, carrots and mushrooms to the pan and stir-fry over a high heat for 2–3 minutes. Add the bean sprouts and the reserved sauce and stir-fry for a further 2–3 minutes.

4 Thinly slice the steak and add it to the pan. Toss everything together and serve immediately.

Luxury Lamb and Leek Hotpot

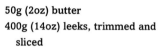

Preparation Time 20 minutes • **Cooking Time** 2 hours 50 minutes • **Serves 6** • **Per Serving** 530 calories, 33g fat (of which 20g saturates), 27g carbohydrate, 0.5g salt • **Easy**

50g (2oz) butter
400g (14oz) leeks, trimmed and
    sliced
1 medium onion, chopped
1 tbsp olive oil
800g (1¾lb) casserole lamb, cubed
    and tossed with 1 tbsp plain flour
2 garlic cloves, crushed
800g (1¾lb) waxy potatoes, such as
    Desirée, sliced
3 tbsp freshly chopped flat-leafed
    parsley
1 tsp freshly chopped thyme
300ml (½ pint) lamb stock
142ml carton double cream
salt and ground black pepper

1 Melt half the butter in a 3.5 litre (6¼ pint) flameproof casserole. Add the leeks and onion, stir to coat, then cover and cook over a low heat for 10 minutes.

2 Transfer the leeks and onion on to a large sheet of greaseproof paper. Add the oil to the casserole and heat, then brown the meat in batches with the garlic and plenty of seasoning. Remove and put to one side on another large sheet of greaseproof paper.

3 Preheat the oven to 170°C (150°C fan oven) mark 3. Put half the potatoes in a layer over the bottom of the casserole and season. Add the meat, then spoon the leek mixture on top. Arrange a layer of overlapping potatoes on top of that, sprinkle with herbs, then pour in the stock.

4 Bring the casserole to the boil, then cover and transfer to a low shelf in the oven and cook for about 1 hour 50 minutes. Remove from the oven, dot with the remaining butter and add the cream. Return to the oven and cook, uncovered, for 30–40 minutes until the potatoes are golden brown.

Lamb with Orange and Mint

Preparation Time 10 minutes • **Cooking Time** 20 minutes • **Serves 4** • **Per Serving** 411 calories, 28g fat
(of which 10g saturates), 6g carbohydrate, 1.1g salt • **Gluten Free** • **Dairy Free** • **Easy**

4 tbsp olive oil
4 lamb steaks, about 700g (1½lb)
  total weight
185g jar chargrilled sweet red
  peppers, drained and roughly
  chopped
50g (2oz) black olives
1 orange
juice of 1 lemon
1 small bunch of mint, roughly
  chopped
salt and ground black pepper

1 Heat 2 tbsp oil in a large non-stick frying pan. Brown the lamb in the hot oil, turning occasionally until the meat has formed a deep golden-brown crust all over.

2 Reduce the heat and add the peppers and olives to the pan. Chop up the orange, squeeze the juice directly into the pan and add the orange pieces for extra flavour. Add the lemon juice and the remaining oil.

3 Simmer for 5 minutes, stirring to break down the peppers a little. Stir the mint into the pan. Season to taste with salt and pepper and serve.

Braised Lamb Shanks with Cannellini Beans

★

Preparation Time 15 minutes • **Cooking Time** 3 hours • **Serves 6** • **Per Serving** 382 calories, 18g fat (of which 6g saturates), 29g carbohydrate, 1.2g salt • **Gluten Free** • **Dairy Free** • **Easy**

3 tbsp olive oil
6 lamb shanks
1 large onion, chopped
3 carrots, sliced
3 celery sticks, sliced
2 garlic cloves, crushed
2 × 400g cans chopped tomatoes
125ml (4fl oz) balsamic vinegar
2 bay leaves
2 × 400g cans cannellini beans,
    drained and rinsed
salt and ground black pepper

1 Preheat the oven to 170°C (150°C fan oven) mark 3. Heat the oil in a large flameproof casserole and brown the lamb shanks, in two batches, all over. Remove and set aside.

2 Add the onion, carrots, celery and garlic to the casserole and cook gently until softened and just beginning to colour.

3 Return the lamb to the casserole and add the chopped tomatoes and balsamic vinegar, giving the mixture a good stir. Season with salt and pepper and add the bay leaves. Bring to a simmer, cover and cook on the hob for 5 minutes.

4 Transfer to the oven and cook for 1½–2 hours or until the lamb shanks are nearly tender.

5 Remove the casserole from the oven and add the cannellini beans. Cover and return to the oven for a further 30 minutes, then serve.

Lamb with Red Wine and Lentils

Preparation Time 15 minutes • **Cooking Time** about 30 minutes • **Serves 4** • **Per Serving** 537 calories, 37g fat (of which 16g saturates), 17g carbohydrate, 0.3g salt • **Gluten Free** • **Dairy Free** • **Easy**

½ tbsp sunflower oil
1 medium onion, sliced
1 garlic clove, crushed
8 lamb cutlets
250g (9oz) puy lentils
150ml (¼ pint) each red wine and
  hot lamb stock
1 bay leaf
12 cherry tomatoes, halved
125g (4oz) roasted yellow or red
  peppers, seeded and roughly
  chopped
2 tbsp freshly chopped curly
  parsley
salt and ground black pepper
extra virgin olive oil for drizzling

1 Heat the sunflower oil in a large frying pan and gently cook the onion for 10 minutes or until softened. Add the garlic and cook for 1 minute. Remove the onion and garlic with a slotted spoon and put to one side.

2 Reheat the pan. Season the cutlets with salt and pepper and fry for 2–3 minutes on each side, depending on their size. Transfer the cutlets to a warmed plate, cover loosely with foil and put into a warm oven.

3 Return the onions and garlic to the same pan and stir in the lentils. Pour in the wine and simmer for 1 minute or until reduced slightly. Add the hot stock and bay leaf and simmer for 5 minutes.

4 Stir in the tomatoes and chopped peppers and simmer for 5 minutes or until warmed through. The lentils should be moist – add a splash of hot water if they look dry. Stir in three-quarters of the parsley and check the seasoning.

5 Divide among four warmed plates, top with the cutlets, garnish with the remaining parsley and drizzle with a little olive oil.

Turkish Lamb Stew

Preparation Time 10 minutes • **Cooking Time** 1½–2 hours • **Serves** 4 • **Per Serving** 389 calories, 20g fat (of which 7g saturates), 28g carbohydrate, 1.2g salt • **Gluten Free** • **Dairy Free** • **Easy**

2 tbsp olive oil
400g (14oz) lean lamb fillet, cubed
1 red onion, sliced
1 garlic clove, crushed
1 potato, quartered
400g can chopped plum tomatoes
1 red pepper, seeded and sliced
200g (7oz) canned chickpeas,
  drained and rinsed
1 aubergine, cut into chunks
200ml (7fl oz) lamb stock
1 tbsp red wine vinegar
1 tsp each freshly chopped thyme,
  rosemary and oregano
8 black olives, halved and pitted
salt and ground black pepper

1 Heat 1 tbsp oil in a flameproof casserole and brown the lamb over a high heat. Reduce the heat and add the remaining oil, the onion and garlic, then cook until soft.

2 Preheat the oven to 170°C (150°C fan oven) mark 3. Add the potato, tomatoes, red pepper, chickpeas, aubergine, stock, vinegar and herbs to the pan. Season, stir and bring to the boil. Cover the pan, transfer to the oven and cook for 1–1½ hours until the lamb is tender.

3 About 15 minutes before the end of the cooking time, add the olives.

Lamb, Prune and Almond Tagine

Preparation Time 20 minutes, plus marinating • **Cooking Time** 2½ hours • **Serves 6** • **Per Serving** 652 calories, 44g fat (of which 16g saturates), 31g carbohydrate, 0.6g salt • **Gluten Free** • **Easy**

2 tsp coriander seeds
2 tsp cumin seeds
2 tsp chilli powder
1 tbsp paprika
1 tbsp ground turmeric
5 garlic cloves, chopped
6 tbsp olive oil
1.4kg (3lb) lamb leg steaks
75g (3oz) ghee or clarified butter
    (see Cook's Tip)
2 large onions, finely chopped
1 carrot, roughly chopped
900ml (1½ pints) lamb stock
300g (11oz) ready-to-eat prunes
4 cinnamon sticks
4 bay leaves

50g (2oz) ground almonds
12 shallots
1 tbsp honey
salt and ground black pepper
toasted blanched almonds and
    freshly chopped flat-leafed
    parsley to garnish
couscous to serve

1 Using a pestle and mortar or a blender, combine the coriander and cumin seeds, chilli powder, paprika, turmeric, garlic and 4 tbsp oil. Coat the lamb with the paste, then cover and chill for at least 5 hours.

2 Preheat the oven to 170°C (150°C fan oven) mark 3. Melt 25g (1oz) ghee or butter in a large flameproof casserole. Add the onions and carrot and cook until soft. Remove and put to one side. Fry the paste-coated lamb on both sides in the remaining ghee or butter. Add a little of the stock and bring to the boil, scraping up the sediment from the bottom. Put the onions and carrot back in the casserole and add 100g (3½oz) prunes. Add the remaining stock with the cinnamon sticks, bay leaves and ground almonds. Season, cover and cook in the oven for 2 hours or until the meat is really tender.

3 Meanwhile, fry the shallots in the remaining oil and the honey until they turn a deep golden brown. Add to the casserole 30–40 minutes before the end of the cooking time.

4 Take the lamb out of the sauce and put to one side. Bring the sauce to the boil, then reduce to a thick consistency. Put the lamb back in the casserole, add the remaining prunes and bubble for 3–4 minutes. Garnish with the almonds and parsley. Serve hot with couscous.

 COOK'S TIP
To make clarified butter, heat butter in a pan without allowing it to colour. Skim off the foam; the solids will sink. Pour the clear butter into a bowl through a lined sieve. Leave for 10 minutes. Pour into a bowl, leaving any sediment behind. Cool. Store in a jar in the fridge for up to six months.

Italian Braised Leg of Lamb

★

Preparation Time 15 minutes • **Cooking Time** about 5 hours • **Serves 6** • **Per Serving** 400 calories, 18g fat (of which 6g saturates), 17g carbohydrate, 0.7g salt • **Gluten Free** • **Dairy Free** • **Easy**

2.3kg (5lb) boned leg of lamb
50ml (2fl oz) olive oil
700g (1½lb) onions, roughly
  chopped
1 each red, orange and yellow
  peppers, seeded and roughly
  chopped
2 red chillies, seeded and finely
  chopped (see page 19)
1 garlic bulb, cloves separated and
  peeled
3 tbsp dried oregano
75cl bottle dry white wine
3 × 400g cans cherry tomatoes
salt and ground black pepper

1 Preheat the oven to 170°C (150°C fan oven) mark 3. Season the lamb with salt and pepper. Heat 2 tbsp oil in a large deep flameproof casserole and brown the meat well. Remove and set aside. Wipe the pan clean.

2 Heat the remaining oil in the casserole and fry the onions, peppers, chillies, garlic and oregano over a medium heat for 10–15 minutes until the onions are translucent and golden brown. Stir in the wine and tomatoes and bring to the boil. Bubble for 10 minutes.

3 Put the lamb on top of the vegetables and season. Baste the meat with the sauce and cover the casserole tightly with foil and a lid. Cook in the oven for 4 hours, basting occasionally.

4 Uncover and cook for a further 30 minutes. Serve the lamb carved into thick slices with the sauce spooned over.

Lamb and Pasta Pot

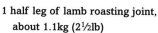

Preparation Time 10 minutes • **Cooking Time** 50 minutes • **Serves 4** • **Per Serving** 686 calories, 36g fat (of which 16g saturates), 18g carbohydrate, 1.4g salt • **Dairy Free** • **Easy**

1 half leg of lamb roasting joint, about 1.1kg (2½lb)

125g (4oz) smoked streaky bacon, chopped

150ml (¼ pint) red wine

400g can chopped tomatoes with chilli, or 400g (14oz) passata

75g (3oz) dried pasta shapes

12 sunblush tomatoes

150g (5oz) chargrilled artichokes in oil, drained and halved

basil leaves to garnish

1 Preheat the oven to 200°C (180°C fan oven) mark 6. Put the lamb and bacon into a small deep flameproof roasting tin and fry for 5 minutes or until the lamb is brown all over and the bacon is beginning to crisp.

2 Remove the lamb and set aside. Pour the wine into the tin with the bacon – it should bubble at once. Stir well, scraping the base to loosen any crusty bits, then leave to bubble until half the wine has evaporated. Stir in 300ml (½ pint) water and add the chopped tomatoes or passata, pasta and sunblush tomatoes.

3 Put the lamb on a rack over the roasting tin so that the juices drip into the pasta. Cook, uncovered, in the oven for about 35 minutes.

4 Stir the artichokes into the pasta and put everything back in the oven for 5 minutes or until the lamb is tender and the pasta cooked. Slice the lamb thickly. Serve with the pasta and scatter the basil on top.

Lamb, Potato and Peanut Curry

Preparation Time 20 minutes • **Cooking Time** about 2 hours • **Serves 8** • **Per Serving** 664 calories, 47g fat
(of which 20g saturates), 19g carbohydrate, 0.5g salt • **Gluten Free** • **Dairy Free** • **Easy**

2 tbsp olive oil

1 medium onion, chopped

1 tbsp peeled and grated fresh root
　ginger

1.6kg (3½lb) leg of lamb, diced

3–4 tbsp Massaman paste (see
　Cook's Tip)

1 tbsp fish sauce

2 tbsp peanut butter

100g (3½oz) ground almonds

400ml can coconut milk

600ml (1 pint) hot chicken stock

1–2 tbsp dry sherry

500g (1lb 2oz) small potatoes,
　quartered

200g (7oz) green beans, trimmed

75g (3oz) toasted peanuts, roughly
　chopped, to garnish

20g pack coriander, finely chopped,
　to garnish

2 limes, quartered, and rice
　(optional) to serve

1 Preheat the oven to 170°C (150°C
fan oven) mark 3. Heat the oil in a
large flameproof casserole. Add the
onion and cook over a medium heat
for 7–8 minutes until golden. Add
the ginger and cook for 1 minute.
Spoon the onion mixture out of the
pan and set aside. Add the lamb
and fry in batches until browned.
Set aside.

2 Add the Massaman paste, fish
sauce and peanut butter to the
casserole dish and fry for 2–3
minutes, then add the reserved
onion and ginger mixture and lamb
pieces, the ground almonds,
coconut milk, hot stock and sherry.

3 Bring to the boil, then cover
with a lid and cook in the oven for
1 hour. Add the potatoes and cook
for a further 40 minutes, uncovered,
adding the green beans for the last
20 minutes. Garnish the curry with
toasted peanuts and coriander.
Serve with freshly cooked rice, if you
like, and lime wedges to squeeze
over the curry.

★ COOK'S TIP
Massaman paste is a Thai curry paste.
The ingredients include red chillies,
roasted shallots, roasted garlic,
galangal, lemongrass, roasted coriander
seeds, roasted cumin, roasted cloves,
white pepper, salt and shrimp paste.
It's available in supermarkets or Asian
food stores.

One-pot Gammon Stew

Preparation Time 15 minutes • **Cooking Time** 1 hour 10 minutes • **Serves 4** • **Per Serving** 680 calories, 30g fat (of which 11g saturates), 41g carbohydrate, 6.3g salt • **Gluten Free** • **Easy**

1 tbsp olive oil
1.1kg (2½lb) smoked gammon joint
8 shallots, blanched in boiling water, drained, peeled and chopped into chunks
3 carrots, chopped into chunks
3 celery sticks, chopped into chunks
4 large Desirée potatoes, unpeeled
450ml (¾ pint) each apple juice and hot vegetable stock
½ small Savoy cabbage
25g (1oz) butter

1 Preheat the oven to 190°C (170°C fan oven) mark 5. Heat the oil in a large flameproof casserole. Add the gammon and cook for 5 minutes or until brown all over. Remove from the pan.

2 Add the shallots, carrots and celery to the pan and fry for 3–4 minutes until starting to soften.

3 Return the gammon to the pan. Chop the potatoes into quarters and add to the pan with the apple juice and hot stock. Cover and bring to the boil, then transfer to the oven and cook for 50 minutes or until the meat is cooked through and the vegetables are tender.

4 Remove from the oven and put the dish back on the hob over a low heat. Shred the cabbage and stir into the pan. Simmer for 2–3 minutes, then stir in the butter and serve.

Honey Pork with Roast Potatoes and Apples

Preparation Time 20 minutes • **Cooking Time** 1 hour 40 minutes, plus resting • **Serves 4** • **Per Serving** 830 calories, 55g fat (of which 19g saturates), 40g carbohydrate, 0.4g salt • **Gluten Free** • **Easy**

1kg (2¼lb) loin of pork, with skin
   and four bones
4 tbsp olive oil
25g (1oz) butter
700g (1½lb) Charlotte potatoes,
   scrubbed and halved
1 large onion, cut into eight wedges
1 tbsp clear honey mixed with
   1 tbsp wholegrain mustard
2 Cox's Orange Pippin apples,
   cored and each cut into six
   wedges
12 fresh sage leaves
175ml (6fl oz) dry cider
salt and ground black pepper

1 Preheat the oven to 240°C (220°C fan oven) mark 9. Put the pork on a board and use a paring knife to score the skin into thin strips, cutting about halfway into the fat underneath. Rub 1 tsp salt and 2 tbsp oil over the skin and season well with pepper. Put the meat on a rack, skin side up, over a large roasting tin (or just put the pork into the tin).

2 Roast for 25 minutes. Turn the oven down to 190°C (170°C fan oven) mark 5 and continue to roast for 15 minutes. Add the remaining oil and the butter to the roasting tin. Scatter the potatoes and onion around the meat, season and continue to roast for 45 minutes.

3 Brush the meat with the honey and mustard mixture. Add the

apples and sage leaves to the tin and roast for a further 15 minutes or until the pork is cooked.

4 Remove the pork from the tin and wrap completely with foil, then leave to rest for 10 minutes. Put the potatoes, onions and apples into a warmed serving dish and put back in the oven to keep warm.

5 Put the roasting tin on the hob, add the cider and stir well to make a thin gravy. Season.

6 Cut the meat away from the bone. Cut between each bone. Pull the crackling away from the meat and cut into strips. Carve the joint, giving each person some crackling and a bone to chew. Serve with the gravy and potatoes, onion and apples.

Spanish-style Pork

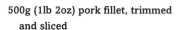

Preparation Time 15 minutes • **Cooking Time** 25 minutes • **Serves 4** • **Per Serving** 349 calories, 12g fat (of which 3g saturates), 26g carbohydrate, 1.2g salt • **Dairy Free** • **Easy**

500g (1lb 2oz) pork fillet, trimmed
and sliced
2 tbsp olive oil
1 Spanish onion, chopped
2 celery sticks, finely chopped
2 tsp smoked paprika
1 tbsp tomato purée
750ml (1¼ pints) hot chicken stock
400g can butter beans, drained and
rinsed
¼ Savoy cabbage, finely shredded
200g (7oz) green beans, trimmed
and halved
salt and ground black pepper

1 tbsp freshly chopped rosemary to
garnish
lemon wedges and crusty bread to
serve

1 Lay the pork out on a board, cover with clingfilm and flatten slightly with a rolling pin. Heat 1 tbsp oil in a frying pan and fry the pork over a medium to high heat until browned. Remove from the pan and set aside.

2 Heat the remaining oil and gently fry the onion and celery for 10 minutes or until softened. Stir in the paprika and tomato purée and cook for 1 minute. Stir in the hot stock, butter beans and cabbage. Season with salt and pepper.

3 Return the pork to the pan and bring to the boil, then simmer for 10 minutes, adding the green beans for the last 4 minutes. Garnish with rosemary and serve with lemon wedges and crusty bread on the side.

Pork and Apple Hotpot

Preparation Time 15 minutes • **Cooking Time** 2–2¼ hours • **Serves 4** • **Per Serving** 592 calories, 18g fat (of which 7g saturates), 56g carbohydrate, 1g salt • **Easy**

1 tbsp olive oil
900g (2lb) pork shoulder steaks
3 onions, cut into wedges
1 large Bramley apple, peeled, cored and thickly sliced
1 tbsp plain flour
600ml (1 pint) hot weak chicken or vegetable stock
¼ Savoy cabbage, sliced
2 fresh thyme sprigs
900g (2lb) large potatoes, cut into 2cm (¾in) slices
25g (1oz) butter
salt and ground black pepper

1 Preheat the oven to 170°C (150°C fan oven) mark 3. Heat the oil in a large non-stick flameproof and freezerproof casserole until very hot, then fry the steaks, two at a time, for 5 minutes or until golden all over. Remove the steaks from the pan and set aside.

2 In the same casserole, fry the onions for 10 minutes or until soft – add a little water if they start to stick. Stir in the apple and cook for 1 minute, then add the flour to soak up the juices. Gradually add the hot stock and stir until smooth. Season with salt and pepper. Stir in the cabbage and add the pork.

3 Throw in the thyme, overlap the potato slices on top, then dot with the butter. Cover with a tight-fitting lid and cook near the top of the oven for 1 hour. Remove the lid and cook for 30–45 minutes until the potatoes are tender and golden.

 COOK'S TIP
Put the hotpot under the grill for 2–3 minutes to crisp up the potatoes, if you like.

 FREEZING TIP
To freeze Cool quickly, then freeze in the casserole for up to three months.
To use Thaw overnight at cool room temperature. Preheat the oven to 180°C (160°C fan oven) mark 4. Pour 50ml (2fl oz) hot stock over the hotpot, then cover and reheat for 30 minutes or until piping hot. Uncover and crisp the potatoes under the grill for 2–3 minutes.

Spicy Pork and Bean Stew

Preparation Time 15 minutes • **Cooking Time** 50–55 minutes • **Serves 4** • **Per Serving** 373 calories, 14g fat
(of which 3g saturates), 32g carbohydrate, 1.2g salt • **Dairy Free** • **Easy**

3 tbsp olive oil
400g (14oz) pork escalopes, cubed
1 red onion, sliced
2 leeks, trimmed and cut into chunks
2 celery sticks, cut into chunks
1 tbsp harissa paste
1 tbsp tomato purée
400g can cherry tomatoes
300ml (½ pint) hot vegetable or
   chicken stock
400g can cannellini beans, drained
   and rinsed
1 marinated red pepper, sliced
salt and ground black pepper

freshly chopped flat-leafed parsley
   to garnish
Greek yogurt and lemon wedges to
   serve

1 Preheat the oven to 180°C (160°C fan oven) mark 4. Heat 2 tbsp oil in a flameproof casserole and fry the pork in batches until golden. Remove from the pan and set aside.

2 Heat the remaining oil in the pan and fry the onion for 5–10 minutes until softened. Add the leeks and celery and cook for about 5 minutes. Return the pork to the pan and add the harissa and tomato purée. Cook for 1–2 minutes, stirring all the time. Add the tomatoes and hot stock. Season well with salt and pepper. Bring to the boil, then transfer to the oven and cook for 25 minutes.

3 Add the drained beans and red pepper to the mixture and put back into the oven for 5 minutes to warm through. Garnish with parsley and serve with a dollop of Greek yogurt and lemon wedges for squeezing over.

★ COOK'S TIP
For a simple accompaniment, serve with chunks of crusty baguette or wholegrain bread.

Spicy Sausage and Pasta Supper

Preparation Time 15 minutes • **Cooking Time** 30 minutes • **Serves 6** • **Per Serving** 629 calories, 39g fat (of which 18g saturates), 36g carbohydrate, 3.1g salt • **Easy**

1 tbsp olive oil
200g (7oz) salami, sliced
225g (8oz) onion, finely chopped
50g (2oz) celery, finely chopped
2 garlic cloves, crushed
400g can pimientos, drained, rinsed and chopped
400g (14oz) passata or 400g can chopped tomatoes
125g (4oz) sun-dried tomatoes in oil, drained
600ml (1 pint) hot chicken or vegetable stock
300ml (½ pint) red wine
1 tbsp sugar
75g (3oz) dried pasta shapes
400g can borlotti beans, drained and rinsed
salt and ground black pepper
freshly chopped flat-leafed parsley to garnish
300ml (½ pint) soured cream and 175g (6oz) Parmesan, freshly grated, to serve

1 Heat the oil in a large pan over a medium heat and fry the salami for 5 minutes or until golden and crisp. Drain on kitchen paper.

2 Fry the onion and celery in the hot oil for 10 minutes or until soft and golden. Add the garlic and fry for 1 minute. Put the salami back into the pan with the pimientos, passata or chopped tomatoes, the sun-dried tomatoes, hot stock, wine and sugar. Bring to the boil.

3 Stir in the pasta, bring back to the boil and cook for about 10 minutes, or according to the pack instructions, until the pasta is almost tender.

4 Stir in the beans and simmer for 3–4 minutes. Top up with more hot stock if the pasta is not tender when the liquid has been absorbed. Season with salt and pepper.

5 Ladle into warmed bowls and serve topped with soured cream and garnished with chopped parsley. Serve the grated Parmesan separately.

 GET AHEAD
To prepare ahead *Complete the recipe to the end of step 2. Cool quickly, cover and chill for up to one day.*
To use *Bring back to the boil, stir in the pasta and complete the recipe.*

Parma Ham and Artichoke Tagliatelle

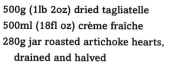

Preparation Time 5 minutes • **Cooking Time** 10–15 minutes • **Serves 4** • **Per Serving** 970 calories, 56g fat (of which 36g saturates), 96g carbohydrate, 1g salt • **Easy**

500g (1lb 2oz) dried tagliatelle
500ml (18fl oz) crème fraîche
280g jar roasted artichoke hearts, drained and halved
80g pack Parma ham (6 slices), torn into strips
2 tbsp freshly chopped sage leaves, plus extra to garnish
40g (1½oz) Parmesan, pared into shavings with a vegetable peeler
salt and ground black pepper

1 Bring a large pan of water to the boil. Add the pasta, bring back to the boil and cook according to the pack instructions.

2 Drain the pasta well, leaving a ladleful of the cooking water in the pan, then put the pasta back in the pan.

3 Add the crème fraîche, artichokes, Parma ham and chopped sage and stir everything together. Season well with salt and pepper.

4 Spoon the pasta into warmed bowls, sprinkle with the Parmesan shavings and garnish with sage. Serve immediately.

Pork and Roasted Vegetable Couscous

★

Preparation Time 20 minutes • **Cooking Time** about 30 minutes • **Serves 2** • **Per Serving** 539 calories, 17g fat (of which 3g saturates), 64g carbohydrate, 0.4g salt • **Dairy Free** • **Easy**

125g (4oz) couscous
150ml (¼ pint) hot chicken stock
1 red onion, cut into six wedges
2 small baby turnips, chopped into
  1cm (½in) chunks
2 carrots, chopped into 2cm (¾in)
  chunks
½ fennel bulb, chopped into small
  bite-size pieces
olive oil spray
4 thick asparagus spears, each cut
  into three pieces
250g (9oz) pork fillet, chopped into
  small bite-size pieces
1 tbsp extra virgin olive oil
zest and juice of 1 lemon
50g (2oz) dried apricots, roughly
  chopped
1 tbsp roasted flaked almonds
a small handful each of fresh
  parsley and mint, roughly
  chopped
salt and ground black pepper

1 Preheat the oven to 200°C (180°C fan oven) mark 6. Put the couscous into a large bowl and pour the hot stock over. Cover with clingfilm and leave to soak.

2 Line a roasting tin with baking parchment. Add the red onion wedges, turnips, carrots and fennel. Spray the vegetables three times with the olive oil spray, then season and toss well to coat. Roast for 10 minutes, then add the asparagus. After another 10 minutes, stir in the pork and continue cooking for 10 minutes or until the meat is

cooked through and the vegetables are tender.

3 Whisk together the extra virgin olive oil, lemon zest and juice and season to taste with salt and plenty of black pepper.

4 Use a fork to fluff up the couscous. Add to the roasted vegetables and meat, along with the apricots and almonds and toss everything together. Stir the fresh herbs and olive oil dressing through and serve immediately.

★ TRY SOMETHING
DIFFERENT
Swap the pork with the same quantity of skinless turkey.

Pork, Garlic and Basil Risotto

Preparation Time 15 minutes • **Cooking Time** 50 minutes • **Serves 6** • **Per Serving** 431 calories, 18g fat (of which 6g saturates), 28g carbohydrate, 0.7g salt • **Easy**

6 thin pork escalopes
150g (5oz) Parma ham
about 6 fresh basil leaves
25g (1oz) plain flour
about 75g (3oz) unsalted butter
175g (6oz) onion, finely chopped
2 garlic cloves, crushed
225g (8oz) risotto (arborio) rice
450ml (¾ pint) white wine
450ml (¾ pint) hot chicken stock
3 tbsp fresh ready-made pesto (see
  page 11)
50g (2oz) grated Parmesan
4 tbsp freshly chopped flat-leafed
  parsley
salt and ground black pepper

1 Preheat the oven to 180°C (160°C fan oven) mark 4. If needed, pound the escalopes carefully with a rolling pin until they are wafer-thin. Lay a slice of Parma ham on each escalope and put a basil leaf on top. Fix in place with a wooden cocktail stick. Season and dip in the flour, dusting off any excess.

2 Melt a small knob of the butter in a deep ovenproof pan and quickly fry the escalopes in batches for 2–3 minutes on each side until lightly golden. Melt a little more butter for each batch. You will need about half the butter at this stage. Remove the escalopes and keep warm, covered, in the oven.

3 Melt about another 25g (1oz) butter in the pan and fry the onion for about 10 minutes or until soft and golden. Add the garlic and rice and stir well. Add the wine and hot stock. Bring to the boil, then put into the oven and cook, uncovered, for 20 minutes.

4 Stir in the pesto, Parmesan and parsley. Push the browned escalopes into the rice, cover and put the pan back in the oven for a further 5 minutes or until the rice has completely absorbed the liquid and the escalopes are cooked through and piping hot.

⭐ TRY SOMETHING DIFFERENT
Use turkey or veal escalopes instead of pork.

Salami and Olive Tart

Preparation Time 10 minutes • **Cooking Time** 25 minutes • **Serves 6** • **Per Serving** 370 calories, 28g fat (of which 1g saturates), 25g carbohydrate, 1.4g salt • **Easy**

375g pack ready-rolled puff pastry
4 tbsp chargrilled aubergine pesto
12 slices Italian salami, thinly sliced
**   (about 70g/scant 3oz)**
2 medium tomatoes, sliced
2 tbsp pitted black olives, sliced
2 large handfuls of rocket
extra virgin olive oil for drizzling

1 Preheat the oven to 200°C (180°C fan oven) mark 6. Unroll the pastry and put on a baking sheet, then fold the edges over by 1cm (½ in) as a border. Prick the base all over with a fork.

2 Spread the pesto over the base inside the border. Arrange the salami and tomatoes in overlapping layers on top. Bake for 20–25 minutes until golden. Garnish with the olives, rocket and a drizzle of olive oil to serve.

Potato and Chorizo Tortilla

Preparation Time 15 minutes • **Cooking Time** about 25 minutes • **Serves 4** • **Per Serving** 566 calories, 42g fat (of which 8g saturates), 23g carbohydrate, 1.2g salt • **Gluten Free** • **Dairy Free** • **Easy**

6 tbsp olive oil

450g (1lb) potatoes, very thinly sliced

225g (8oz) onions, thinly sliced

2 garlic cloves, chopped

50g (2oz) chorizo sausage, cut into strips

6 large eggs

salt and ground black pepper

1 Heat the oil in an 18cm (7in) non-stick frying pan. Add the potatoes, onion and garlic and stir to coat. Cover the pan, then cook gently for 15 minutes, stirring occasionally, or until the potato is soft. Season with salt.

2 Add the chorizo to the pan. Beat the eggs and season with salt and pepper, then pour into the pan and cook for about 5 minutes or until the edges are beginning to brown and the egg looks about three-quarters set.

3 Put the tortilla under a preheated grill and quickly brown the top. Remove from the heat and leave to cool. Loosen the edges and serve cut into wedges.

Pan-fried Chorizo and Potato

Preparation Time 10 minutes • **Cooking Time** 30 minutes • **Serves 4** • **Per Serving** 553 calories, 36g fat (of which 12g saturates), 32g carbohydrate, 3.4g salt • **Gluten Free** • **Dairy Free** • **Easy**

2 tbsp olive oil

450g (1lb) potatoes, cut into 2.5cm (1in) cubes

2 red onions, sliced

1 red pepper, seeded and chopped

1 tsp paprika

300g (11oz) piece of chorizo sausage, skinned and cut into chunky slices

250g (9oz) cherry tomatoes

100ml (3½fl oz) dry sherry

2 tbsp freshly chopped flat-leafed parsley

1 Heat the oil in a large heavy-based frying pan over a medium heat. Add the potatoes and fry for 7–10 minutes until lightly browned, turning regularly.

2 Reduce the heat, add the onions and red pepper and continue to cook for 10 minutes, stirring from time to time, or until they have softened but not browned.

3 Add the paprika and chorizo and cook for 5 minutes, stirring from time to time.

4 Add the cherry tomatoes and pour in the sherry. Stir everything together and cook for 5 minutes, or until the sherry has reduced and the tomatoes have softened and warmed through.

5 Sprinkle the chopped parsley over the top and serve.

Spiced Salad

Preparation Time 5 minutes • **Serves 4** • **Per Serving** 210 calories, 17g fat (of which 2g saturates), 10g carbohydrate, 0.6g salt • **Gluten Free** • **Dairy Free** • **Easy**

4 tbsp olive oil
4 tsp lime juice
large pinch of golden caster sugar
50g (2oz) chorizo sausage, thinly
    shredded
2 mild red chillies, seeded and
    chopped (see page 19)
2 red peppers, seeded and sliced
2 shallots, finely chopped
4 tomatoes, chopped
large bag mixed crisp lettuce leaves
salt and crushed black peppercorns
wholemeal rolls or rye bread to
    serve

1 Put the oil, lime juice, sugar, some salt and crushed black peppercorns into a bowl and stir to combine.

2 Add the chorizo, chillies, red peppers, shallots, tomatoes and lettuce leaves and turn in the dressing.

3 Serve with wholemeal rolls or slices of rye bread.

Stir-fried Pork with Chinese Greens

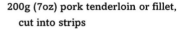

Preparation Time 15 minutes, plus marinating • **Cooking Time** about 15 minutes • **Serves 4** • **Per Serving** 234 calories, 15g fat (of which 2g saturates), 6g carbohydrate, 1.8g salt • **Dairy Free** • **Easy**

200g (7oz) pork tenderloin or fillet, cut into strips

2 tbsp finely chopped fresh root ginger

3 tbsp soy sauce

2 garlic cloves, crushed

700g (1½lb) mixed vegetables, such as pak choi, broccoli, carrots, bean sprouts and sugarsnap peas

3 tbsp vegetable oil

5 spring onions, cut into four lengthways

1 red chilli, seeded and sliced (see page 19)

1 tbsp sesame oil

2 tbsp dry sherry

2 tbsp oyster sauce

salt and ground black pepper

1 Put the pork into a non-metallic dish with the ginger, 2 tbsp soy sauce and the garlic. Set aside to marinate for at least 30 minutes.

2 Meanwhile, prepare the vegetables. Cut the pak choi into quarters, separate the broccoli into florets and cut the carrots into ribbons, using a vegetable peeler.

3 Heat a wok or large frying pan over a high heat and add the vegetable oil. Stir-fry the pork in two batches, cooking each batch for 2–3 minutes until the meat is browned.

Season the pork with salt and pepper, set aside and keep warm.

4 Add the spring onions and chilli to the pan and cook for 30 seconds. Add all the vegetables and stir-fry for 4–5 minutes. Return the pork to the pan. Add the remaining soy sauce, the sesame oil, sherry and oyster sauce, then stir-fry for 2 minutes or until the sauce is syrupy. Serve immediately.

 GET AHEAD

To prepare ahead *Complete the recipe to the end of step 3, then cool, wrap and chill the pork and vegetables separately for up to four hours.*

To use *Complete the recipe until the pork is piping hot.*

Savoury Pudding

Preparation Time 15 minutes, plus soaking • **Cooking Time** 1–1¼ hours • **Serves 6** • **Per Serving** 397 calories, 27g fat (of which 15g saturates), 17g carbohydrate, 2.2g salt • **Easy**

150–175g (5–6oz) thickly sliced white bread (such as sourdough), crusts left on
75g (3oz) butter, softened
Dijon mustard
200g (7oz) sliced ham, very roughly chopped
150g (5oz) mature Cheddar, grated
600ml (1 pint) full-fat milk
5 large eggs, beaten
a pinch of freshly grated nutmeg
2 tbsp freshly chopped herbs, such as parsley, marjoram or thyme
salt and ground black pepper
green salad to serve

1 Spread the bread generously with butter and sparingly with mustard. Put half the slices into the base of a 2 litre (3½ pint) ovenproof dish. Top with the ham and half the cheese, then with the remaining bread, butter side up.

2 Whisk together the milk, eggs, nutmeg and plenty of salt and pepper. Stir in the herbs, then slowly pour the mixture over the bread. Scatter the remaining cheese on top and leave to soak for 15 minutes. Meanwhile, preheat the oven to 180°C (160°C fan oven) mark 4.

3 Put the dish into a roasting tin and fill halfway up the sides with hand-hot water, then cook for 1–1¼ hours until puffed up, golden brown and just set to the centre. Serve immediately, with a green salad.

★ TRY SOMETHING DIFFERENT
For a vegetarian alternative, leave out the ham and use 250g (9oz) cheese, such as Gruyère. Add three-quarters of the cheese over the first layer of bread and scatter the remaining cheese on top.

Pot-roasted Pheasant with Red Cabbage

Preparation Time 15 minutes • Cooking Time about 1 hour • Serves 4 • Per Serving 659 calories, 21g fat (of which 12g saturates), 11g carbohydrate, 1.4g salt • Gluten Free • Easy

25g (1oz) butter
1 tbsp oil
2 oven-ready young pheasants, halved
2 onions, sliced
450g (1lb) red cabbage, cored and finely shredded
1 tsp cornflour
250ml (9fl oz) red wine
2 tbsp redcurrant jelly
1 tbsp balsamic vinegar
4 rindless smoked streaky bacon rashers, halved
salt and ground black pepper

1 Preheat the oven to 200°C (180°C fan oven) mark 6. Melt the butter with the oil in a large flameproof casserole over a medium to high heat. Add the pheasant and brown on all sides, then remove and put to one side. Add the onions and cabbage to the casserole and fry for 5 minutes, stirring frequently, or until softened.

2 Blend the cornflour with a little water to make a paste. Add to the casserole with the wine, redcurrant jelly and vinegar. Season with salt and pepper. Bring to the boil, stirring.

3 Arrange the pheasant halves, skin side up, on the cabbage. Put the halved bacon rashers on top. Cover the casserole and cook in the oven for 30 minutes or until the birds are tender (older pheasants would take an extra 10–20 minutes).

4 Serve the pot-roasted pheasant and red cabbage with the cooking juices spooned over.

★ TRY SOMETHING DIFFERENT
Pot-roasted Pigeon with Red Cabbage
Instead of the pheasant, use oven-ready pigeons; put an onion wedge inside each bird before browning to impart extra flavour.

Rabbit Casserole with Prunes

Preparation Time 20 minutes, plus soaking • **Cooking Time** 1¼ hours • **Serves 6** • **Per Serving** 538 calories, 26g fat (of which 13g saturates), 11g carbohydrate, 0.5g salt • **Gluten Free** • **Easy**

175g (6oz) ready-to-eat pitted
  prunes
300ml (½ pint) red wine
3–4 tbsp olive oil
about 2.3kg (5lb) rabbit joints
1 large onion, chopped
2 large garlic cloves, crushed
5 tbsp Armagnac
450ml (¾ pint) light stock
a few fresh thyme sprigs, tied
  together, or 1 tsp dried thyme,
  plus extra sprigs to garnish
2 bay leaves
150ml (¼ pint) double cream

125g (4oz) brown-cap mushrooms,
  sliced
salt and ground black pepper

1 Put the prunes and wine into a bowl. Cover and leave for about 4 hours, then strain, keeping the wine and prunes to one side.

2 Preheat the oven to 170°C (150°C fan oven) mark 3. Heat 3 tbsp oil in a flameproof casserole. Brown the rabbit joints a few at a time, then remove from the casserole. Add the onion and garlic with a little more oil, if needed, and brown lightly. Put the rabbit back into the casserole, add the Armagnac and warm through. Carefully light the Armagnac with a taper or long match, then shake the pan gently until the flames subside.

3 Pour in the stock and the wine from the prunes and bring to the boil. Add the thyme sprigs or dried thyme to the casserole with the bay leaves and plenty of salt and pepper. Cover tightly and cook in the oven for about 1 hour or until tender.

4 Lift the rabbit out of the juices and keep warm. Boil the cooking juices until reduced by half. Add the cream and mushrooms and continue boiling for 2–3 minutes. Stir in the prunes and warm through. Adjust the seasoning, then spoon the sauce over the rabbit to serve. Garnish with sprigs of fresh thyme.

★ TRY SOMETHING
DIFFERENT
Use chicken joints instead of rabbit.

Braised Guinea Fowl and Red Cabbage

Preparation Time 30 minutes • Cooking Time 2 hours 20 minutes • Serves 8 • Per Serving 373 calories, 17g fat (of which 6g saturates), 12g carbohydrate, 0.9g salt • **Dairy Free** • **Easy**

2 tbsp rapeseed oil
2 oven-ready guinea fowl
150g (5oz) smoked lardons
400g (14oz) whole shallots, peeled
1 small red cabbage, cored and
    finely sliced
12 juniper berries, crushed
2 tsp dark brown sugar
1 tbsp red wine vinegar
2 fresh thyme sprigs
150ml (¼ pint) hot chicken stock
salt and ground black pepper

1 Preheat the oven to 180°C (160°C fan oven) mark 4. Heat 1 tbsp oil in a flameproof casserole large enough for both birds and brown the guinea fowl over a medium to high heat. Remove from the casserole and set aside.

2 Add the remaining oil to the casserole with the lardons. Fry gently to release the fat, then add the shallots and cook over a medium heat until lightly browned.

3 Stir in the red cabbage and cook for 5 minutes, stirring, or until the cabbage has softened slightly. Add the juniper berries, sugar, vinegar, thyme and hot stock. Season with salt and pepper.

4 Put the guinea fowl on top of the cabbage mixture, then cover the casserole tightly with a lid or double thickness of foil and braise in the oven for 1½ hours. Remove the lid and continue cooking for 30 minutes or until the birds are cooked through – the juices should run clear when you pierce the thighs with a skewer.

5 Transfer the guinea fowl to a board and spoon the cabbage and juices on to a serving platter. Keep warm. Joint the birds into eight, as you would a chicken, then arrange the guinea fowl on the platter on top of the cabbage. Serve at once.

Vegetarian and
Vegetables

One-pot Vegetable Rice

Preparation Time 15 minutes • **Cooking Time** about 30 minutes • **Serves 4** • **Per Serving** 572 calories, 6g fat (of which 1g saturates), 103g carbohydrate, 0.2g salt • **Vegetarian** • **Gluten Free** • **Dairy Free** • **Easy**

1 tbsp sunflower oil

1 large onion, thinly sliced

200g (7oz) basmati rice

1 tbsp curry paste, mild, medium or hot

800ml (1 pint 7fl oz) hot vegetable stock

400g can green lentils, drained

550g (1¼lb) vegetables, such as diced carrots, courgettes, fennel and red pepper

mango chutney and mini poppadums to serve

1 Heat the oil in a large pan and fry the onion for 10 minutes, stirring, or until golden. Set half the onion aside. Add the rice to the pan and stir into the onion, then cook for 1 minute to coat with the oil. Stir in the curry paste and fry for another minute.

2 Pour in the hot stock, lentils and vegetables and bring to the boil. Reduce the heat, cover the pan and simmer for 20 minutes or until the stock has been absorbed and the rice is tender.

3 Leave to stand for 5 minutes, then fluff up with a fork. Garnish with the reserved onion and serve with mango chutney and mini poppadums.

Pumpkin Risotto with Hazelnut Butter

Preparation Time 15 minutes • **Cooking Time** 40 minutes • **Serves 4** • **Per Serving** 706 calories, 50g fat (of which 27g saturates), 51g carbohydrate, 1.1g salt • **Vegetarian** • **Gluten Free** • **Easy**

50g (2oz) butter
175g (6oz) onion, finely chopped
900g (2lb) pumpkin, halved, peeled, seeded and cut into small cubes
2 garlic cloves, crushed
225g (8oz) risotto (arborio) rice
600ml (1 pint) hot chicken stock
grated zest of ½ orange
40g (1½oz) freshly shaved vegetarian Parmesan (see Cook's Tips)
salt and ground black pepper

FOR THE HAZELNUT BUTTER
50g (2oz) hazelnuts
125g (4oz) softened butter
2 tbsp freshly chopped flat-leafed parsley

1 To make the hazelnut butter, spread the hazelnuts on a baking sheet and toast under a hot grill until golden brown, turning frequently. Put the nuts in a clean teatowel and rub off the skins, then chop finely. Put the nuts, butter and parsley on a piece of non-stick baking parchment. Season with pepper and mix together. Mould into a sausage shape, twist at both ends and chill.

2 To make the risotto, melt the butter in a large pan and fry the onion until soft but not coloured.

Add the pumpkin and sauté over a low heat for 5–8 minutes until just beginning to soften. Add the garlic and rice and stir until well mixed. Increase the heat to medium and add the hot stock a little at a time, allowing the liquid to be absorbed after each addition. This will take about 25 minutes.

3 Stir in the orange zest and Parmesan and season with salt and pepper. Serve the risotto with a slice of the hazelnut butter melting on top.

★ COOK'S TIPS
● *If you can't find pumpkin, use butternut squash.*
● Vegetarian cheeses: *some vegetarians prefer to avoid cheeses that have been produced by the traditional method, because this uses animal-derived rennet. Most supermarkets and cheese shops now stock an excellent range of vegetarian cheeses, produced using vegetarian rennet, which comes from plants, such as thistle and mallow, that contain enzymes capable of curdling milk.*

Aubergine and Chickpea Pilau

Preparation Time 10 minutes • **Cooking Time** 20 minutes, plus standing • **Serves 4** • **Per Serving** 462 calories, 20g fat (of which 5g saturates), 58g carbohydrate, 0.9g salt • **Vegetarian** • **Gluten Free** • **Easy**

4–6 tbsp olive oil
275g (10oz) aubergine, roughly chopped
225g (8oz) onions, finely chopped
25g (1oz) butter
½ tsp cumin seeds
175g (6oz) long-grain rice
600ml (1 pint) vegetable or chicken stock
400g can chickpeas, drained and rinsed
225g (8oz) baby spinach leaves
salt and ground black pepper

1 Heat half the oil in a large pan or flameproof casserole over a medium heat. Fry the aubergine for 4–5 minutes, in batches, until deep golden brown. Remove from the pan with a slotted spoon and put to one side. Add the remaining oil to the pan and cook the onions for 5 minutes or until golden and soft.

2 Add the butter to the pan, then stir in the cumin seeds and rice. Fry for 1–2 minutes, then pour in the stock, season with salt and pepper and bring to the boil. Reduce the heat, then simmer, uncovered, for 10–12 minutes until most of the liquid has evaporated and the rice is tender.

3 Remove the pan from the heat. Stir in the chickpeas, spinach and reserved aubergine. Cover with a tight-fitting lid and leave to stand for 5 minutes or until the spinach has wilted and the chickpeas are heated through. Adjust the seasoning to taste. Fork through the rice grains to separate and make them fluffy before serving.

★ GET AHEAD
To prepare ahead Complete the recipe to the end of step 1. Cover and keep in a cool place for 1½ hours.
To use Complete the recipe.

Warm Spiced Rice Salad

Preparation Time 10 minutes • Cooking Time 20–30 minutes • Serves 4 • Per Serving 700 calories, 27g fat (of which 6g saturates), 88g carbohydrate, 0.7g salt • **Vegetarian** • **Gluten Free** • **Easy**

½ tbsp ground cumin
½ tsp ground cinnamon
2 tbsp sunflower oil
2 large red onions, sliced
250g (9oz) basmati rice
600ml (1 pint) hot vegetable or
   chicken stock
400g can lentils, drained and rinsed
salt and ground black pepper

FOR THE SALAD
75g (3oz) watercress
250g (9oz) broccoli, steamed and
   chopped into 2.5cm (1in) pieces
25g (1oz) sultanas
75g (3oz) dried apricots, chopped
75g (3oz) mixed nuts and seeds
2 tbsp freshly chopped flat-leafed
   parsley
100g (3½oz) goat's cheese,
   crumbled

1 Put the cumin and cinnamon into a large deep frying pan and heat gently for 1–2 minutes. Add the oil and onions and fry over a low heat for 8–10 minutes until the onions are soft. Add the rice, toss to coat in the spices and onions, then add the hot stock. Cover and cook for 12–15 minutes until the stock has been absorbed and the rice is cooked. Season, tip into a serving bowl and add the lentils.

2 To make the salad, add the watercress, broccoli, sultanas, apricots and mixed nuts and seeds to the bowl. Scatter with the parsley, then toss together, top with the cheese and serve immediately.

★TRY SOMETHING DIFFERENT
Replace the goat's cheese with two roasted, skinless chicken breasts, which have been shredded.

Curried Coconut and Vegetable Rice

★

Preparation Time 15 minutes • **Cooking Time** 30 minutes, plus standing • **Serves 6** • **Per Serving** 413 calories, 17g fat (of which 2g saturates), 57g carbohydrate, 0.4g salt • **Vegetarian** • **Gluten Free** • **Dairy Free** • **Easy**

1 large aubergine, about 300g (11oz)
1 large butternut squash, about 500g (1lb 2oz), peeled and seeded
250g (9oz) dwarf green beans, trimmed
100ml (3½fl oz) vegetable oil
1 large onion, chopped
1 tbsp black mustard seeds
3 tbsp korma paste
350g (12oz) basmati rice
400ml can coconut milk
200g (7oz) baby spinach leaves
salt and ground black pepper

1 Cut the aubergine and butternut squash into 2cm (¾in) cubes. Slice the green beans into 2cm (¾in) pieces.

2 Heat the oil in a large pan. Add the onion and cook for about 5 minutes or until a light golden colour. Add the mustard seeds and cook, stirring, until they begin to pop. Stir in the korma paste and cook for 1 minute.

3 Add the aubergine and cook, stirring, for 5 minutes. Add the butternut squash, beans, rice and 2 tsp salt, mixing well. Pour in the coconut milk and add 600ml (1 pint) water. Bring to the boil, then reduce the heat, cover the pan and simmer for 15–18 minutes.

4 When the rice and vegetables are cooked, remove the lid and put the spinach leaves on top. Cover and leave, off the heat, for 5 minutes. Gently stir the wilted spinach through the rice, check the seasoning and serve immediately.

Chickpea Curry

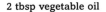

Preparation Time 20 minutes • **Cooking Time** 40–45 minutes • **Serves 6** • **Per Serving** 291 calories, 8g fat (of which 1g saturates), 46g carbohydrate, 1.3g salt • **Vegetarian** • **Gluten Free** • **Dairy Free** • **Easy**

2 tbsp vegetable oil
2 onions, finely sliced
2 garlic cloves, crushed
1 tbsp ground coriander
1 tsp mild chilli powder
1 tbsp black mustard seeds
2 tbsp tamarind paste (see Cook's
   Tip)
2 tbsp sun-dried tomato paste
750g (1lb 11oz) new potatoes,
   quartered
400g can chopped tomatoes
1 litre (1¾ pints) hot vegetable
   stock
250g (9oz) green beans, trimmed
2 × 400g cans chickpeas, drained
   and rinsed
2 tsp garam masala
salt and ground black pepper

1 Heat the oil in a pan and fry the onions for 10–15 minutes until golden – when they have a good colour they will add depth of flavour. Add the garlic, coriander, chilli powder, mustard seeds, tamarind paste and sun-dried tomato paste. Cook for 1–2 minutes until the aroma from the spices is released.

2 Add the potatoes and toss in the spices for 1–2 minutes. Add the tomatoes and hot stock and season with salt and pepper. Cover and bring to the boil, then reduce the heat and simmer, half covered, for 20 minutes or until the potatoes are just cooked.

3 Add the beans and chickpeas and continue to cook for 5 minutes or until the beans are tender and the chickpeas are warmed through. Stir in the garam masala and serve.

⭐ COOK'S TIP
Tamarind paste has a very sharp, sour flavour and is widely used in Asian and South-east Asian cooking.

Spiced Chickpeas with Spinach

Preparation Time 10 minutes • **Cooking Time** 20–30 minutes • **Serves 4** • **Per Serving** 306 calories, 12g fat (of which 2g saturates), 45g carbohydrate, 0.7g salt • **Vegetarian** • **Gluten Free** • **Dairy Free** • **Easy**

3 sweet potatoes, chopped into
   chunks
½ tsp cumin seeds, roasted and
   ground
1 tsp olive oil
3 tbsp extra virgin olive oil
1 tbsp red wine vinegar
1 red chilli, chopped (see page 19)
4 spring onions, sliced
400g cans chickpeas, drained and
   rinsed (see Cook's Tip)
a handful of spinach leaves
salt and ground black pepper

1 Preheat the oven to 200°C (180°C fan oven) mark 6. Put the sweet potatoes into a roasting tin and toss in the ground cumin and olive oil. Season with salt and pepper and roast for 20–30 minutes until tender.

2 Mix the extra virgin olive oil with the vinegar, chilli and spring onions. Stir into the sweet potatoes with the chickpeas, then check the seasoning. Stir in the spinach until it just wilts, then serve.

★ COOK'S TIP
Allow half a can of chickpeas per person if you're serving them as a main meal, and a quarter of a can per person if they're part of a side dish. They are a rich source of protein and high in fibre too.

Veggie Curry

Preparation Time 5 minutes • **Cooking Time** 12 minutes • **Serves 1** • **Per Serving** 468 calories, 20g fat (of which 3g saturates), 58g carbohydrate, 1.4g salt • **Vegetarian** • **Gluten Free** • **Dairy Free** • **Easy**

1 tbsp medium curry paste
227g can chopped tomatoes
150ml (¼ pint) hot vegetable stock
200g (7oz) vegetables, such as
   broccoli, courgettes and
   sugarsnap peas, roughly chopped
½ × 410g can chickpeas, drained
   and rinsed
griddled wholemeal pitta and
   yogurt to serve

1 Heat the curry paste in a large heavy-based pan for 1 minute, stirring the paste to warm the spices. Add the tomatoes and hot stock. Bring to the boil, then reduce the heat to a simmer and add the vegetables. Simmer for 5–6 minutes until the vegetables are tender.

2 Stir in the chickpeas and heat for 1–2 minutes until hot. Serve the vegetable curry with a griddled wholemeal pitta and yogurt.

Tofu Laksa Curry

Preparation Time 15 minutes • Cooking Time 22 minutes • Serves 4 • Per Serving 349 calories, 7g fat
(of which 1g saturates), 59g carbohydrate, 1.4g salt • **Vegetarian** • **Dairy Free** • **Easy**

2 tbsp light soy sauce
½ red chilli, seeded and chopped
 (see page 19)
5cm (2in) piece fresh root ginger,
 peeled and grated
250g pack fresh tofu
1 tbsp olive oil
1 onion, finely sliced
3 tbsp laksa paste (see page 220)
200ml (7fl oz) coconut milk
900ml (1½ pints) hot vegetable
 stock
200g (7oz) baby sweetcorn, halved
 lengthways
200g (7oz) fine green beans,
 trimmed

250g pack medium rice noodles
salt and ground black pepper
2 spring onions, sliced diagonally,
 2 tbsp chopped coriander and
 1 lime, cut into four wedges, to
 garnish

1 Put the soy sauce, chilli and ginger into a bowl, add the tofu and leave to marinate while you cook the onion.

2 Heat the oil in a large pan. Add the onion and fry over a medium heat for 10 minutes, stirring, or until golden. Add the laksa paste and cook for 2 minutes. Add the tofu, coconut milk, hot stock and sweetcorn and season. Bring to the boil, add the green beans, reduce the heat and simmer for 8–10 minutes.

3 Meanwhile, put the noodles into a large bowl, pour boiling water over them and soak for 30 seconds. Drain, then stir into the curry. Pour into bowls and garnish with the spring onions, coriander and lime wedges. Serve immediately.

Aubergine and Lentil Curry

Preparation Time 10 minutes • **Cooking Time** 40–45 minutes • **Serves 4** • **Per Serving** 335 calories, 15g fat (of which 3g saturates), 39g carbohydrate, 0.2g salt • **Vegetarian** • **Easy**

3 tbsp olive oil
2 aubergines, cut into 2.5cm (1in) chunks
1 onion, chopped
2 tbsp mild curry paste
3 × 400g cans chopped tomatoes
200ml (7fl oz) hot vegetable stock
150g (5oz) red lentils, rinsed
100g (3½oz) spinach leaves
25g (1oz) fresh coriander, roughly chopped
2 tbsp fat-free Greek yogurt
rice to serve (optional)

1 Heat 2 tbsp oil in a large pan over a low heat and fry the aubergine chunks until golden. Remove from the pan and put to one side.

2 Heat the remaining oil in the same pan and fry the onion for 8–10 minutes until soft. Add the curry paste and stir-fry for a further 2 minutes.

3 Add the tomatoes, hot stock, lentils and reserved aubergines to the pan. Bring to the boil, then reduce the heat to a low simmer, half-cover the pan with a lid and simmer for 25 minutes or according to the lentils' pack instructions.

4 At the end of cooking, stir the spinach, coriander and yogurt through the curry. Serve with rice, if you like.

★ COOK'S TIP
Choose aubergines that are firm, shiny and blemish-free, with a bright green stem.

Mauritian Vegetable Curry

Preparation Time 15 minutes • **Cooking Time** 30 minutes • **Serves 4** • **Per Serving** 184 calories, 11g fat (of which 1g saturates), 18g carbohydrate, 1.7g salt • **Vegetarian** • **Dairy Free** • **Easy**

3 tbsp vegetable oil

1 onion, finely sliced

4 garlic cloves, crushed

2.5cm (1in) piece fresh root ginger, peeled and grated

3 tbsp medium curry powder

6 fresh curry leaves

150g (5oz) potatoes, cut into 1cm (½in) cubes

125g (4oz) aubergine, cut into 2cm (¾in) sticks, 5mm (¼in) wide

150g (5oz) carrots, cut into 5mm (¼in) dice

900ml (1½ pints) hot vegetable stock

a pinch of saffron threads

1 tsp salt

150g (5oz) green beans, trimmed

75g (3oz) frozen peas

ground black pepper

3 tbsp freshly chopped coriander to garnish

1 Heat the oil in a large heavy-based pan over a low heat. Add the onion and fry for 5–10 minutes until golden. Add the garlic, ginger, curry powder and curry leaves and fry for a further minute.

2 Add the potatoes and aubergine to the pan and fry, stirring, for 2 minutes. Add the carrots, hot stock, saffron and salt. Season with plenty of pepper. Cover and cook for 10 minutes or until the vegetables are almost tender.

3 Add the beans and peas to the pan and cook for a further 4 minutes. Sprinkle with the chopped coriander and serve.

★ GET AHEAD

To prepare ahead *Complete the recipe, without the garnish, and chill quickly. Keep in the fridge for up to two days.*
To use *Put into a pan, cover and bring to the boil, then simmer for 10–15 minutes. Complete the recipe.*

Saag Aloo

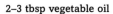

Preparation Time 15 minutes • **Cooking Time** 55 minutes • **Serves 4** • **Per Serving** 295 calories, 10g fat (of which 1g saturates), 47g carbohydrate, 0.2g salt • **Vegetarian** • **Gluten Free** • **Dairy Free** • **Easy**

2–3 tbsp vegetable oil
1 onion, finely sliced
2 garlic cloves, finely chopped
1 tbsp black mustard seeds
2 tsp ground turmeric
900g (2lb) potatoes, cut into 4cm
   (½in) chunks
1 tsp salt
4 handfuls of baby spinach leaves

1 Heat the oil in a pan and fry the onion over a medium heat for 10 minutes or until golden, taking care not to burn it.

2 Add the garlic, mustard seeds and turmeric and cook for 1 minute. Add the potatoes, salt and 150ml (¼ pint) water. Cover the pan and bring to the boil, then reduce the heat and cook gently for 35–40 minutes or until tender. Add the spinach and cook until the leaves just wilt. Serve immediately.

Lentil Chilli

Preparation Time 10 minutes • **Cooking Time** 30 minutes • **Serves 6** • **Per Serving** 191 calories, 2g fat (of which trace saturates), 30g carbohydrate, 0g salt • **Vegetarian** • **Dairy Free** • **Easy**

oil-water spray (see Cook's Tip)
2 red onions, chopped
1½ tsp each ground coriander and ground cumin
½ tsp ground paprika
2 garlic cloves, crushed
2 sun-dried tomatoes, chopped
¼ tsp crushed dried chilli flakes
125ml (4fl oz) red wine
300ml (½ pint) hot vegetable stock
2 × 400g cans brown or green lentils, drained and rinsed
2 × 400g cans chopped tomatoes
sugar to taste
salt and ground black pepper
plain low-fat yogurt and rice (optional) to serve

1 Spray a pan with the oil-water spray and cook the onions for 5 minutes or until softened. Add the coriander, cumin and paprika. Combine the garlic, sun-dried tomatoes, chilli flakes, wine and hot stock and add to the pan. Cover and simmer for 5–7 minutes. Uncover and simmer until the onions are very tender and the liquid is almost gone.

2 Stir in the lentils and canned tomatoes and season with salt and pepper. Simmer, uncovered, for 15 minutes or until thick. Stir in sugar to taste. Remove from the heat.

3 Ladle out a quarter of the mixture and whiz in a food processor or blender. Combine the puréed and unpuréed portions. Serve with yogurt, and rice, if you like.

★ COOK'S TIP

Oil-water spray is far lower in calories than oil alone and, as it sprays on thinly and evenly, you'll use less. Fill one-eighth of a travel-size spray bottle with oil such as sunflower, light olive or vegetable (rapeseed) oil – then top up with water. To use, shake well before spraying.

Black-eye Bean Chilli

Preparation Time 10 minutes • **Cooking Time** 20 minutes • **Serves 4** • **Per Serving** 245 calories, 5g fat (of which 1g saturates), 39g carbohydrate, 1.8g salt • **Vegetarian** • **Easy**

1 tbsp olive oil
1 onion, chopped
3 celery sticks, finely chopped
2 × 400g cans black-eye beans, drained
2 × 400g cans chopped tomatoes
2 or 3 splashes of Tabasco sauce
3 tbsp freshly chopped coriander
warm tortillas and soured cream to serve

1 Heat the oil in a heavy-based frying pan over a low heat. Add the onion and celery and fry for 10 minutes or until softened.

2 Add the black-eye beans to the pan with the tomatoes and Tabasco sauce. Bring to the boil, then reduce the heat and simmer for 10 minutes.

3 Just before serving, stir in the chopped coriander. Spoon the chilli on to warm tortillas and serve with a spoonful of soured cream.

★ TRY SOMETHING DIFFERENT
Replace half the black-eye beans with red kidney beans.

Chilli Bean Cake

Preparation Time 10 minutes • **Cooking Time** 20 minutes • **Serves 4** • **Per Serving** 265 calories, 6g fat (of which 1g saturates), 41g carbohydrate, 2.1g salt • **Vegetarian** • **Dairy Free** • **Easy**

3 tbsp olive oil
75g (3oz) wholemeal breadcrumbs
1 bunch of spring onions, finely chopped
1 orange pepper, seeded and chopped
1 small green chilli, seeded and finely chopped (see page 19)
1 garlic clove, crushed
1 tsp ground turmeric (optional)
400g can mixed beans, drained and rinsed
3 tbsp mayonnaise
a small handful of fresh basil, chopped
salt and ground black pepper
soured cream, freshly chopped coriander and lime wedges to serve (optional)

1 Heat 2 tbsp oil in a non-stick frying pan over a medium heat and fry the breadcrumbs until golden and beginning to crisp. Remove and put to one side.

2 Using the same pan, add the remaining oil and fry the spring onions until soft and golden. Add the orange pepper, chilli, garlic and turmeric, if using, and cook, stirring, for 5 minutes.

3 Tip in the beans, mayonnaise, two-thirds of the fried breadcrumbs and the basil. Season with salt and pepper, mash roughly with a fork, then press down the mixture to flatten it. Sprinkle with the remaining breadcrumbs. Fry the bean cake over a medium heat for 4–5 minutes until the base is golden. Remove from the heat, cut into wedges and serve with soured cream, coriander and lime wedges, if you like.

Lentil Casserole

Preparation Time 20 minutes • **Cooking Time** 1 hour • **Serves 6** • **Per Serving** 239 calories, 6g fat (of which 1g saturates), 36g carbohydrate, 0.4g salt • **Vegetarian** • **Gluten Free** • **Dairy Free** • **Easy**

2 tbsp olive oil
2 onions, sliced
4 carrots, sliced
3 leeks, trimmed and sliced
450g (1lb) button mushrooms
2 garlic cloves, crushed
2.5cm (1in) piece fresh root ginger,
   peeled and grated
1 tbsp ground coriander
225g (8oz) split red lentils
750ml (1¼ pints) hot vegetable
   stock
4 tbsp freshly chopped coriander
salt and ground black pepper

1 Preheat the oven to 180°C (160°C fan oven) mark 4. Heat the oil in a flameproof ovenproof casserole, add the onions, carrots and leeks and fry, stirring, for 5 minutes. Add the mushrooms, garlic, ginger and ground coriander and fry for 2–3 minutes.

2 Rinse and drain the lentils, then stir into the casserole with the hot stock. Season with salt and pepper and return to the boil. Cover and cook in the oven for 45–50 minutes until the vegetables and lentils are tender. Stir in the chopped coriander before serving.

Moroccan Chickpea Stew

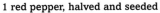

Preparation Time 10 minutes • **Cooking Time** 40 minutes • **Serves 4** • **Per Serving** 232 calories, 9g fat (of which 1g saturates), 29g carbohydrate, 0.6g salt • **Vegetarian** • **Dairy Free** • **Easy**

1 red pepper, halved and seeded
1 green pepper, halved and seeded
1 yellow pepper, halved and seeded
2 tbsp olive oil
1 onion, finely sliced
2 garlic cloves, crushed
1 tbsp harissa paste
2 tbsp tomato purée
½ tsp ground cumin
1 aubergine, diced
400g can chickpeas, drained and
   rinsed
450ml (¾ pint) vegetable stock
4 tbsp roughly chopped fresh flat-
   leafed parsley, plus a few sprigs
   to garnish
salt and ground black pepper

1 Preheat the grill and lay the peppers, skin side up, on a baking sheet. Grill for around 5 minutes until the skin begins to blister and char. Put the peppers into a plastic bag, seal and put to one side for a few minutes. When cooled a little, peel off the skins and discard, then slice the peppers and put to one side.

2 Heat the oil in a large heavy-based frying pan over a low heat, add the onion and cook for 5–10 minutes until soft. Add the garlic, harissa, tomato purée and cumin and cook for 2 minutes.

3 Add the peppers to the pan with the aubergine. Stir everything to coat evenly with the spices and cook for 2 minutes. Add the chickpeas and stock, season well with salt and pepper and bring to the boil. Reduce the heat and simmer for 20 minutes.

4 Just before serving, stir the parsley through the chickpea stew. Serve in warmed bowls, garnished with parsley sprigs.

Tomato and Butter Bean Stew

Preparation Time 10 minutes • **Cooking Time** 50–55 minutes • **Serves 4** • **Per Serving** 286 calories, 8g fat (of which 1g saturates), 41g carbohydrate, 1.8g salt • **Vegetarian** • **Dairy Free** • **Easy**

2 tbsp olive oil
1 onion, finely sliced
2 garlic cloves, finely chopped
2 large leeks, trimmed and sliced
2 × 400g cans cherry tomatoes
2 × 400g cans butter beans, drained
   and rinsed
150ml (¼ pint) hot vegetable stock
1–2 tbsp balsamic vinegar
salt and ground black pepper

1 Preheat the oven to 180°C (160°C fan oven) mark 4. Heat the oil in a flameproof casserole over a medium heat. Add the onion and garlic and cook for 10 minutes or until golden and soft. Add the leeks and cook, covered, for 5 minutes.

2 Add the tomatoes, beans and hot stock and season well with salt and pepper. Bring to the boil, then cover and cook in the oven for 35–40 minutes until the sauce has thickened. Remove from the oven, stir in the vinegar and spoon into warmed bowls.

Italian Bean Stew

Preparation Time 15 minutes • **Cooking Time** 15 minutes • **Serves 4** • **Per Serving** 405 calories, 10g fat (of which 1g saturates), 35g carbohydrate, 1.3g salt • **Vegetarian** • **Easy**

1 tbsp olive oil

2 large shallots, finely sliced

2 medium carrots, finely diced

1 celery stick, finely diced

1.5 litres (2½ pints) hot vegetable stock

250g (9oz) asparagus, cut into 2cm (¾in) lengths

75g (3oz) tiny soup pasta, such as ditalini or stellete

2 × 400g cans flageolet beans, drained and rinsed

2 tbsp fresh ready-made pesto (see page 11), made with vegetarian Parmesan, to serve

1 Heat the oil in a large pan. Add the shallots and fry gently for 3 minutes or until softened but not coloured.

2 Add the carrots, celery and hot stock and bring to the boil. Reduce the heat and simmer for 10 minutes. Add the asparagus and pasta and cook for a further 7 minutes.

3 Stir in the flageolet beans and heat for 2–3 minutes. Divide among the serving bowls and serve with a swirl of pesto on top.

Pea, Mint and Ricotta Pasta

Preparation Time 5 minutes • **Cooking Time** 10 minutes • **Serves 4** • **Per Serving** 426 calories, 14g fat (of which 5g saturates), 63g carbohydrate, 0g salt • **Vegetarian** • **Easy**

300g (11oz) farfalle pasta
200g (7oz) frozen peas
175g (6oz) vegetarian ricotta
3 tbsp freshly chopped mint
2 tbsp extra virgin olive oil
salt and ground black pepper

1 Cook the pasta according to the pack instructions. Add the frozen peas for the last 4 minutes of cooking.

2 Drain the pasta and peas, reserving the water, then return to the pan. Stir in the ricotta and mint with a ladleful of pasta cooking water. Season well, drizzle with the oil and serve at once.

Pasta with Pesto and Beans

Preparation Time 5 minutes • **Cooking Time** 15 minutes • **Serves 4** • **Per Serving** 738 calories, 38g fat (of which 10g saturates), 74g carbohydrate, 1g salt • **Vegetarian** • **Easy**

350g (12oz) dried pasta shapes
175g (6oz) fine green beans,
roughly chopped
175g (6oz) small salad potatoes,
such as Anya, thickly sliced
250g (9oz) fresh ready-made pesto
(see page 11), made with
vegetarian Parmesan
Parmesan shavings to serve
(optional, see page 155)

1 Bring a large pan of water to the boil. Add the pasta, bring back to the boil and cook for 5 minutes.

2 Add the beans and potatoes to the pan and continue to boil for a further 7–8 minutes until the potatoes are just tender.

3 Drain the pasta, beans and potatoes in a colander, then tip everything back into the pan and stir in the pesto sauce. Serve scattered with Parmesan shavings, if you like.

★ COOK'S TIP
Use leftover cooked pasta, beans or potatoes: tip the pasta into a pan of boiling water and bring back to the boil for 30 seconds. Bring the beans or potatoes to room temperature, but there's no need to reboil them.

Spinach and Cheese Lasagne

Preparation Time 30 minutes • **Cooking Time** 50–55 minutes • **Serves 6** • **Per Serving** 442 calories, 27g fat (of which 14g saturates), 32g carbohydrate, 1.6g salt • **Vegetarian** • **Easy**

- **125g (4oz) fresh or frozen leaf spinach, thawed**
- **40g (1½oz) fresh basil, roughly chopped**
- **250g (9oz) ricotta cheese**
- **5 pieces marinated artichokes, drained and chopped**
- **350g carton cheese sauce**
- **175g (6oz) Dolcelatte cheese, roughly diced**
- **9 sheets fresh egg lasagne**
- **25g (1oz) pinenuts, toasted**
- **tomato salad to serve**

1 Preheat the oven to 180°C (160°C fan oven) mark 4. Chop the spinach finely (if it was frozen, squeeze out the excess liquid first). Put into a bowl with the basil, ricotta cheese, artichokes and 6 tbsp cheese sauce. Mix well.

2 Beat the Dolcelatte into the remaining cheese sauce. Layer the ricotta mixture, lasagne, then cheese sauce into a 23 x 23cm (9 x 9in) ovenproof dish. Repeat to use up the remainder.

3 Cook the lasagne for 40 minutes. Sprinkle the pinenuts over and put back in the oven for a further 10–15 minutes until golden. Serve with a tomato salad.

★COOK'S TIP
Italian Dolcelatte cheese has a much milder flavour than Stilton or Roquefort; it also has a deliciously rich, creamy texture.

Baked Tomatoes and Fennel

Preparation Time 10 minutes • **Cooking Time** 1¼ hours • **Serves 6** • **Per Serving** 127 calories, 9g fat (of which 1g saturates), 7g carbohydrate, 0.1g salt • **Vegetarian** • **Gluten Free** • **Dairy Free** • **Easy**

900g (2lb) fennel, trimmed and cut into quarters
75ml (2½fl oz) white wine
5 thyme sprigs
75ml (2½fl oz) olive oil
900g (2lb) ripe beef or plum tomatoes

1 Preheat the oven to 200°C (180°C fan oven) mark 6. Put the fennel into a roasting tin and pour the wine over it. Snip the thyme sprigs over the fennel, drizzle with the oil and roast for 45 minutes.

2 Halve the tomatoes, add to the roasting tin and continue to roast for 30 minutes or until tender, basting with the juices halfway through.

 COOK'S TIP
This is an ideal accompaniment to grilled fish or meat, or a vegetarian frittata.

Mushrooms with Cashew Nuts

Preparation Time 5 minutes • **Cooking Time** 5–8 minutes • **Serves 4** • **Per Serving** 75 calories, 6g fat
(of which 1g saturates), 2g carbohydrate, 0.1g salt • **Vegetarian** • **Gluten Free** • **Easy**

1 tbsp vegetable oil
25g (1oz) unsalted cashew nuts
225g (8oz) brown-cap mushrooms,
   sliced
1 tbsp lemon juice
4 tbsp freshly chopped coriander,
   plus fresh sprigs to garnish
1 tbsp single cream (optional)
salt and ground black pepper

1 Heat the oil in a wok or large frying pan. Add the cashew nuts and cook over a high heat for 2–3 minutes until golden. Add the mushrooms and cook for a further 2–3 minutes until tender, stirring frequently.

2 Stir in the lemon juice and chopped coriander and season to taste with salt and pepper. Heat until bubbling. Remove the pan from the heat and stir in the cream, if using. Adjust the seasoning if necessary and serve immediately, garnished with coriander sprigs.

★ TRY SOMETHING
DIFFERENT
Chinese Garlic Mushrooms
Replace the nuts with 2 crushed garlic cloves and stir-fry for only 20 seconds before adding the mushrooms. Replace the lemon juice with rice wine or dry sherry.

Courgettes with Sesame Seeds

Preparation Time 5 minutes • **Cooking Time** 12 minutes • **Serves 6** • **Per Serving** 107 calories, 9g fat (of which 1g saturates), 3g carbohydrate, 0.4g salt • **Vegetarian** • **Gluten Free** • **Dairy Free** • **Easy**

2 tbsp sesame seeds
2 tbsp vegetable oil
4 garlic cloves, crushed
900g (2lb) courgettes, thinly sliced
1 spring onion, thickly sliced
½ tsp salt
1 tbsp sesame oil
ground black pepper
banana leaves to serve (optional, see Cook's Tip)

1 Toast the sesame seeds in a hot wok or large frying pan until golden. Tip on to a plate.

2 Heat the vegetable oil in the wok or frying pan. Add the garlic and fry for 2 minutes.

3 Add the courgettes and stir-fry for 7–8 minutes. Stir in the spring onion, salt and sesame oil. Season to taste with pepper. Cook for a further 1 minute, then add the toasted sesame seeds. Stir once and serve hot or cold on a bed of banana leaves, if you like.

★ COOK'S TIP
Banana leaves are sometimes used instead of plates in South-east Asia; they make an unusual presentation and are available from some Asian food shops.

Roasted Ratatouille

Preparation Time 15 minutes **Cooking Time** 1½ hours • **Serves 6** • **Per Serving** 224 calories, 18g fat (of which 3g saturates), 14g carbohydrate, 0g salt • **Vegetarian** • **Gluten Free** • **Dairy Free** • **Easy**

400g (14oz) red peppers, seeded and roughly chopped
700g (1½lb) aubergines, cut into chunks
450g (1lb) onions, cut into wedges
4 or 5 garlic cloves, unpeeled and left whole
150ml (¼ pint) olive oil
1 tsp fennel seeds
200ml (7fl oz) passata
sea salt flakes and ground black pepper
a few fresh thyme sprigs to garnish

1 Preheat the oven to 240°C (220°C fan oven) mark 9. Put the peppers, aubergines, onions, garlic, oil and fennel seeds into a roasting tin. Season with sea salt flakes and pepper and toss together.

2 Transfer to the oven and cook for 30 minutes (tossing frequently during cooking) or until the vegetables are charred and beginning to soften.

3 Stir the passata through the vegetables and put the roasting tin back in the oven for 50–60 minutes, stirring occasionally. Garnish with the thyme sprigs and serve.

★ TRY SOMETHING DIFFERENT
Replace half the aubergines with 400g (14oz) courgettes; use a mix of green and red peppers; garnish with fresh basil instead of thyme.

Roasted Summer Vegetables

Preparation Time 10 minutes, plus salting and cooling • **Cooking Time** 40 minutes • **Serves 6** • **Per Serving** 137 calories, 6g fat (of which 1g saturates), 18g carbohydrate, 0g salt • **Vegetarian** • **Gluten Free** • **Dairy Free** • **Easy**

1 aubergine, cut into chunks
2 large courgettes, trimmed and thickly sliced
550g (1¼lb) new potatoes, halved if large
4 garlic cloves, unpeeled
3 tbsp extra virgin olive oil
1 tbsp balsamic vinegar
75g (3oz) sunblush tomatoes, roughly chopped
salt and ground black pepper
a small handful of basil leaves, roughly torn, to garnish

1 Put the aubergine and courgettes into a colander. Sprinkle with salt to draw out excess juices – this firms up the flesh so that it absorbs less oil during roasting. Cover with a plate and weigh down with cans for 30 minutes. Rinse and pat dry with kitchen paper.

2 Preheat the oven to 200°C (180°C fan oven) mark 6. Put the potatoes and garlic into a roasting pan with the oil and season well with salt and pepper. Cook for 15 minutes, then add the aubergine, courgettes and vinegar and toss well. Roast for 20–25 minutes until the vegetables are tender.

3 Tip the vegetables into a serving bowl and leave to cool – they're best at room temperature. Stir in the tomatoes and garnish with basil just before serving.

★ COOK'S TIP
To make this a more substantial meal, stir in a 400g can of drained chickpeas and 75g (3oz) marinated artichokes before serving.

Leek and Broccoli Bake

Preparation Time 20 minutes • **Cooking Time** 45–55 minutes • **Serves 4** • **Per Serving** 245 calories, 13g fat (of which 4g saturates), 18g carbohydrate, 0.4g salt • **Vegetarian** • **Gluten Free** • **Easy**

2 tbsp olive oil

1 large red onion, cut into wedges

1 aubergine, chopped

2 leeks, trimmed and cut into chunks

1 broccoli head, cut into florets and stalks chopped

3 large flat mushrooms, chopped

2 × 400g cans cherry tomatoes

3 rosemary sprigs, chopped

50g (2oz) vegetarian Parmesan, freshly grated (optional, see page 155)

salt and ground black pepper

1 Preheat the oven to 200°C (180°C fan oven) mark 6. Heat the oil in a large flameproof dish, add the onion, aubergine and leeks and cook for 10–12 minutes until golden and softened.

2 Add the broccoli, mushrooms, cherry tomatoes, half the rosemary and 300ml (½ pint) boiling water. Season with salt and pepper. Stir well, then cover and cook in the oven for 30 minutes.

3 Meanwhile, put the Parmesan into a bowl, if using. Add the remaining rosemary and season with pepper. When the vegetables are cooked, remove the lid and sprinkle the Parmesan mixture on top. Cook, uncovered, in the oven for a further 5–10 minutes until the topping is golden.

★ TRY SOMETHING DIFFERENT
Use sliced courgettes instead of aubergine.

Easy Veggie Pad Thai

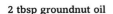

Preparation Time 15 minutes • **Cooking Time** 10 minutes • **Serves 2** • **Per Serving** 766 calories, 41g fat (of which 8g saturates), 84g carbohydrate, 0.7g salt • **Vegetarian** • **Dairy Free** • **Easy**

2 tbsp groundnut oil

2 medium eggs, beaten

2 spring onions, cut into chunks

¼ red chilli, finely chopped (see page 19)

1 red pepper, seeded and finely sliced

1 carrot, finely sliced

1 garlic clove, crushed

juice of ½ lime

1 tbsp tamarind paste (see page 159)

125g (4oz) bean sprouts

200g (7oz) straight-to-wok ribbon noodles

a handful each of freshly chopped coriander and mint

2 tbsp roasted peanuts, chopped

salt and ground black pepper

1 Heat 1 tbsp oil in a wok or non-stick pan. Add the eggs, then stir-fry until just set. Season, scoop out and put to one side.

2 Heat the remaining 1 tbsp oil in the wok and add the spring onions, chilli, red pepper, carrot and garlic. Stir-fry for 3–5 minutes, adding a splash of water if you need to.

3 Stir in the lime juice and tamarind, then add the bean sprouts, cooked egg and noodles. Mix well and heat through. Sprinkle with the herbs and peanuts and serve.

Stir-fried Green Vegetables

Preparation Time 5 minutes • Cooking Time 3–4 minutes • Serves 6 • Per Serving 100 calories, 8g fat
(of which 3g saturates), 5g carbohydrate, 0.1g salt • **Vegetarian** • **Gluten Free** • **Easy**

2 tbsp vegetable oil
225g (8oz) courgettes, thinly sliced
175g (6oz) mangetouts
25g (1oz) butter
175g (6oz) frozen peas, thawed
salt and ground black pepper

1 Heat the oil in a wok or large frying pan, add the courgettes and stir-fry for 1–2 minutes. Add the mangetouts and cook for 1 minute. Add the butter and peas and cook for 1 minute. Season to taste with salt and pepper and serve immediately.

★ TRY SOMETHING DIFFERENT
Try other vegetables, such as thinly sliced leeks, spring onions or pak choi.

Chilli Vegetable and Coconut Stir-fry

★

Preparation Time 25 minutes • **Cooking Time** about 10 minutes • **Serves 4** • **Per Serving** 220 calories, 12g fat
(of which 2g saturates), 22g carbohydrate, 1.7g salt • **Vegetarian** • **Dairy Free** • **Easy**

2 tbsp sesame oil
2 green chillies, seeded and finely
    chopped (see page 19)
2.5cm (1in) piece fresh root ginger,
    peeled and finely grated
2 garlic cloves, crushed
1 tbsp Thai green curry paste
125g (4oz) carrots, cut into fine
    matchsticks
125g (4oz) baby sweetcorn, halved
125g (4oz) mangetouts, halved on
    the diagonal
2 large red peppers, seeded and
    finely sliced
2 small pak choi, quartered
4 spring onions, finely chopped
300ml (½ pint) coconut milk
2 tbsp peanut satay sauce
2 tbsp light soy sauce
1 tsp soft brown sugar
4 tbsp freshly chopped coriander,
    plus extra sprigs to garnish
ground black pepper
roasted peanuts to garnish
rice or noodles to serve (optional)

1 Heat the oil in a wok or large non-stick frying pan over a medium heat, add the chillies, ginger and garlic and stir-fry for 1 minute. Add the curry paste and fry for a further 30 seconds.

2 Add the carrots, sweetcorn, mangetouts and red peppers. Stir-fry over a high heat for 3–4 minutes, then add the pak choi and spring onions. Cook, stirring, for a further 1–2 minutes.

3 Pour in the coconut milk, satay sauce, soy sauce and sugar. Season with pepper, bring to the boil and cook for 1–2 minutes, then add the chopped coriander. Garnish with the peanuts and coriander sprigs and serve with rice or noodles, if you like.

★ COOK'S TIP
Check the ingredients in the Thai curry paste: some contain shrimp and are therefore not suitable for vegetarians.

Sweet Chilli Tofu Stir-fry

Preparation Time 5 minutes, plus marinating • Cooking Time 12 minutes • Serves 4 • Per Serving 167 calories, 11g fat (of which 2g saturates), 5g carbohydrate, 1.6g salt • **Vegetarian** • **Dairy Free** • **Easy**

200g (7oz) firm tofu
4 tbsp sweet chilli sauce
2 tbsp light soy sauce
1 tbsp sesame seeds
2 tbsp toasted sesame oil
600g (1lb 5oz) ready-prepared mixed stir-fry vegetables, such as carrots, broccoli, mangetouts and bean sprouts
a handful of pea shoots or young salad leaves to garnish

1 Drain the tofu, pat it dry and cut it into large cubes. Put the tofu into a shallow container and pour over 1 tbsp sweet chilli sauce and 1 tbsp light soy sauce. Cover and marinate for 10 minutes.

2 Meanwhile, toast the sesame seeds in a hot wok or large frying pan until golden. Tip on to a plate.

3 Return the wok or frying pan to the heat and add 1 tbsp oil. Add the marinated tofu and stir-fry for 5 minutes or until golden. Remove and set aside.

4 Heat the remaining 1 tbsp oil in the pan, add the vegetables and stir-fry for 3–4 minutes until just tender. Stir in the cooked tofu.

5 Pour the remaining sweet chilli sauce and soy sauce into the pan, toss well and cook for a further 1 minute or until heated through. Sprinkle with the toasted sesame seeds and pea shoots or salad leaves and serve immediately.

Chickpea and Chilli Stir-fry

Preparation Time 10 minutes • **Cooking Time** 15–20 minutes • **Serves 4** • **Per Serving** 258 calories, 11g fat (of which 1g saturates), 30g carbohydrate, 1g salt • **Vegetarian** • **Gluten Free** • **Dairy Free** • **Easy**

2 tbsp olive oil
1 tsp ground cumin
1 red onion, sliced
2 garlic cloves, finely chopped
1 red chilli, seeded and finely chopped (see page 19)
2 × 400g cans chickpeas, drained and rinsed
400g (14oz) cherry tomatoes
125g (4oz) baby spinach leaves
salt and ground black pepper
brown rice or pasta to serve (optional)

1 Heat the oil in a wok or large frying pan. Add the cumin and fry for 1–2 minutes. Add the onion and stir-fry for 5–7 minutes.

2 Add the garlic and chilli and stir-fry for 2 minutes.

3 Add the chickpeas to the wok with the tomatoes. Reduce the heat and simmer until the chickpeas are hot. Season with salt and pepper, then add the spinach and stir until just wilted. Serve with brown rice or pasta, if you like.

Stir-fried Veg with Crispy Crumbs

Preparation Time 10 minutes • **Cooking Time** 15–20 minutes • **Serves 4** • **Per Serving** 145 calories, 8g fat (of which 1g saturates), 13g carbohydrate, 0.5g salt • **Dairy Free** • **Easy**

- 1 thick slice wholemeal bread, crusts removed
- 2 tbsp olive oil
- 1 broccoli head, chopped into florets
- 1 large carrot, cut into thin strips
- 1 red pepper, seeded and cut into thin strips
- 4 anchovy fillets, chopped

1 Whiz the bread in a food processor to make breadcrumbs. Heat 1 tbsp oil in a large non-stick frying pan or wok. Add the breadcrumbs and stir-fry for 4–5 minutes until crisp. Remove from the pan and set aside on a piece of kitchen paper.

2 Heat the remaining oil in the frying pan until hot. Add the broccoli, carrot and red pepper and stir-fry over a high heat for 4–5 minutes until they're starting to soften. Add the anchovies and continue to cook for a further 5 minutes or until slightly softened. Serve the vegetables immediately, scattered with the breadcrumbs.

★TRY SOMETHING DIFFERENT
Use other vegetables in season: try 400g (14oz) cauliflower florets instead of the broccoli.

Summer Vegetable Stir-fry

Preparation Time 15 minutes • **Cooking Time** 7–8 minutes • **Serves 4** • **Per Serving** 78 calories, 4g fat (of which 1g saturates), 7g carbohydrate, 0g salt • **Vegetarian** • **Gluten Free** • **Dairy Free** • **Easy**

125g (4oz) baby carrots, scrubbed and trimmed
1 tbsp sesame seeds
2 tbsp sunflower oil
2 garlic cloves, roughly chopped
125g (4oz) baby courgettes, halved lengthways
1 large yellow pepper, seeded and cut into thick strips
125g (4oz) thin asparagus spears, trimmed
125g (4oz) cherry tomatoes, halved
2 tbsp balsamic or sherry vinegar
1 tsp sesame oil
salt and ground black pepper

1 Blanch the carrots in lightly salted boiling water for 2 minutes, then drain and pat dry.

2 Toast the sesame seeds in a hot dry wok or large frying pan over a medium heat, stirring until they turn golden. Tip on to a plate.

3 Return the wok or frying pan to the heat, add the sunflower oil and heat until it is smoking. Add the garlic to the oil and stir-fry for 20 seconds. Add the carrots, courgettes, yellow pepper and asparagus and stir-fry over a high heat for 1 minute.

4 Add the tomatoes and season to taste with salt and pepper. Stir-fry for 3–4 minutes until the vegetables are just tender. Add the vinegar and sesame oil, toss well and sprinkle with the toasted sesame seeds. Serve immediately.

⭐ TRY SOMETHING DIFFERENT
Vary the vegetables, but always blanch the harder ones first. For a winter vegetable stir-fry, use cauliflower and broccoli florets, carrot sticks, 2–3 sliced spring onions and a little chopped fresh root ginger.

Courgette and Parmesan Frittata

Preparation Time 10 minutes • **Cooking Time** 15–20 minutes • **Serves 4** • **Per Serving** 229 calories, 19g fat (of which 9g saturates), 2g carbohydrate, 0.6g salt • **Vegetarian** • **Gluten Free** • **Easy**

40g (1½oz) butter
1 small onion, finely chopped
225g (8oz) courgettes, trimmed and finely sliced
6 medium eggs, beaten
25g (1oz) vegetarian Parmesan, freshly grated, plus shavings to garnish (optional, see page 155)
salt and ground black pepper
green salad to serve (optional)

1 Melt 25g (1oz) butter in an 18cm (7in) non-stick frying pan and cook the onion for about 10 minutes or until softened. Add the courgettes and fry gently for 5 minutes or until they begin to soften.

2 Beat the eggs in a bowl and season with salt and pepper.

3 Add the remaining butter to the pan and heat, then pour in the eggs. Cook for 2–3 minutes or until golden underneath and cooked around the edges. Meanwhile, preheat the grill to medium.

4 Sprinkle the grated cheese, if using, over the frittata and grill for 1–2 minutes until just set. Scatter with Parmesan shavings, if you like, cut into quarters and serve with a green salad, if you like.

★ TRY SOMETHING DIFFERENT
Cherry Tomato and Rocket Frittata
Replace the courgettes with 175g (6oz) ripe cherry tomatoes, frying them for 1 minute only, until they begin to soften. Immediately after pouring in the eggs, scatter 25g (1oz) rocket leaves over the surface. Continue cooking as in step 3.

Creamy Baked Eggs

Preparation Time 5 minutes • Cooking Time 15–18 minutes • Serves 4 • Per Serving 161 calories, 14g fat
(of which 7g saturates), 3g carbohydrate, 0.2g salt • Vegetarian • Easy

butter to grease
4 sun-dried tomatoes
4 medium eggs
4 tbsp double cream
salt and ground black pepper

1 Preheat the oven to 180°C (160°C fan oven) mark 4. Grease four individual ramekins.

2 Put a tomato in each ramekin and season with salt and pepper. Carefully break an egg on top of each, then drizzle 1 tbsp cream over each egg.

3 Bake for 15–18 minutes – the eggs will continue to cook once they have been taken out of the oven.

4 Leave to stand for 2 minutes before serving.

Egg Fu Yung

Preparation Time 10 minutes • **Cooking Time** about 5 minutes • **Serves 4** • **Per Serving** 232 calories, 18g fat (of which 4g saturates), 6g carbohydrate, 0.9g salt • **Vegetarian** • **Dairy Free** • **Easy**

3 tbsp groundnut or vegetable oil

8 spring onions, finely sliced, plus extra spring onion curls to garnish (see Cook's Tip)

125g (4oz) shiitake or oyster mushrooms, sliced

125g (4oz) canned bamboo shoots, drained and chopped

½ green pepper, seeded and finely chopped

125g (4oz) frozen peas, thawed

6 medium eggs, beaten

2 good pinches of chilli powder

1 tbsp light soy sauce

a pinch of salt

1 Heat the oil in a wok or large frying pan, add the spring onions, mushrooms, bamboo shoots, green pepper and peas and stir-fry for 2–3 minutes.

2 Season the eggs with salt and chilli powder. Pour the eggs into the pan and continue to cook, stirring, until the egg mixture is set.

3 Sprinkle the soy sauce over and stir well. Serve immediately, garnished with spring onion curls.

★ COOK'S TIP

To make spring onion curls, trim spring onions into 7.5cm (3in) lengths, shred finely, then place in a bowl of water with ice cubes for 30 minutes.

★ TRY SOMETHING DIFFERENT

This serves four with other dishes as part of a Chinese meal, but for a quick (non-vegetarian) supper for two, add 75g (3oz) cooked peeled prawns.

Piperade

★

Preparation Time 20 minutes • **Cooking Time** 20 minutes • **Serves 4** • **Per Serving** 232 calories, 17g fat (of which 4g saturates), 7g carbohydrate, 0.4g salt • **Vegetarian** • **Gluten Free** • **Dairy Free** • **Easy**

2 tbsp olive oil
1 medium onion, finely chopped
1 garlic clove, finely chopped
1 red pepper, seeded and chopped
375g (13oz) tomatoes, peeled, seeded and chopped
a pinch of cayenne pepper
8 large eggs
salt and ground black pepper
freshly chopped flat-leafed parsley to garnish
fresh bread to serve

1 Heat the oil in a heavy-based frying pan. Add the onion and garlic and cook gently for 5 minutes. Add the red pepper and cook for 10 minutes or until softened.

2 Add the tomatoes, increase the heat and cook until they are reduced to a thick pulp. Season well with cayenne pepper, salt and pepper.

3 Lightly whisk the eggs and add to the frying pan. Using a wooden spoon, stir gently until they've just begun to set but are still creamy. Garnish with parsley and serve with bread.

Caramelised Onion and Goat's Cheese Tart

★

Preparation Time 10 minutes • **Cooking Time** 1 hour • **Serves 6** • **Per Serving** 480 calories, 28g fat (of which 14g saturates), 44g carbohydrate, 1.5g salt • **Vegetarian** • **Easy**

230g ready-made shortcrust pastry
   case
275g jar onion confit
300g (11oz) mild soft goat's cheese
1 medium egg, beaten
25g (1oz) freshly grated vegetarian
   Parmesan (see page 155)
50g (2oz) wild rocket
balsamic vinegar and extra virgin
   olive oil to drizzle
salt and ground black pepper

1 Preheat the oven to 200°C (180°C fan oven) mark 6. Line the pastry case with greaseproof paper, fill with baking beans and bake blind (see Cook's Tip) for 10 minutes. Remove the paper and beans, prick the pastry base all over with a fork and cook for a further 15–20 minutes until golden.

2 Spoon the onion confit into the pastry case. Beat the goat's cheese and egg together in a bowl until smooth, season with salt and pepper, then spoon on top of the onions. Level the surface with a

knife and sprinkle the Parmesan over. Cook the tart for 25–30 minutes until the filling is set and just beginning to turn golden.

3 Leave to cool for 15 minutes, then cut away the sides of the foil case and carefully slide the tart on to a plate. Just before serving, arrange the rocket on top of the tart and drizzle with balsamic vinegar and olive oil. Serve warm.

★ COOK'S TIP
Baking blind
Cooking the pastry before filling gives a crisp result. Preheat the oven according to the recipe. Prick the pastry base with a fork. Cover with foil or greaseproof paper 7.5cm (3in) larger than the tin. Spread baking beans on top. Bake for 15–20 minutes. Remove the foil or paper and beans and bake for 5–10 minutes until the pastry is light golden. When cooked and while still hot, brush the base of the pastry with a little beaten egg, to seal the fork pricks or any cracks. This will prevent any filling leaking, which can make it difficult to remove the pie or tart from the tin.

Egg and Pepper Pizza

Preparation Time 15 minutes • **Cooking Time** 12 minutes • **Serves 4** • **Per Serving** 403 calories, 13g fat (of which 2g saturates), 61g carbohydrate, 1g salt • **Vegetarian** • **Gluten Free** • **Easy**

150g (5oz) red and yellow
  marinated peppers in oil
8 tbsp passata
4 small wheat-free pizza bases
4 medium eggs
125g (4oz) watercress, washed and
  stalks removed

1 Preheat the oven to 220°C (200°C fan oven) mark 7 and preheat two large baking sheets, big enough to hold two pizzas each.

2 Drain the peppers, reserving the oil. Chop into thin strips. Spoon 2 tbsp passata over each pizza base and scatter strips of the chopped peppers around the edges. Make a dip in the passata in the middle of each pizza and break an egg into it. Carefully slide the pizzas on to the preheated baking sheets. Place in the oven and cook for 12 minutes until the egg is thoroughly cooked.

3 Top the pizzas with the watercress, drizzle with a little of the reserved oil from the peppers and serve.

★COOK'S TIP
Watercress is the salad superfood par excellence. It has been shown to have anti-cancer and health-enhancing properties and is a good source of iron, and vitamins C and E.

Roast Mushrooms with Pesto

★

Preparation Time 5 minutes • **Cooking Time** 15 minutes • **Serves 4** • **Per Serving** 258 calories, 23g fat (of which 6g saturates), 1g carbohydrate, 0.5g salt • **Vegetarian** • **Easy**

8 portabello mushrooms
8 tbsp fresh ready-made pesto (see page 11)
toasted ciabatta, salad and basil leaves to serve

1 Preheat the oven to 200°C (180°C fan oven) mark 6. Put the mushrooms into an ovenproof dish, then spoon 1 tbsp fresh pesto on top of each one.

2 Pour 150ml (¼ pint) boiling water into the tin, then cook for 15 minutes until the mushrooms are soft and the topping is hot. Serve with toasted ciabatta and salad, and scatter a few small basil leaves over.

Roasted Vegetable Salad with Mustard Mayonnaise

★

Preparation Time 15 minutes • **Cooking Time** 40 minutes • **Serves 4** • **Per Serving** 420 calories, 43g fat (of which 6g saturates), 5g carbohydrate, 1g salt • **Vegetarian** • **Gluten Free** • **Dairy Free** • **Easy**

900g (2lb) mixed vegetables, such as fennel, courgettes, leeks, aubergines, baby turnips, new potatoes and red onions
2 garlic cloves, unpeeled
4–5 fresh marjoram or rosemary sprigs
5 tbsp olive oil
1 tsp sea salt flakes
mixed crushed peppercorns to taste
4 tsp balsamic vinegar
warm crusty bread to serve

FOR THE MUSTARD MAYONNAISE
150ml (¼ pint) mayonnaise
2 tbsp Dijon mustard
salt and ground black pepper

1 Preheat the oven to 220°C (200°C fan oven) mark 7. For the vegetables, quarter the fennel, chop the courgettes, leeks and aubergines, trim the turnips and cut the onions into petals. Place the vegetables, garlic, marjoram or rosemary, the oil, salt and peppercorns in a roasting tin and toss well (see Cook's Tip).

2 Cook in the oven for 30–35 minutes or until the vegetables are golden, tossing frequently. Sprinkle the vinegar over and return to the oven for a further 5 minutes.

3 To make the mustard mayonnaise, mix the mayonnaise with the mustard, then season with salt and pepper and set aside.

4 Arrange the vegetable salad on a serving dish and serve with the mustard mayonnaise and crusty bread.

★ COOK'S TIP
It's best to roast vegetables in a single layer or they will steam and become soggy. Use two tins if necessary.

Add a Little Extra ...

Mulligatawny Soup

★

Preparation Time 5 minutes • **Cooking Time** 40 minutes • **Serves 4** • **Per Serving** 252 calories, 13g fat
(of which 4g saturates), 7g carbohydrate, 0.9g salt • **Easy**

3 rashers streaky bacon, rinded and
  finely chopped
550g (1¼lb) chicken portions
600ml (1 pint) hot chicken stock
1 carrot, sliced
1 celery stick, chopped
1 apple, cored and chopped
2 tsp curry powder
4 peppercorns, crushed
1 clove
1 bay leaf
1 tbsp plain flour
150ml (¼ pint) milk
50g (2oz) long-grain rice, cooked,
  and crusty bread to serve

1 Fry the bacon in a large pan until
the fat begins to run. Do not allow
the bacon to become brown.

2 Add the chicken and brown well.
Drain the meat on kitchen paper
and pour off the fat.

3 Return the bacon and chicken
to the pan and add the hot stock
and next seven ingredients. Cover
the pan and simmer for about
30 minutes or until the chicken
is tender.

4 Remove the chicken and allow to
cool a little. Cut off the meat and
return it to the soup. Discard the
clove and bay leaf and reheat the
soup gently.

5 Mix the flour with a little cold
water. Add to the soup with the
milk and reheat without boiling.

6 Ladle the soup into warmed
bowls, spoon a mound of rice into
each one and serve immediately
with crusty bread.

Chicken Cacciatore

Preparation Time 5 minutes • **Cooking Time** 40 minutes • **Serves 4** • **Per Serving** 327 calories, 17g fat (of which 4g saturates), 3g carbohydrate, 1.3g salt • **Gluten Free** • **Dairy Free** • **Easy**

2 tbsp olive oil
8 boneless, skinless chicken thighs
2 garlic cloves, crushed
1 tsp dried thyme
1 tsp dried tarragon
150ml (¼ pint) white wine
400g can chopped tomatoes
12 pitted black olives
12 capers, rinsed and drained
ground black pepper
brown rice and broad beans or peas
   to serve

1 Heat the oil in a flameproof casserole over a high heat. Add the chicken and brown all over. Reduce the heat and add the garlic, thyme, tarragon and wine to the casserole. Stir for 1 minute, then add the tomatoes and season with pepper.

2 Bring to the boil, then reduce the heat, cover the casserole and simmer for 20 minutes or until the chicken is tender.

3 Lift the chicken out of the casserole and put to one side. Bubble the sauce for 5 minutes or until thickened, add the olives and capers, stir well and cook for a further 2–3 minutes.

4 Put the chicken into the sauce. Serve with brown rice and broad beans or peas.

Alsace Chicken

★

Preparation Time 20 minutes • **Cooking Time** 1 hour 20 minutes • **Serves 4** • **Per Serving** 484 calories, 24g fat (of which 8g saturates), 11g carbohydrate, 1.4g salt • **Easy**

2 tbsp vegetable oil

8 chicken pieces (such as breasts, thighs and drumsticks)

125g (4oz) rindless smoked streaky bacon rashers, cut into strips

12 shallots, peeled but left whole

3 fresh tarragon sprigs

1 tbsp plain flour

150ml (¼ pint) Alsace Riesling white wine

500ml (18fl oz) hot chicken stock

3 tbsp crème fraîche

salt and ground black pepper

new potatoes (optional) and green vegetables to serve

1 Heat half the oil in a frying pan over a medium heat. Fry the chicken, in batches, until golden, adding more oil to the pan as necessary. Set aside.

2 Put the bacon into the same pan and fry gently to release its fat. Add the shallots and cook for 5 minutes, stirring occasionally, or until both the shallots and bacon are lightly coloured.

3 Strip the leaves from the tarragon and set both the leaves and stalks aside. Sprinkle the flour over the shallots and bacon and stir to absorb the juices. Cook for 1 minute, then gradually add the wine, hot stock and tarragon stalks. Put the chicken back into the pan, cover and simmer over a gentle heat for 45 minutes– 1 hour until the chicken is cooked through.

4 Remove the chicken, bacon and shallots with a slotted spoon and keep warm. Discard the tarragon stalks. Bubble the sauce until reduced by half. Stir in the crème fraîche and tarragon leaves. Season with salt and pepper.

5 Turn off the heat, put the chicken, bacon and shallots back into the pan and stir to combine. Serve with new potatoes, if you like, and green vegetables.

Chicken with Fennel and Tarragon

Preparation Time 10 minutes • **Cooking Time** 45–55 minutes • **Serves 4** • **Per Serving** 334 calories, 26g fat (of which 15g saturates), 3g carbohydrate, 0.5g salt • **Gluten Free** • **Easy**

1 tbsp olive oil
4 chicken thighs
1 onion, finely chopped
1 fennel bulb, sliced
juice of ½ lemon
200ml (7fl oz) hot chicken stock
200g (7oz) half-fat crème fraîche
1 small bunch of tarragon, roughly chopped
wild rice to serve

1 Preheat the oven to 200°C (180°C fan oven) mark 6. Heat the oil in a large flameproof casserole. Add the chicken thighs and fry for 5 minutes or until brown, then remove and set them aside to keep warm.

2 Add the onion to the pan and fry for 5 minutes, then add the fennel and cook for 5–10 minutes until softened.

3 Add the lemon juice to the pan, then add the hot stock. Bring to a simmer and cook until the liquid is reduced by half.

4 Stir in the crème fraîche and return the chicken to the pan. Stir once to mix, then cover and cook in the oven for 25–30 minutes. Stir the tarragon into the sauce and serve with wild rice.

Mediterranean Chicken

Preparation Time 5 minutes • **Cooking Time** 20 minutes • **Serves 4** • **Per Serving** 223 calories, 7g fat (of which 1g saturates), 3g carbohydrate, 0.2g salt • **Gluten Free** • **Dairy Free** • **Easy**

1 red pepper, seeded and chopped
2 tbsp capers
2 tbsp freshly chopped rosemary
2 tbsp olive oil
4 skinless chicken breasts, about
   125g (4oz) each
salt and ground black pepper
rice or new potatoes to serve

1 Preheat the oven to 200°C (180°C fan oven) mark 6. Put the red pepper into a bowl with the capers, rosemary and oil. Season with salt and pepper and mix well.

2 Put the chicken breasts into an ovenproof dish and spoon the pepper mixture over the top. Roast for 15–20 minutes until the chicken is cooked through and the topping is hot. Serve with rice or new potatoes.

Marinated Poussins

Preparation Time 30 minutes, plus overnight marinating • **Cooking Time** 30 minutes • **Serves 4** • **Per Serving** 508 calories, 30g fat (of which 8g saturates), 10g carbohydrate, 1.6g salt • **Gluten Free** • **Dairy Free** • **Easy**

150ml (¼ pint) bourbon
15g (½oz) soft brown sugar
50ml (2fl oz) clear honey
50ml (2fl oz) tomato ketchup
2 tbsp wholegrain mustard
1 tbsp white wine vinegar
3 garlic cloves, crushed
1 tsp each salt and ground black
  pepper
4 poussins
chargrilled peppers, tomatoes and
  onions, garnished with flat-leafed
  parsley, to serve

1 Mix the bourbon, sugar, honey, tomato ketchup and mustard together. Stir in the vinegar, garlic, salt and pepper.

2 Put the poussins breast down on a chopping board, then cut through either side of the backbone with poultry shears or a pair of strong sharp scissors and remove it. Open out the poussins, cover them with clingfilm and flatten them slightly by tapping them with the base of a heavy pan. Put the poussins in a shallow glass dish and pour the bourbon marinade over the top, then cover and chill overnight.

3 Preheat the barbecue or grill. Soak eight wooden skewers in water for 20 minutes. Thread the skewers through the legs and breasts of the poussins, keeping the marinade to one side. Cook the poussins for 30 minutes or until cooked through, basting from time to time with the reserved marinade. Serve with the peppers, tomatoes and onions garnished with the parsley.

 TRY SOMETHING DIFFERENT
Use chicken joints instead of the poussins.

Chicken with Peanut Sauce

Preparation Time 10 minutes, plus marinating • **Cooking Time** about 10 minutes • **Serves 4** • **Per Serving** 408 calories, 20g fat (of which 3g saturates), 19g carbohydrate, 0.5g salt • **Gluten Free** • **Dairy Free** • **Easy**

4 boneless, skinless chicken
   breasts, cut into strips
1 tbsp ground coriander
2 garlic cloves, finely chopped
4 tbsp vegetable oil
2 tbsp clear honey
fresh coriander sprigs to garnish
Thai fragrant rice to serve

FOR THE PEANUT SAUCE
1 tbsp vegetable oil
2 tbsp curry paste
2 tbsp brown sugar
2 tbsp peanut butter
200ml (7fl oz) coconut milk

1 Mix the chicken with the ground coriander, garlic, oil and honey. Cover, chill and leave to marinate for 15 minutes.

2 To make the peanut sauce, heat the oil in a pan, add the curry paste, brown sugar and peanut butter and fry for 1 minute. Add the coconut milk and bring to the boil, stirring all the time, then simmer for 5 minutes.

3 Meanwhile, heat a wok or large frying pan and, when hot, stir-fry the chicken and its marinade in batches for 3–4 minutes or until cooked, adding more oil if needed.

4 Serve the chicken on a bed of Thai fragrant rice, with the peanut sauce poured over. Garnish with coriander sprigs.

★ TRY SOMETHING DIFFERENT
Replace the chicken with pork escalopes or rump steak, cut into thin strips.

Chicken with Vegetables and Noodles

Preparation Time 10 minutes • Cooking Time about 12 minutes • Serves 2 • Per Serving 584 calories, 19g fat (of which 3g saturates), 67g carbohydrate, 4.1g salt • **Dairy Free** • **Easy**

225g (8oz) fine egg noodles
about 2 tbsp vegetable oil
1 large boneless, skinless chicken breast, about 150g (5oz), cut into very thin strips
2.5cm (1in) piece fresh root ginger, peeled and finely chopped
1 garlic clove, finely chopped
1 red pepper, seeded and thinly sliced
4 spring onions, thinly sliced
2 carrots, thinly sliced
125g (4oz) shiitake or button mushrooms, halved
a handful of beansprouts (optional)
3 tbsp hoisin sauce
2 tbsp light soy sauce
1 tbsp chilli sauce
shredded spring onion and sesame seeds to garnish

1 Bring a large pan of water to the boil and cook the noodles for about 3 minutes or according to the pack instructions. Drain thoroughly and toss with a little of the oil to prevent them sticking together. Set aside.

2 Heat the remaining oil in a wok or large frying pan. Add the chicken, ginger and garlic and stir-fry over a very high heat for about 5 minutes or until the chicken is browned on the outside and cooked right through.

3 Add all the vegetables to the pan and stir-fry over a high heat for about 2 minutes or until they are just cooked, but still crunchy.

4 Stir in the hoisin, soy and chilli sauces and mix well. Add the noodles, toss well to mix and cook for a couple of minutes until heated through. Serve immediately, sprinkled with shredded spring onion and sesame seeds.

★ TRY SOMETHING DIFFERENT
● *Replace the chicken with thinly sliced turkey escalopes.*
● *Increase the heat of the dish by frying a chopped chilli with the garlic and ginger.*

Warming Winter Casserole

Preparation Time 20 minutes • **Cooking Time** 1 hour • **Serves 4** • **Per Serving** 407 calories, 16g fat (of which 3g saturates), 32g carbohydrate, 1g salt • **Gluten Free** • **Dairy Free** • **Easy**

2 tbsp olive oil
500g (1lb 2oz) pork fillet, cubed
1 onion, finely chopped
2 garlic cloves, finely chopped
1 tsp ground cinnamon
1 tbsp ground coriander
1 tsp ground cumin
2.5cm (1in) piece fresh root ginger, peeled and grated
400g can mixed beans or chickpeas, drained
1 red pepper, seeded and sliced
50g (2oz) ready-to-eat dried apricots, roughly chopped
300ml (½ pint) chicken stock

25g (1oz) flaked almonds, toasted
salt and ground black pepper
freshly chopped flat-leafed parsley to garnish
brown basmati rice to serve

1 Heat 1 tbsp oil in a flameproof casserole, add the pork and fry, in batches, until brown all over. Remove and set aside. Add the remaining oil, then add the onion and cook for 10 minutes or until softened. Return the pork to the casserole, add the garlic, spices and ginger and cook for 2 minutes.

2 Add the mixed beans, red pepper, apricots and stock. Season well with salt and pepper, then stir and bring to the boil. Reduce the heat to the lowest setting and simmer, covered, for 40 minutes, adding a little extra stock if it begins to look dry.

3 Check the seasoning and sprinkle with the almonds, then garnish with the parsley and serve with brown basmati rice.

★ TRY SOMETHING DIFFERENT
Instead of pork, use the same quantity of lean lamb, such as leg, trimmed of excess fat and cut into cubes.

Pork Chops with Mustard Sauce

Preparation Time 15 minutes • **Cooking Time** 30 minutes • **Serves 6** • **Per Serving** 503 calories, 29g fat (of which 14g saturates), 21g carbohydrate, 1g salt • **Gluten Free** • **Easy**

25g (1oz) butter
6 spare-rib pork chops, trimmed of
    fat (see Cook's Tip)
700g (1½lb) onions, chopped
700g (1½lb) trimmed leeks,
    chopped
1 garlic clove, crushed
900ml (1½ pints) milk
1 bay leaf
1 fresh thyme sprig
125ml (4fl oz) double cream or
    crème fraîche
3 tbsp English mustard
salt and ground black pepper
flat noodles, such as tagliatelle, to
    serve

1 Heat the butter in a flameproof casserole. When the butter is foaming, fry the chops briskly until very light golden brown, then put to one side. Add the onions and leeks and cook gently until soft. Add the garlic and cook for 30 seconds.

2 Pour in the milk and bring to the boil. Put the chops back into the casserole, add the herbs and reduce the heat; bubble gently for 10 minutes. When the pork is tender, transfer to serving plates and keep warm.

3 Bubble the sauce until reduced almost to nothing, then add the cream or crème fraîche and the mustard. Season well with salt and pepper, then pour over the chops. Serve with noodles.

★ COOK'S TIP
It's important to use spare-rib chops for this recipe, as loin chops won't be tender enough.

Quick Beef Stroganoff

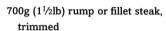

Preparation Time 10 minutes • **Cooking Time** 20 minutes • **Serves 4** • **Per Serving** 750 calories, 60g fat (of which 35g saturates), 3g carbohydrate, 0.5g salt • **Gluten Free** • **Easy**

700g (1½lb) rump or fillet steak, trimmed
50g (2oz) unsalted butter or 4 tbsp olive oil
1 onion, thinly sliced
225g (8oz) brown-cap mushrooms, sliced
3 tbsp brandy
1 tsp French mustard
200ml (7fl oz) crème fraîche
100ml (3½fl oz) double cream
3 tbsp freshly chopped flat-leafed parsley
salt and ground black pepper
rice or noodles to serve

1 Cut the steak into strips about 5mm (¼in) wide and 5cm (2in) long.

2 Heat half the butter or oil in a large heavy frying pan over a medium heat. Add the onion and cook gently for 10 minutes or until soft and golden. Remove with a slotted spoon and set aside. Add the mushrooms to the pan and cook, stirring, for 2–3 minutes until golden brown. Remove and set aside.

3 Increase the heat and add the remaining butter or oil to the pan. Quickly fry the meat, in two or three batches, for 2–3 minutes, stirring constantly to ensure even browning. Add the brandy and allow it to bubble to reduce.

4 Put the meat, onion and mushrooms back into the pan. Reduce the heat and stir in the mustard, crème fraîche and cream. Heat through, stir in most of the parsley and season with salt and pepper. Serve with rice or noodles, with the remaining parsley scattered over the top.

 FREEZING TIP
To freeze Complete the recipe, transfer to a freezerproof container, cool, label and freeze for up to three months.
To use Thaw overnight in the fridge. Put in a pan, cover and bring to the boil; reduce the heat to low and simmer until piping hot.

Braised Beef with Mustard and Capers

Preparation Time 15 minutes • Cooking Time 2 hours 20 minutes, plus cooling • Serves 4 • Per Serving 391 calories, 19g fat (of which 7g saturates), 10g carbohydrate, 1.5g salt • Gluten Free • Dairy Free • Easy

50g (2oz) can anchovy fillets in oil, drained, chopped and oil put to one side
olive oil
700g (1½lb) braising steak, cut into small strips
2 large Spanish onions, peeled and thinly sliced
2 tbsp capers
1 tsp English mustard
6 fresh thyme sprigs
20g pack fresh flat-leafed parsley, roughly chopped
salt and ground black pepper
green salad and crusty bread or mashed potato to serve

1 Preheat the oven to 170°C (150°C fan oven) mark 3. Measure the anchovy oil into a deep flameproof casserole, then make up to 3 tbsp with the olive oil. Heat the oil and fry the meat, a few pieces at a time, until well browned. Remove with a slotted spoon and set aside. When all the meat has been browned, pour 4 tbsp cold water into the empty casserole and stir to loosen any bits on the bottom.

2 Put the meat back into the pan and add the onions, anchovies, capers, mustard, half the thyme and all but 1 tbsp of the parsley. Stir until thoroughly mixed.

3 Tear off a sheet of greaseproof paper big enough to cover the pan. Crumple it up and wet it under the cold tap. Squeeze out most of the water, open it out and press down over the surface of the meat.

4 Cover with a tight-fitting lid and cook in the oven for 2 hours or until the beef is meltingly tender. Check the casserole after 1 hour to make sure it's still moist. If it looks dry, add a little water.

5 Adjust for seasoning, then stir in the remaining parsley and thyme. Serve with a green salad and crusty bread or mashed potato.

★ COOK'S TIP
To make a deliciously easy mash, put four baking potatoes into the oven when you put in the casserole. Leave to bake for 2 hours. Cut each potato in half and use a fork to scrape out the flesh into a bowl. Add 50g (2oz) butter and season well with salt and pepper – the potato will be soft enough to mash with the fork.

Braised Lamb Shanks

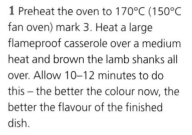

Preparation Time 20–25 minutes • **Cooking Time** 2¾ hours • **Serves 6** • **Per Serving** 355 calories, 16g fat (of which 6g saturates), 23g carbohydrate, 1.2g salt • **Gluten Free** • **Dairy Free** • **Easy**

6 small lamb shanks
450g (1lb) shallots, peeled but left
    whole
2 medium aubergines, cut into
    small dice
2 tbsp olive oil
3 tbsp harissa paste
pared zest of 1 orange and juice of
    3 large oranges
200ml (7fl oz) medium sherry
700g (1½lb) passata
300ml (½ pint) hot vegetable or
    lamb stock
75g (3oz) ready-to-eat dried
    apricots

75g (3oz) cherries (optional)
a large pinch of saffron threads
couscous and French beans
    (optional) to serve

1 Preheat the oven to 170°C (150°C fan oven) mark 3. Heat a large flameproof casserole over a medium heat and brown the lamb shanks all over. Allow 10–12 minutes to do this – the better the colour now, the better the flavour of the finished dish.

2 Remove the lamb and put to one side. Add the shallots, aubergines and oil to the casserole and cook over a high heat, stirring from time to time, until the shallots and aubergines are golden and beginning to soften.

3 Reduce the heat and add the lamb and all the other ingredients except the couscous and beans. The liquid should come halfway up the shanks. Bring to the boil, then cover tightly and put into the oven for 2½ hours. Test the lamb with a fork – it should be so tender that it almost falls off the bone.

4 If the cooking liquid looks too thin, remove the lamb to a heated serving plate, then bubble the sauce on the hob until reduced and thickened. Put the lamb back into the casserole. Serve with couscous and French beans, if you like.

 COOK'S TIP
Cooking lamb shanks in a rich sauce in the oven at a low temperature makes the meat meltingly tender.

Moroccan Lamb Stew

Preparation Time 20 minutes • **Cooking Time** about 1 hour 20 minutes • **Serves 6** • **Per Serving** 274 calories, 11g fat (of which 5g saturates), 25g carbohydrate, 0.2g salt • **Dairy Free** • **Easy**

500g (1lb 2oz) lamb shoulder, well trimmed to remove excess fat, then roughly cubed
15g (½oz) plain flour
½ tbsp sunflower oil
1 onion, thickly sliced
2 carrots, roughly chopped
2 garlic cloves, crushed
2 tsp harissa paste
1 tsp ground cinnamon
2 × 400g cans chopped tomatoes
75g (3oz) dried apricots, roughly chopped
100g (3½oz) couscous
a large handful of curly parsley, roughly chopped
salt and ground black pepper

1 Dust the lamb with the flour. Heat the oil in a large pan and brown the lamb in batches. Set aside. In the same pan, add the onions and carrots and gently fry for 10 minutes. Add a splash of water if they start to stick to the pan.

2 Stir in the garlic, harissa and cinnamon and cook for 1 minute. Add a splash of water and use a wooden spoon to help scrape any goodness from the bottom of the pan, then stir it in. Pour in the tomatoes and return the lamb to the pan. Stir in the apricots and season. Cover and simmer for 1 hour or until the lamb is tender. Season to taste.

3 Meanwhile, put the couscous into a bowl and add boiling water according to the pack instructions. Cover with clingfilm and leave for 10 minutes. When ready, fluff up the grains with a fork, then stir in the parsley. Season. Serve the lamb topped with spoonfuls of couscous (see Cook's Tip).

 COOK'S TIP
Watching your carb intake? Serving the couscous as a garnish on the stew rather than as a substantial side dish is a satisfying alternative.

Lamb and Bamboo Shoot Red Curry

Preparation Time 10 minutes • **Cooking Time** 45 minutes • **Serves 4** • **Per Serving** 397 calories, 25g fat (of which 8g saturates), 17g carbohydrate, 0.4g salt • **Gluten Free** • **Dairy Free** • **Easy**

2 tbsp sunflower oil

1 large onion, cut into wedges

2 garlic cloves, finely chopped

450g (1lb) lean boneless lamb, cut into 3cm (1¼in) cubes

2 tbsp Thai red curry paste

150ml (¼ pint) lamb or beef stock

2 tbsp Thai fish sauce

2 tsp soft brown sugar

200g can bamboo shoots, drained and thinly sliced

1 red pepper, seeded and thinly sliced

2 tbsp freshly chopped mint

1 tbsp freshly chopped basil

25g (1oz) unsalted peanuts, toasted

rice to serve

1 Heat the oil in a wok or large frying pan, add the onion and garlic and fry over a medium heat for 5 minutes.

2 Add the lamb and the curry paste and stir-fry for 5 minutes. Add the stock, fish sauce and sugar and bring to the boil, then reduce the heat, cover the pan and simmer gently for 20 minutes.

3 Stir the bamboo shoots, red pepper and herbs into the curry and cook, uncovered, for a further 10 minutes. Stir in the peanuts and serve immediately, with rice.

Chicken and Coconut Curry

Preparation Time 15 minutes • Cooking Time 35 minutes • Serves 6 • Per Serving 204 calories, 6g fat (of which 1g saturates), 10g carbohydrate, 1.5g salt • **Gluten Free** • **Dairy Free** • **Easy**

2 garlic cloves, peeled
1 onion, quartered
1 lemongrass stalk, trimmed and halved
2.5cm (1in) piece fresh root ginger, peeled and halved
2 small hot chillies (see page 19)
a small handful of fresh coriander
1 tsp ground coriander
grated zest and juice of 1 lime
2 tbsp vegetable oil
6 boneless, skinless chicken breasts, each cut into three pieces
2 large tomatoes, skinned and chopped
2 tbsp Thai fish sauce
900ml (1½ pints) coconut milk
salt and ground black pepper
finely sliced red chilli to garnish
basmati rice to serve

1 Put the garlic, onion, lemongrass, ginger, chillies, fresh coriander, ground coriander and lime zest and juice into a food processor and whiz to a paste. Add a little water if the mixture gets stuck under the blades.

2 Heat the oil in a wok or large frying pan, add the spice paste and cook over a fairly high heat for 3–4 minutes, stirring constantly. Add the chicken and cook for 5 minutes, stirring to coat in the spice mixture.

3 Add the tomatoes, fish sauce and coconut milk. Simmer, covered, for about 25 minutes or until the chicken is cooked. Season with salt and pepper, garnish with red chilli and serve with basmati rice.

Chicken Tikka Masala

★

Preparation Time 15 minutes • **Cooking Time** 30 minutes • **Serves 4** • **Per Serving** 297 calories, 17g fat (of which 4g saturates), 4g carbohydrate, 0.6g salt • **Dairy Free** • **Easy**

2 tbsp vegetable oil
1 onion, finely sliced
2 garlic cloves, crushed
6 boneless, skinless chicken thighs, cut into strips
2 tbsp tikka masala curry paste
200g can chopped tomatoes
450ml (¾ pint) hot vegetable stock
225g (8oz) baby spinach leaves
fresh coriander leaves to garnish
rice, mango chutney and poppadoms to serve

1 Heat the oil in a large pan, add the onion and fry over a medium heat for 5–7 minutes until golden. Add the garlic and chicken and stir-fry for about 5 minutes or until golden.

2 Stir in the curry paste, then add the tomatoes and hot stock. Bring to the boil, then reduce the heat, cover the pan and simmer over a low heat for 15 minutes or until the chicken is cooked through.

3 Add the spinach to the curry, stir and cook until the leaves have just wilted. Garnish with coriander and serve with rice, mango chutney and poppadoms.

Easy Thai Red Chicken Curry

Preparation Time 5 minutes • **Cooking Time** 20 minutes • **Serves 4** • **Per Serving** 248 calories, 8g fat (of which 1g saturates), 16g carbohydrate, 1g salt • **Dairy Free** • **Easy**

1 tbsp vegetable oil

3 tbsp Thai red curry paste

4 boneless, skinless chicken breasts, about 600g (1lb 5oz) total weight, sliced

400ml can coconut milk

300ml (½ pint) hot chicken or vegetable stock

juice of 1 lime, plus lime halves to serve

200g pack mixed baby sweetcorn and mangetouts

2 tbsp freshly chopped coriander, plus sprigs to garnish

rice or rice noodles to serve

1 Heat the oil in a wok or large pan over a low heat. Add the curry paste and cook for 2 minutes or until fragrant.

2 Add the chicken and fry gently for about 10 minutes or until browned.

3 Add the coconut milk, hot stock, lime juice and sweetcorn to the pan and bring to the boil. Add the mangetouts, reduce the heat and simmer for 4–5 minutes until the chicken is cooked.

4 Stir in the chopped coriander, garnish with coriander sprigs and serve immediately with rice or noodles and lime halves to squeeze over.

Grilled Spicy Chicken

Preparation Time 10 minutes, plus marinating • **Cooking Time** about 20 minutes • **Serves 4** • **Per Serving** 157 calories, 2g fat (of which 1g saturates), 3g carbohydrate, 0.2g salt • **Gluten Free** • **Easy**

4 boneless, skinless chicken breasts
1 tbsp coriander seeds, crushed
1 tsp ground cumin
2 tsp mild curry paste
1 garlic clove, crushed
450g (1lb) yogurt
3 tbsp freshly chopped coriander
salt and ground black pepper
coriander sprigs to garnish
mixed salad and rice to serve

1 Prick the chicken breasts all over with a fork, cover with clingfilm and lightly beat with a rolling pin to flatten them slightly.

2 Mix the coriander seeds with the cumin, curry paste, garlic and yogurt in a large shallow dish. Season with salt and pepper and stir in the chopped coriander.

3 Add the chicken and turn to coat with the spiced yogurt. Cover and leave to marinate in the fridge for at least 30 minutes or overnight.

4 Preheat the barbecue or griddle. Lift the chicken out of the marinade and cook over a medium-high heat, turning occasionally, for about 20 minutes or until cooked through. Serve immediately, with rice and a mixed salad, garnished with coriander sprigs.

Kerala Fish Curry

Preparation Time 10 minutes • **Cooking Time** about 20 minutes • **Serves 4** • **Per Serving** 189 calories, 9g fat (of which 1g saturates), 5g carbohydrate, 0.5g salt • **Gluten Free** • **Dairy Free** • **A Little Effort**

4 skinless sole or plaice fillets, about 125g (4oz) each
2 tbsp light olive oil
1 onion, thinly sliced
1 large garlic clove, crushed
1 green chilli, slit lengthways, seeds in (see page 19)
2.5cm (1in) piece fresh root ginger, peeled and grated
1 tsp ground turmeric
1 tbsp garam masala or about 12 curry leaves (see Cook's Tip)
200ml (7fl oz) coconut milk
1 tbsp freshly squeezed lime juice, white wine vinegar or tamarind paste (see page 159)
salt and ground black pepper

TO SERVE
basmati rice
fresh banana leaves (optional, see Cook's Tip)
1 lime, cut into wedges

1 Roll up the fish fillets from head to tail and put to one side.

2 Heat the oil in a deep frying pan over a medium heat and stir in the onion, garlic, chilli and ginger. Keep stirring for 5–7 minutes until the onion is soft. Add the turmeric and garam masala (or curry leaves, if using) and fry for a further 1–2 minutes until aromatic.

3 Pour the coconut milk into the pan along with 200ml (7fl oz) water and bring to the boil. Reduce the heat and simmer very gently, uncovered, for 7–10 minutes until slightly thickened. The sauce should be the consistency of single cream. Stir in the lime juice, vinegar or tamarind. Check the seasoning and adjust if necessary.

4 When you're ready to serve, lower the rolls of fish into the hot sauce gently to avoid splashing and simmer very gently for 1–2 minutes until just cooked. Serve on a bed of basmati rice, in deep bowls lined with strips of banana leaves, if you like, with a wedge of lime to squeeze over.

 GET AHEAD
To prepare ahead *Make the sauce up to 4 hours ahead.*
To use *Gently reheat to simmering point before you add the fish.*

 COOK'S TIP
Buy curry leaves and banana leaves from Asian shops.

Salmon Laksa Curry

Preparation Time 10 minutes • **Cooking Time** about 20 minutes • **Serves 4** • **Per Serving** 570 calories, 22g fat (of which 3g saturates), 55g carbohydrate, 1.9g salt • **Gluten Free** • **Dairy Free** • **Easy**

1 tbsp olive oil
1 onion, thinly sliced
3 tbsp laksa paste (see Cook's Tip)
200ml (7fl oz) coconut milk
900ml (1½ pints) hot vegetable stock
200g (7oz) baby sweetcorn, halved lengthways
600g (1lb 5oz) piece skinless salmon fillet, cut into 1cm (½in) slices
225g (8oz) baby leaf spinach, washed
250g (9oz) medium rice noodles

salt and ground black pepper
2 spring onions, sliced diagonally, and 2 tbsp freshly chopped coriander, to garnish
1 lime, cut into wedges, to serve

1 Heat the oil in a wok or large frying pan, then add the onion and fry over a medium heat for 10 minutes, stirring, or until golden. Add the laksa paste and cook for 2 minutes.

2 Add the coconut milk, hot stock and sweetcorn and season with salt and pepper. Bring to the boil, then reduce the heat and simmer for 5 minutes.

3 Add the salmon slices and spinach, stirring to immerse them in the liquid. Cook for 4 minutes or until the fish is opaque all the way through.

4 Meanwhile, put the noodles into a large heatproof bowl, pour boiling water over to cover and soak for 30 seconds. Drain well, then stir them into the curry. Pour the curry into four serving bowls and garnish with the spring onions and coriander. Serve immediately with lime wedges.

★ COOK'S TIP
Laksa paste is a hot and spicy paste; you could use Thai curry paste instead.

Thai Curry with Prawns and Aubergines

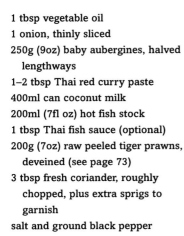

Preparation Time 10 minutes • Cooking Time 20 minutes • Serves 4 • Per Serving 101 calories, 4g fat (of which 1g saturates), 5g carbohydrate, 0.4g salt • **Gluten Free • Dairy Free • Easy**

1 tbsp vegetable oil

1 onion, thinly sliced

250g (9oz) baby aubergines, halved lengthways

1–2 tbsp Thai red curry paste

400ml can coconut milk

200ml (7fl oz) hot fish stock

1 tbsp Thai fish sauce (optional)

200g (7oz) raw peeled tiger prawns, deveined (see page 73)

3 tbsp fresh coriander, roughly chopped, plus extra sprigs to garnish

salt and ground black pepper

1 Heat the oil in a wok or large frying pan. Add the onion and fry over a medium heat until golden. Add the aubergines and fry for a further 5 minutes or until pale brown.

2 Add the curry paste and stir to coat the vegetables, then continue to cook for 1 minute.

3 Add the coconut milk, hot stock and fish sauce, if using, then bring to the boil and simmer for 5 minutes.

4 Add the prawns and season generously with salt and pepper. Simmer until the prawns have turned pink – a couple of minutes.

5 Stir in the chopped coriander, then transfer to four large warmed serving bowls and serve immediately, garnished with coriander sprigs.

★ COOK'S TIP
In Thailand, this might be made with tiny pea aubergines – look out for them in Thai food shops.

Squid and Vegetables in Black Bean Sauce

Preparation Time 35 minutes • **Cooking Time** 10–15 minutes • **Serves 4** • **Per Serving** 274 calories, 15g fat (of which 2g saturates), 12g carbohydrate, 1g salt • **Gluten Free** • **Dairy Free** • **A Little Effort**

450g (1lb) cleaned squid

2 tbsp sesame seeds

2 tbsp sunflower oil

1 tbsp sesame oil

2 garlic cloves

2 dried red chillies

50g (2oz) broccoli, cut into florets

50g (2oz) mangetouts, trimmed

50g (2oz) carrots, thinly sliced

75g (3oz) cauliflower, cut into small florets

1 small green or red pepper, seeded and thinly sliced

50g (2oz) Chinese cabbage or pak choi, shredded

25g (1oz) bean sprouts

2 tbsp fresh coriander, roughly torn

FOR THE SAUCE

2 tbsp black bean sauce

1 tbsp Thai fish sauce

2–3 tsp clear honey

75ml (2½fl oz) fish or vegetable stock

1 tbsp tamarind juice

2 tsp cornflour

1 First, prepare the sauce. In a small bowl, mix together the black bean sauce, fish sauce, honey and stock. Add the tamarind juice and cornflour and whisk until smooth. Set aside.

2 Wash and dry the squid and halve the tentacles if large. Open out the body pouches, score diagonally, then cut into large squares. Set aside.

3 Toast the sesame seeds in a dry wok or large frying pan over a medium heat, stirring until they turn golden. Tip on to a plate.

4 Heat the sunflower and sesame oils in the same pan. Add the garlic and chillies and fry gently for 5 minutes. Remove the garlic and chillies with a slotted spoon and discard.

5 Add all the vegetables to the pan and stir-fry for 3 minutes. Add the squid, increase the heat and stir-fry for a further 2 minutes or until the squid curls up and turns opaque. Add the sauce and allow to simmer for 1 minute.

6 Scatter the sesame seeds and coriander over and serve immediately.

★ TRY SOMETHING DIFFERENT

Instead of squid, try 400g (14oz) rump steak, cut into thin strips.

Thai Green Shellfish Curry

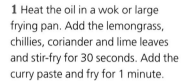

Preparation Time 10 minutes • **Cooking Time** 10–15 minutes • **Serves 6** • **Per Serving** 156 calories, 5g fat (of which 1g saturates), 6g carbohydrate, 0.8g salt • **Gluten Free** • **Dairy Free** • **Easy**

1 tbsp vegetable oil

1 lemongrass stalk, trimmed and chopped

2 small red chillies, chopped (see page 19)

a handful of coriander leaves, chopped, plus extra to serve

2 kaffir lime leaves, chopped

1–2 tbsp Thai green curry paste

400ml can coconut milk

450ml (¾ pint) vegetable stock

375g (13oz) queen scallops with corals

250g (9oz) raw tiger prawns, peeled and deveined (see page 73), with tails intact

salt and ground black pepper

jasmine rice to serve

1 Heat the oil in a wok or large frying pan. Add the lemongrass, chillies, coriander and lime leaves and stir-fry for 30 seconds. Add the curry paste and fry for 1 minute.

2 Add the coconut milk and stock and bring to the boil, then reduce the heat and simmer for 5–10 minutes until slightly reduced. Season well with salt and pepper.

3 Add the scallops and tiger prawns and bring to the boil, then reduce the heat and simmer gently for 2–3 minutes until cooked. Divide the jasmine rice among six serving bowls and spoon the curry over the top. Sprinkle with coriander and serve immediately.

★ TRY SOMETHING DIFFERENT

Use cleaned squid or mussels instead of scallops and prawns.

Tofu Noodle Curry

★

Preparation Time 15 minutes, plus marinating • **Cooking Time** about 25 minutes • **Serves 4** • **Per Serving** 367 calories, 7g fat (of which 1g saturates), 60g carbohydrate, 2g salt • **Vegetarian** • **Dairy Free** • **Easy**

250g (9oz) fresh tofu
2 tbsp light soy sauce
½ red chilli, chopped (see page 19)
5cm (2in) piece fresh root ginger, peeled and grated
1 tbsp olive oil
1 onion, finely sliced
2 tbsp Thai red curry paste (see page 185)
200ml (7fl oz) coconut milk
900ml (1½ pints) hot vegetable stock
200g (7oz) baby sweetcorn, halved lengthways
200g (7oz) fine green beans
250g (9oz) medium rice noodles
salt and ground black pepper
2 spring onions, sliced diagonally, and 2 tbsp freshly chopped coriander to garnish
1 lime, cut into wedges, to serve

1 Drain the tofu, pat it dry and cut it into large cubes. Put the tofu into a shallow dish with the soy sauce, chilli and ginger. Toss to coat, then leave to marinate for 30 minutes.

2 Heat the oil in a large pan over a medium heat, then add the onion and fry for 10 minutes, stirring, or until golden. Add the curry paste and cook for 2 minutes.

3 Add the tofu and marinade, coconut milk, hot stock and sweetcorn and season with salt and pepper. Bring to the boil, add the green beans, then reduce the heat and simmer for 8–10 minutes.

4 Meanwhile, put the noodles into a large bowl, pour boiling water over them and soak for 30 seconds. Drain the noodles, then stir into the curry. Pour into bowls and garnish with the spring onions and coriander. Serve immediately, with lime wedges.

Aubergines in a Hot Sweet and Sour Sauce

★

Preparation Time 10 minutes • **Cooking Time** 35 minutes • **Serves 4** • **Per Serving** 136 calories, 7g fat (of which 1g saturates), 17g carbohydrate, 2.5g salt • **Vegetarian** • **Gluten Free** • **Dairy Free** • **Easy**

3 tbsp vegetable oil
200g (7oz) onions, thinly sliced
2.5cm (1in) piece fresh root ginger, peeled and finely chopped
2 red chillies, finely chopped (see page 19), plus extra whole red chillies to garnish (optional)
1½ tsp cumin seeds
1½ tsp coriander seeds
3 cloves
5cm (2in) cinnamon stick
1 tbsp paprika
juice of 2 limes
3–4 tbsp dark muscovado sugar
1–2 tsp salt

450g (1lb) aubergines, cut into 2.5cm (1in) pieces
rice to serve

1 Heat the oil in a wok or large frying pan, add the onions, ginger and chopped chillies and stir-fry for about 4 minutes or until softened. Add the cumin and coriander seeds, cloves and cinnamon and cook for 2–3 minutes.

2 Add 300ml (½ pint) water to the pan, then stir in the paprika, lime juice, sugar, salt and aubergines. Bring to the boil, then reduce the heat and simmer, covered, for about 20 minutes or until the aubergines are tender.

3 Uncover the pan and bring the sauce back to the boil. Bubble for 3–4 minutes until the liquid is thick enough to coat the aubergine pieces. Serve with rice, garnished with whole red chillies, if you like.

★ TRY SOMETHING DIFFERENT
Braised Aubergines
Omit the cumin, coriander, cloves, cinnamon and paprika. Add the aubergines to the onion mixture at the end of step 1 and stir-fry for 1–2 minutes. Add 1 tbsp sugar, 1 tsp salt, 3–4 tbsp yellow bean sauce and the water, then complete the recipe.

Stir-fried Salmon and Broccoli

★

Preparation Time 10 minutes • **Cooking Time** 5–6 minutes • **Serves 2** • **Per Serving** 90 calories, 4g fat (of which 1g saturates), 9g carbohydrate, 2.7g salt • **Dairy Free** • **Easy**

2 tsp sesame oil

1 red pepper, seeded and thinly sliced

½ red chilli, thinly sliced (see page 19)

1 garlic clove, crushed

125g (4oz) broccoli florets

2 spring onions, sliced

2 salmon fillets, about 125g (4oz) each, cut into strips

1 tsp Thai fish sauce

2 tsp soy sauce

wholewheat noodles to serve

1 Heat the oil in a wok or large frying pan and add the red pepper, chilli, garlic, broccoli florets and spring onions. Stir-fry over a high heat for 3–4 minutes.

2 Add the salmon, fish sauce and soy sauce and cook for 2 minutes, stirring gently. Serve immediately with wholewheat noodles.

Steamed Sesame Salmon

★

Preparation Time 20 minutes • **Cooking Time** 15–18 minutes • **Serves 4** • **Per Serving** 312 calories, 19g fat (of which 3g saturates), 2g carbohydrate, 1.5g salt • **Dairy Free** • **Easy**

8–12 large Chinese leaves or lettuce leaves
4 salmon steaks, about 150g (5oz) each
½ tsp sesame oil
2 tbsp dry sherry
2 tbsp light soy sauce, plus extra to serve
4 spring onions, shredded, plus extra spring onion curls (see page 192) to garnish
3 tsp sesame seeds, lightly toasted in a dry wok or heavy-based pan
ground white pepper

1 Steam the Chinese leaves or lettuce leaves for 1–2 minutes until soft and pliable. Discard about 2.5cm (1in) of the firm stalk end from each leaf to neaten and place 2–3 leaves together, slightly overlapping. Put the salmon steaks on top.

2 Mix the sesame oil with the sherry and soy sauce and drizzle the mixture over the salmon. Sprinkle with the shredded spring onions, 2 tsp sesame seeds and white pepper to taste.

3 Fold the leaves over the salmon to form neat parcels. Steam for 5–7 minutes or until the fish is cooked and flakes easily.

4 Serve the salmon parcels with the juices spooned over. Sprinkle with the remaining sesame seeds and a little extra soy sauce and garnish with spring onion curls.

Sweet and Sour Duck

★

Preparation Time 15 minutes, plus marinating • **Cooking Time** about 15 minutes • **Serves 4** • **Per Serving** 278 calories, 13g fat (of which 2g saturates), 29g carbohydrate, 1.9g salt • **Dairy Free** • **Easy**

3 tbsp dark soy sauce

1 tbsp dry sherry

1 tsp sesame oil

225g (8oz) duck breast fillets, thinly sliced

1 tbsp sugar

2 tsp cornflour

3 tbsp distilled malt vinegar

1 tbsp tomato ketchup

4 tbsp vegetable oil

125g (4oz) aubergines, sliced

1 red onion, sliced

1 garlic clove, sliced

125g (4oz) carrots, sliced lengthways into strips

125g (4oz) sugarsnap peas or mangetouts

1 mango, peeled, stoned and thinly sliced

noodles to serve

1 Mix 1 tbsp soy sauce with the sherry and sesame oil. Pour the mixture over the duck, cover and marinate for at least 30 minutes.

2 Mix together the sugar, cornflour, vinegar, ketchup and remaining 2 tbsp soy sauce. Set aside.

3 Heat 2 tbsp vegetable oil in a wok or large non-stick frying pan. Drain the duck from the marinade and reserve the marinade. Fry the duck over a high heat for 3–4 minutes until golden and the fat is crisp. Remove from the pan and set aside.

4 Add 1 tbsp more oil to the pan and fry the aubergines for about 2 minutes on each side until golden. Add the remaining 1 tbsp oil and fry the onion, garlic and carrots for 2–3 minutes, then add the sugarsnap peas or mangetouts and fry for a further 1–2 minutes. Add the mango to the pan along with the duck, the soy sauce mixture and the reserved marinade. Bring to the boil, stirring gently all the time and allow to bubble for 2–3 minutes until slightly thickened. Serve immediately, with noodles.

Quick Chicken Stir-fry

Preparation Time 10 minutes • Cooking Time 12 minutes • Serves 4 • Per Serving 316 calories, 3g fat
(of which 1g saturates), 46g carbohydrate, 0.5g salt • **Gluten Free** • **Dairy Free** • **Easy**

1 tsp groundnut oil
300g (11oz) boneless, skinless
   chicken breasts, sliced
4 spring onions, chopped
200g (7oz) medium rice noodles
100g (3½oz) mangetouts
200g (7oz) purple sprouting
   broccoli, chopped
2–3 tbsp sweet chilli sauce
freshly chopped coriander and lime
   wedges (optional) to garnish

1 Heat the oil in a wok or large frying pan and add the chicken and spring onions. Stir-fry over a high heat for 5–6 minutes until the chicken is golden.

2 Meanwhile, soak the rice noodles in boiling water for 4 minutes or according to the pack instructions.

3 Add the mangetouts, broccoli and chilli sauce to the chicken. Continue to stir-fry for 4 minutes.

4 Drain the noodles and add them to the pan. Toss everything together. Scatter the chopped coriander over the top and serve with lime wedges to squeeze over, if you like.

★ TRY SOMETHING DIFFERENT
Other vegetables are just as good in this dish: try pak choi, button mushrooms, carrots cut into matchsticks, or baby sweetcorn.

Pork and Vegetable Stir-fry

Preparation Time 15 minutes, plus marinating • **Cooking Time** about 15 minutes • **Serves 4** • **Per Serving** 220 calories, 8g fat (of which 2g saturates), 7g carbohydrate, 1.6g salt • **Dairy Free** • **Easy**

2 tbsp light soy sauce
2 tbsp dry sherry
2 garlic cloves, crushed
5cm (2in) piece fresh root ginger, peeled and grated
1 tsp cornflour
450g (1lb) pork tenderloin, cut into thin slices
1 tbsp groundnut oil
1 large carrot, cut into matchsticks
225g (8oz) broccoli, cut into small florets
8 spring onions, shredded
150g (5oz) bean sprouts
salt and ground black pepper
rice to serve

1 Put 1 tbsp soy sauce, 1 tbsp sherry, the garlic, ginger and cornflour into a large bowl and mix well. Add the pork to the soy sauce mixture and stir thoroughly, then set aside to marinate for 15 minutes.

2 Heat a wok or large non-stick frying pan until very hot and add the oil. Stir-fry the pork slices in two batches, cooking each batch for 2–3 minutes until the meat is browned. Set aside and keep warm.

3 Reheat the pan, then add the carrot and broccoli and stir-fry for 5 minutes. Add the remaining sherry and soy sauce and 4 tbsp cold water and bring just to the boil. Return the pork to the pan and stir-fry for 2–3 minutes until heated through. Add the spring onions and bean sprouts and stir-fry for 1 minute. Season with salt and pepper, then serve with rice.

Teriyaki Beef Stir-fry

★

Preparation Time 20 minutes, plus marinating • **Cooking Time** 5 minutes • **Serves 4** • **Per Serving** 275 calories, 16g fat (of which 5g saturates), 6g carbohydrate, 2g salt • **Gluten Free** • **Dairy Free** • **Easy**

450g (1lb) beef fillet, sliced as
    thinly as possible, then cut into
    1cm (½in) wide strips
2 tbsp vegetable or groundnut oil
225g (8oz) carrots, cut into
    matchsticks
½ cucumber, cut in half
    lengthways, seeded and cut into
    matchsticks
4–6 spring onions, thinly sliced
    diagonally
noodles tossed in a little sesame oil
    and wasabi paste (optional, see
    Cook's Tips) to serve

FOR THE TERIYAKI
    MARINADE
4 tbsp tamari (see Cook's Tips)
4 tbsp mirin or medium sherry
1 garlic clove, finely chopped
2.5cm (1in) piece fresh root ginger,
    peeled and finely chopped

1 First, make the marinade. Put all the ingredients for the marinade into a shallow bowl and mix well. Add the beef and turn to coat, then cover and chill for at least 30 minutes, preferably overnight.

2 Drain the beef, reserving any marinade. Heat a wok or large frying pan, then add the oil and heat until it is smoking. Add the carrots, cucumber and spring onions and fry over a high heat for 2 minutes or until the edges are well browned. Remove from the pan and set aside.

3 Add the beef to the pan and stir-fry over a very high heat for 2 minutes.

4 Return the vegetables to the pan and add the reserved marinade. Stir-fry for 1–2 minutes until heated through. Serve immediately with noodles tossed in a little sesame oil and a small amount of wasabi paste, if you like.

★ COOK'S TIPS
● *Wasabi paste is a Japanese condiment, green in colour and extremely hot – a little goes a long way. It is available from some supermarkets.*
● *Tamari is a type of Japanese soy sauce; it is not made with wheat and is gluten free.*

Thai Vegetable Curry

Preparation Time 10 minutes • Cooking Time 15 minutes • Serves 4 • Per Serving 200 calories, 10g fat (of which 2g saturates), 19g carbohydrate, 0.7g salt • **Vegetarian** • **Gluten Free** • **Dairy Free** • **Easy**

2–3 tbsp Thai red curry paste
2.5cm (1in) piece fresh root ginger, peeled and finely chopped
50g (2oz) cashew nuts
400ml can coconut milk
3 carrots, cut into thin batons
1 broccoli head, cut into florets
20g (¾oz) fresh coriander, roughly chopped
zest and juice of 1 lime
2 large handfuls of washed spinach leaves
basmati rice to serve

1 Put the curry paste into a large pan. Add the ginger and cashew nuts to the pan and stir over a medium heat for 2–3 minutes.

2 Add the coconut milk, cover and bring to the boil. Stir the carrots into the pan, then reduce the heat and simmer for 5 minutes. Add the broccoli florets and simmer for a further 5 minutes or until tender.

3 Stir the coriander and lime zest into the pan with the spinach. Squeeze the lime juice over and serve with basmati rice.

⭐ TRY SOMETHING DIFFERENT
Replace the carrots and / or broccoli with alternative vegetables: try baby sweetcorn, sugarsnap peas or mangetouts and simmer for only 5 minutes until tender.

Bean Sprouts with Peppers and Chillies

Preparation Time 10 minutes • Cooking Time 4 minutes • Serves 4 • Per Serving 149 calories, 9g fat (of which 1g saturates), 14g carbohydrate, 0.7g salt • **Vegetarian** • **Dairy Free** • **Easy**

3 tbsp vegetable oil
2 garlic cloves, chopped
2.5cm (1in) piece fresh root ginger, peeled and chopped
6 spring onions, cut into 2.5cm (1in) pieces
1 red pepper, seeded and thinly sliced
1 yellow pepper, seeded and thinly sliced
2 green chillies, seeded and finely chopped (see page 19)
350g (12oz) bean sprouts
1 tbsp dark soy sauce
1 tbsp sugar
1 tbsp malt vinegar
a few drops of sesame oil (optional)
boiled rice with 2 tbsp freshly chopped coriander stirred through to serve

1 Heat the oil in a wok or large frying pan. Add the garlic, ginger, spring onions, sliced peppers, chillies and bean sprouts and stir-fry over a medium heat for 3 minutes.

2 Add the soy sauce, sugar and vinegar and fry, stirring, for a further 1 minute.

3 Sprinkle with a few drops of sesame oil, if you like, then serve immediately with coriander rice.

For the Slow Cooker ★

Mexican Bean Soup

Preparation Time 15 minutes • **Cooking Time** 2–3 hours on High • **Serves 6** • **Per Serving** without lime butter 184 calories, 8g fat (of which 1g saturates), 21g carbohydrate, 1.3g salt • **Vegetarian** • **Dairy Free** • **Easy**

4 tbsp olive oil
1 onion, chopped
2 garlic cloves, chopped
a pinch of crushed red chillies
1 tsp ground coriander
1 tsp ground cumin
½ tsp ground cinnamon
600ml (1 pint) hot vegetable stock
300ml (½ pint) tomato juice
1–2 tsp chilli sauce
2 × 400g cans red kidney beans,
    drained and rinsed
2 tbsp freshly chopped coriander
salt and ground black pepper

coriander leaves, roughly torn, to
    garnish
lime butter to serve (optional, see
    Cook's Tip)

1 Heat the oil in a large pan, add the onion, garlic, chillies and spices and fry gently for 5 minutes or until lightly golden.

2 Add the hot stock, the tomato juice, chilli sauce and beans and bring to the boil, then transfer to the slow cooker, cover and cook High for 2–3 hours.

3 Leave the soup to cool a little, then whiz in batches in a blender or food processor until very smooth. Pour the soup into a pan, stir in the chopped coriander and heat through, then season to taste with salt and pepper.

4 Ladle the soup into warmed bowls. Top each portion with a few slices of lime butter, if you like, and scatter with torn coriander leaves.

★ COOK'S TIP
Lime Butter
Beat the grated zest and juice of ½ lime into 50g (2oz) softened butter and season to taste with salt and pepper. Shape into a log, wrap in clingfilm and chill until needed. To serve, unwrap and slice thinly.

Scotch Broth

Preparation Time 15 minutes • **Cooking Time** 8–10 hours on Low • **Serves 8** • **Per Serving** 173 calories, 2g fat (of which trace saturates), 35g carbohydrate, 2.3g salt • **Dairy Free** • **Easy**

- 1.4kg (3lb) piece beef skirt (ask your butcher for this)
- 300g (11oz) broth mix (to include pearl barley, red lentils, split peas and green peas), soaked according to the pack instructions
- 2 carrots, finely chopped
- 1 parsnip, finely chopped
- 2 onions, finely chopped
- ¼ white cabbage, finely chopped
- 1 leek, trimmed and finely chopped
- 1 piece marrow bone, about 350g (12oz)
- ½ tbsp salt
- ground black pepper
- 2 tbsp freshly chopped parsley to serve

1 Put the beef into a large pan and cover with water. Slowly bring to the boil, then reduce the heat and simmer for 10 minutes, using a slotted spoon to remove any scum that comes to the surface. Drain.

2 Put the broth mix and all the vegetables into the slow cooker, then place the beef and marrow bone on top. Add 1.5 litres (2½ pints) boiling water – there should be enough to just cover the meat. Cover and cook on Low for 8–10 hours until the meat is tender.

3 Remove the marrow bone and beef from the broth. Add a few shreds of beef to the broth, if you like. Season the broth well with the salt and some pepper, stir in the chopped parsley and serve hot.

★ COOK'S TIP
This can be two meals in one: a starter and a main course. The beef flavours the stock and is removed before serving. You can then divide up the meat and serve it with mashed potatoes, swedes or turnips.

Split Pea and Ham Soup

Preparation Time 15 minutes, plus overnight soaking • **Cooking Time** 3–4 hours on High • **Serves 6** •
Per Serving 400 calories, 10g fat (of which 5g saturates), 53g carbohydrate, 1.5g salt • **Gluten Free** • **Easy**

500g pack dried yellow split peas, soaked overnight (see Cook's Tip)
25g (1oz) butter
1 large onion, finely chopped
125g (4oz) rindless smoked streaky bacon rashers, roughly chopped
1 garlic clove, crushed
1.7 litres (3 pints) well-flavoured ham or vegetable stock
1 bouquet garni
1 tsp dried oregano
125g (4oz) chopped cooked ham
salt and ground black pepper
cracked black pepper to serve

1 Drain the soaked split peas. Melt the butter in a large pan, add the onion, bacon and garlic and cook over a low heat for about 10 minutes or until the onion is soft.

2 Add the drained split peas to the pan with the stock. Bring to the boil and use a slotted spoon to remove any scum that comes to the surface. Add the bouquet garni and oregano, then season with salt and pepper. Transfer to the slow cooker, cover and cook on High for 3–4 hours until the peas are very soft.

3 Leave the soup to cool a little, then whiz half the soup in a blender or food processor until smooth. Pour the soup into a pan and reheat, then add the ham and check the seasoning. Ladle into warmed bowls and sprinkle with cracked black pepper to serve.

★ COOK'S TIP
Dried peas form the base of this comforting soup. First, you need to soak them overnight in about 1 litre (1³/₄ pints) cold water. If you forget, put them straight into a pan with the water, bring to the boil and cook for 1–2 minutes, then leave to stand for 2 hours before using.

Easy Chicken Casserole

Preparation Time 15 minutes • Cooking Time 5–6 hours on Low • Serves 6 • Per Serving 323 calories, 18g fat (of which 5g saturates), 17g carbohydrate, 0.9g salt • Gluten Free • Dairy Free • Easy

1 tbsp sunflower oil
1 small chicken, about 1.4kg (3lb)
1 fresh rosemary sprig
2 bay leaves
1 red onion, cut into wedges
2 carrots, cut into chunks
2 leeks, trimmed and cut into chunks
2 celery sticks, cut into chunks
12 baby new potatoes, halved if large
900ml (1½ pints) hot chicken stock
200g (7oz) green beans, trimmed
salt and ground black pepper

1 Heat the oil in a large pan over a medium heat. Add the chicken and fry until browned all over. Put the chicken into the slow cooker, along with the herbs and all the vegetables except the green beans. Season well.

2 Pour in the hot stock, cover and cook on Low for 5–6 hours until the chicken is cooked through. Add the beans for the last hour or cook separately in lightly salted boiling water and stir into the casserole once it's cooked. To test the chicken is cooked, pierce the thickest part of the leg with a knife: the juices should run clear.

3 Remove the chicken and spoon the vegetables into six bowls. Carve the chicken and divide among the bowls, then ladle the cooking liquid over.

★ TRY SOMETHING DIFFERENT
Omit the baby new potatoes and serve with mashed potatoes.

Spanish Chicken

Preparation Time 25 minutes, plus infusing • **Cooking Time** 1–2 hours on Low • **Serves 4** • **Per Serving** 671 calories, 28g fat (of which 5g saturates), 70g carbohydrate, 0.8g salt • **Gluten Free** • **Dairy Free** • **Easy**

1 tsp ground turmeric

1.1 litres (2 pints) hot chicken stock

2 tbsp vegetable oil

4 boneless, skinless chicken thighs,
   roughly diced

1 onion, chopped

1 red pepper, seeded and sliced

50g (2oz) chorizo sausage, diced

2 garlic cloves, crushed

300g (11oz) long-grain rice

125g (4oz) frozen peas

salt and ground black pepper

3 tbsp chopped flat-leafed parsley
   to garnish

crusty bread to serve

1 Add the turmeric to the hot stock and leave to infuse for at least 5 minutes. Meanwhile, heat the oil in a large frying pan over a medium heat. Add the chicken and fry for 10 minutes or until golden, then transfer to the slow cooker.

2 Add the onion to the pan and cook over a medium heat for 5 minutes or until soft. Add the red pepper and chorizo and cook for a further 5 minutes, then add the garlic and cook for 1 minute.

3 Add the rice and mix well. Pour in the stock and peas and season, then transfer to the slow cooker and stir together. Cover and cook on Low for 1–2 hours until the rice is tender and the chicken is cooked through.

4 Check the seasoning and garnish with the parsley. Serve with some crusty bread.

Chicken Tagine with Apricots and Almonds

Preparation Time 10 minutes • **Cooking Time** 4–5 hours on Low • **Serves 4** • **Per Serving** 376 calories, 22g fat (of which 4g saturates), 19g carbohydrate, 0.5g salt • **Gluten Free** • **Dairy Free** • **Easy**

2 tbsp olive oil
4 chicken thighs
1 onion, chopped
2 tsp ground cinnamon
2 tbsp runny honey
150g (5oz) dried apricots
75g (3oz) blanched almonds
125ml (4fl oz) hot chicken stock
salt and ground black pepper
flaked almonds to garnish
couscous to serve

1 Heat 1 tbsp oil in a large pan over a medium heat. Add the chicken and fry for 5 minutes or until brown, then transfer to the slow cooker.

2 Add the onion to the pan with the remaining oil and fry for 10 minutes or until softened.

3 Add the cinnamon, honey, apricots, almonds and hot stock to the onion and season well. Bring to the boil, then transfer to the slow cooker, cover and cook on Low for 4–5 hours until the chicken is tender and cooked through. Garnish with the flaked almonds and serve hot with couscous.

Chicken with Chorizo and Beans

Preparation Time 10 minutes • **Cooking Time** 4–5 hours on Low • **Serves 6** • **Per Serving** 690 calories, 41g fat (of which 12g saturates), 33g carbohydrate, 2.6g salt • **Dairy Free** • **Easy**

1 tbsp olive oil

12 chicken pieces (6 drumsticks and 6 thighs)

175g (6oz) chorizo sausage, cubed

1 onion, finely chopped

2 large garlic cloves, crushed

1 tsp mild chilli powder

3 red peppers, seeded and roughly chopped

400g (14oz) passata

2 tbsp tomato purée

150ml (¼ pint) hot chicken stock

2 × 400g cans butter beans, drained and rinsed

200g (7oz) new potatoes, quartered

1 small bunch of thyme

1 bay leaf

200g (7oz) baby leaf spinach

1 Heat the oil in a large pan over a medium heat. Add the chicken and fry until browned all over, then transfer to the slow cooker.

2 Add the chorizo to the pan and fry for 2–3 minutes until its oil starts to run. Add the onion, garlic and chilli powder and fry over a low heat for 5 minutes or until the onion is soft.

3 Add the red peppers and cook for 2–3 minutes until soft. Stir in the passata, tomato purée, hot stock, butter beans, potatoes, thyme sprigs and bay leaf. Bring to the boil, then add to the chicken. Cover and cook on Low for 4–5 hours until the chicken is cooked through.

4 Remove the thyme and bay leaf, then stir in the spinach until it wilts. Serve immediately.

★ TRY SOMETHING DIFFERENT
Use mixed beans instead of the butter beans.

Mexican Chilli Con Carne

Preparation Time 5 minutes • Cooking Time 4–5 hours on Low • Serves 4 • Per Serving 408 calories, 19g fat (of which 7g saturates), 28g carbohydrate, 1.1g salt • **Gluten Free** • **Dairy Free** • **Easy**

2 tbsp olive oil

450g (1lb) minced beef

1 large onion, finely chopped

½–1 tsp each hot chilli powder and ground cumin

3 tbsp tomato purée

150ml (¼ pint) hot beef stock

400g can chopped tomatoes with garlic (see Cook's Tips)

25g (1oz) dark chocolate

400g can red kidney beans, drained and rinsed

2 × 20g packs coriander, chopped

salt and ground black pepper

guacamole, salsa, soured cream, grated cheese, tortilla chips and pickled chillies to serve

1 Heat 1 tbsp oil in a large pan and fry the beef for 10 minutes or until well browned, stirring to break up any lumps. Remove from the pan with a slotted spoon and transfer to the slow cooker.

2 Add the remaining oil to the pan, then fry the onion, stirring, for 10 minutes or until soft and golden.

3 Add the spices and fry for 1 minute, then add the tomato purée, hot stock and the tomatoes. Bring to the boil, then stir into the mince in the slow cooker. Cover and cook on Low for 4–5 hours.

4 Stir in the chocolate, kidney beans and coriander and season with salt and pepper, then leave to stand for 10 minutes.

5 Serve with guacamole, salsa, soured cream, grated cheese, tortilla chips and pickled chillies.

★ COOK'S TIPS

● *Instead of a can of tomatoes with garlic, use a can of chopped tomatoes and 1 crushed garlic clove.*

● *Adding a little dark chocolate to chilli con carne brings out the flavours of this tasty dish.*

Beef Goulash

Preparation Time 30 minutes • **Cooking Time** 8–10 hours on Low • **Serves 6** • **Per Serving** 726 calories, 44g fat (of which 16g saturates), 21g carbohydrate, 1.6g salt • **Easy**

1kg (2¼lb) stewing steak
2 tbsp seasoned plain flour
3 tbsp vegetable oil
700g (1½lb) onions, chopped
225g (8oz) pancetta cubes or bacon
    lardons
2 garlic cloves, crushed
4 tbsp paprika
2 tsp dried mixed herbs
400g can peeled plum tomatoes
150ml (¼ pint) hot beef stock
150ml (¼ pint) soured cream
salt and ground black pepper
chopped parsley, to garnish
noodles to serve

1 Cut the beef into 3cm (1¼in) cubes, then toss the cubes in the flour to coat and shake off any excess.

2 Heat 2 tbsp oil in a large pan and quickly fry the meat in small batches until browned on all sides. Transfer to the slow cooker.

3 Heat the remaining oil in the pan, add the onions and fry gently for 5–7 minutes until starting to soften and turn golden. Add the pancetta or lardons and fry over a high heat until crispy. Stir in the garlic and paprika and cook, stirring, for 1 minute.

4 Add the herbs, tomatoes and hot stock and bring to the boil. Stir into the beef in the slow cooker, cover and cook on Low for 8–10 hours until tender.

5 Check the seasoning, then stir in the soured cream. Garnish with parsley and serve with noodles.

Beef and Guinness Stew

★

Preparation Time 15 minutes • **Cooking Time** 8–10 hours on Low • **Serves 6** • **Per Serving** 526 calories, 29g fat (of which 10g saturates), 10g carbohydrate, 0.4g salt • **Dairy Free** • **Easy**

1.4kg (3lb) shin of beef or braising steak, cut into 3cm (1¼in) cubes
2 tbsp seasoned plain flour
4 tbsp vegetable oil
2 medium onions, sliced
4 medium carrots, cut into chunks
225ml (8fl oz) Guinness
300ml (½ pint) hot beef stock
2 bay leaves
700g (1½lb) baby potatoes, halved if large
2 tbsp freshly chopped flat-leafed parsley
salt and ground black pepper

1 Toss the beef in the flour to coat and shake off any excess. Heat the oil in a large pan until hot. Add a handful of beef and cook until well browned. Remove with a slotted spoon, transfer to the slow cooker and repeat until all the meat is browned.

2 Add the onions and carrots to the pan and cook for 10 minutes or until browned. Add the Guinness, scraping the base to loosen the goodness, then stir in the hot stock. Add the bay leaves and potatoes and bring to the boil. Pour over the beef in the slow cooker, cover and cook on Low for 8–10 hours until the meat is tender.

3 Stir in the parsley, season to taste and serve.

Pheasant Casserole with Cider and Apples

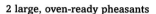

Preparation Time 50 minutes • **Cooking Time** 6–7 hours on Low • **Serves 8** • **Per Serving** 478 calories, 28g fat (of which 16g saturates), 12g carbohydrate, 0.7g salt • **Easy**

2 large, oven-ready pheasants
2 tbsp plain flour, plus extra to dust
50g (2oz) butter
4 rindless streaky bacon rashers, halved
2 onions, chopped
2 celery sticks, chopped
1 tbsp dried juniper berries, lightly crushed
2.5cm (1in) piece fresh root ginger, peeled and finely chopped
150ml (¼ pint) hot pheasant or chicken stock
350ml (12fl oz) dry cider
150ml (¼ pint) double cream
4 crisp eating apples, such as Granny Smith
1 tbsp lemon juice
salt and ground black pepper

1 Cut each pheasant into four portions, season with salt and pepper and dust with flour.

2 Melt three-quarters of the butter in a large pan and brown the pheasant portions, in batches, over a high heat until deep golden brown on all sides. Transfer to the slow cooker.

3 Add the bacon to the pan and fry for 2–3 minutes until golden. Add the onions, celery, juniper and ginger and cook for 8–10 minutes.

4 Stir in the flour and cook, stirring, for 2 minutes, then add the hot stock and the cider and bring to the boil, stirring. Pour into the slow cooker and season well, then cover and cook on Low for 6–7 hours or until the pheasant is tender.

5 Lift out the pheasant and put into a warmed dish and keep it warm. Strain the sauce through a sieve into a pan. Stir in the cream, bring to the boil and bubble for 10 minutes or until syrupy.

6 Quarter, core and cut the apples into wedges, then toss in the lemon juice. Melt the remaining butter in a small pan and fry the apple wedges for 2–3 minutes until golden. Return the pheasant to the sauce, along with the apples, and check the seasoning before serving.

Curried Lamb with Lentils

★

Preparation Time 15 minutes, plus marinating • **Cooking Time** 5–6 hours on Low • **Serves 4** • **Per Serving** 478 calories, 22g fat (of which 7g saturates), 36g carbohydrate, 0.3g salt • **Gluten Free** • **Dairy Free** • **Easy**

500g (1lb 2oz) lean stewing lamb on the bone, cut into 8 pieces (ask your butcher to do this), trimmed of fat
1 tsp ground cumin
1 tsp ground turmeric
2 garlic cloves, crushed
1 medium red chilli, seeded and chopped (see page 19)
2.5cm (1in) piece fresh root ginger, peeled and grated
2 tbsp vegetable oil
1 onion, chopped
400g can chopped tomatoes
2 tbsp vinegar
175g (6oz) red lentils, rinsed

salt and ground black pepper
coriander sprigs to garnish
rocket salad to serve

1 Put the lamb into a shallow sealable container and add the spices, garlic, chilli, ginger, salt and pepper. Stir well to mix, then cover and chill for at least 30 minutes.

2 Heat the oil in a large pan, add the onion and cook over a low heat for 5 minutes. Add the lamb and cook for 10 minutes, turning regularly, or until the meat is evenly browned.

3 Add the tomatoes, vinegar, lentils and 225ml (8fl oz) boiling water and bring to the boil. Season well. Transfer to the slow cooker, cover and cook on Low for 5–6 hours until the lamb is tender.

4 Serve hot, garnished with coriander, with a rocket salad.

Spiced Bean and Vegetable Stew

Preparation Time 15 minutes • **Cooking Time** 2–3 hours on Low • **Serves 6** • **Per Serving** 262 calories, 7g fat (of which 1g saturates), 44g carbohydrate, 1.3g salt • **Vegetarian** • **Gluten Free** • **Dairy Free** • **Easy**

3 tbsp olive oil
2 small onions, sliced
2 garlic cloves, crushed
1 tbsp sweet paprika
1 small dried red chilli, seeded and finely chopped
700g (1½lb) sweet potatoes, cubed
700g (1½lb) pumpkin, cut into chunks
125g (4oz) okra, trimmed
500g jar passata
400g can haricot or cannellini beans, drained and rinsed
450ml (¾ pint) hot vegetable stock
salt and ground black pepper

1 Heat the oil in a large pan over a very gentle heat. Add the onions and garlic and cook for 5 minutes.

2 Stir in the paprika and chilli and cook for 2 minutes, then add the sweet potatoes, pumpkin, okra, passata, beans and hot stock. Season generously with salt and pepper and bring to the boil.

3 Transfer to the slow cooker, cover and cook on Low for 2–3 hours until the vegetables are tender.

★ TRY SOMETHING DIFFERENT
Instead of paprika, use 1 tsp each ground cumin and ground coriander. Garnish with freshly chopped coriander.

Mushroom and Bean Hotpot

Preparation Time 15 minutes • **Cooking Time** 2–3 hours on Low • **Serves 6** • **Per Serving** 280 calories, 10g fat
(of which 1g saturates), 34g carbohydrate, 1.3g salt • **Vegetarian** • **Dairy Free** • **Easy**

3 tbsp olive oil

700g (1½lb) chestnut mushrooms,
   roughly chopped

1 large onion, finely chopped

2 tbsp plain flour

2 tbsp mild curry paste

150ml (¼ pint) dry white wine

400g can chopped tomatoes

2 tbsp sun-dried tomato paste

2 × 400g cans mixed beans, drained
   and rinsed

3 tbsp mango chutney

3 tbsp roughly chopped fresh
   coriander and mint

1 Heat the oil in a large pan over a low heat and fry the mushrooms and onion until the onion is soft and dark golden. Stir in the flour and curry paste and cook for 1–2 minutes, then add the wine, tomatoes, sun-dried tomato paste and beans.

2 Bring to the boil, then transfer to the slow cooker. Cover and cook on Low for 2–3 hours.

3 Stir in the chutney and herbs and serve.

Lentils with Red Pepper

★

Preparation Time 10 minutes • **Cooking Time** 3–4 hours on High • **Serves 4** • **Per Serving** 296 calories, 5g fat
(of which 1g saturates), 47g carbohydrate, 0.1g salt • **Vegetarian** • **Gluten Free** • **Dairy Free** • **Easy**

1 tbsp olive oil
1 large onion, finely chopped
2 celery sticks, diced
2 carrots, diced
2 bay leaves, torn
300g (11oz) Puy lentils
600ml (1 pint) hot vegetable stock
1 marinated red pepper, drained
   and chopped
2 tbsp chopped flat-leafed parsley,
   plus extra to garnish
ground black pepper

1 Heat the oil in a pan, add the onion and cook over a low heat for 15 minutes or until soft. Add the celery, carrots and bay leaves and cook for 2 minutes.

2 Add the lentils with the hot stock and stir everything together. Transfer to the slow cooker, cover and cook on High for 3–4 hours.

3 Stir in the red pepper and parsley and season with pepper. Leave to stand for 10 minutes, then garnish with extra parsley and serve as an accompaniment.

Ratatouille

Preparation Time 20 minutes • **Cooking Time** 3–4 hours on High • **Serves 6** • **Per Serving** 150 calories, 9g fat (of which 1g saturates), 15g carbohydrate, 0.1g salt • **Vegetarian** • **Gluten Free** • **Dairy Free** • **Easy**

4 tbsp olive oil
2 onions, thinly sliced
1 large garlic clove, crushed
350g (12oz) small aubergines, thinly
  sliced
450g (1lb) small courgettes, thinly
  sliced
450g (1lb) tomatoes, skinned,
  seeded and roughly chopped
1 green and 1 red pepper, each
  cored, seeded and sliced
1 tbsp chopped basil
2 tsp freshly chopped thyme
2 tbsp freshly chopped flat-leafed
  parsley

2 tbsp sun-dried tomato paste
salt and ground black pepper

1 Heat the oil in a large pan, add the onions and garlic and fry gently for 10 minutes or until softened and golden.

2 Add the aubergines, courgettes, tomatoes, sliced peppers, herbs, tomato paste and seasoning. Fry, stirring, for 2–3 minutes.

3 Transfer to the slow cooker and cover. Cook on High for 3–4 hours until all the vegetables are tender. Taste and adjust the seasoning. Serve the ratatouille hot or at room temperature.

Braised Red Cabbage

★

Preparation Time 10 minutes • **Cooking Time** 2–3 hours on Low • **Serves 8** • **Per Serving** 50 calories, trace fat, 11g carbohydrate, 0g salt • **Vegetarian** • **Gluten Free** • **Dairy Free** • **Easy**

½ medium red cabbage, about 500g (1lb 2oz), shredded
1 red onion, finely chopped
1 Bramley apple, peeled, cored and chopped
25g (1oz) light muscovado sugar
1 cinnamon stick
a pinch of ground cloves
¼ tsp freshly grated nutmeg
2 tbsp each red wine vinegar and red wine
juice of 1 orange
salt and ground black pepper

1 Put all the ingredients into the slow cooker and stir to mix well. Cover and cook on Low for 2–3 hours.

2 When the cabbage is tender, remove the pan from the heat and discard the cinnamon stick. Serve at once, or cool, put into a bowl, cover and chill the cabbage overnight.

3 To reheat, put the cabbage into a pan, add 2 tbsp cold water and cover with a tight-fitting lid. Bring to the boil, then reduce the heat and simmer for 25 minutes.

Fruity Rice Pudding

Preparation Time 10 minutes, plus cooling and chilling (optional) • **Cooking Time** 2–3 hours on Low • **Serves 6** •
Per Serving 323 calories, 17g fat (of which 10g saturates), 36g carbohydrate, 0.2g salt • **Vegetarian** • **Gluten Free** • **Easy**

125g (4oz) pudding rice
1.1 litres (2 pints) full-fat milk
1 tsp vanilla extract
3–4 tbsp caster sugar
200ml (7fl oz) whipping cream
6 tbsp wild lingonberry sauce

1 Put the rice into the slow cooker with the milk, vanilla extract and sugar. Cover and cook on Low for 2–3 hours. You can enjoy the pudding hot now or leave to cool and continue the recipe.

2 Lightly whip the cream and fold through the pudding. Chill for 1 hour.

3 Divide the rice mixture among six glass dishes and top with 1 tbsp lingonberry sauce.

★ **TRY SOMETHING DIFFERENT**
● *Although wild lingonberry sauce is used here, a spoonful of any fruit sauce or compote, such as strawberry or blueberry, will taste delicious.*
● *For an alternative presentation, serve in tumblers, layering the rice pudding with the fruit sauce; you will need to use double the amount of fruit sauce.*

Winter Fruit Compote

★

Preparation Time 10 minutes • **Cooking Time** 3–4 hours on Low • **Serves 6** • **Per Serving** 139 calories, trace fat, 26g carbohydrate, 0.1g salt • **Vegetarian** • **Gluten Free** • **Dairy Free** • **Easy**

75g (3oz) ready-to-eat dried pears
75g (3oz) ready-to-eat dried figs
75g (3oz) ready-to-eat dried apricots
75g (3oz) ready-to-eat prunes
1 star anise
½ cinnamon stick
300ml (½ pint) apple juice
300ml (½ pint) dry white wine
light muscovado sugar, to taste
crème fraîche or thick Greek-style yogurt to serve

1 Put the dried fruits into the slow cooker with the star anise and cinnamon stick.

2 Put the apple juice and wine into a pan and bring to the boil. Pour over the fruit, cover and cook on Low for 3–4 hours until plump and tender.

3 Turn the compote into a bowl. Taste the cooking liquid for sweetness, adding a little sugar if necessary. Leave to cool to room temperature.

4 Serve the compote with crème fraîche or thick Greek-style yogurt.

★ TRY SOMETHING DIFFERENT
Replace the figs with dried apple rings and the pears with raisins.

Puddings ★

Quick Apple Tart

★

Preparation Time 10 minutes • **Cooking Time** 20–25 minutes • **Serves 8** • **Per Serving** 221 calories, 12g fat (of which 0g saturates), 29g carbohydrate, 0.4g salt • **Vegetarian** • **Easy**

375g pack all-butter ready-rolled puff pastry
500g (1lb 2oz) Cox's Orange Pippin apples, cored, thinly sliced and tossed in the juice of 1 lemon
golden icing sugar to dust

1 Preheat the oven to 200°C (180°C fan oven) mark 6. Put the pastry on a 28 x 38cm (11 x 15in) baking sheet and roll lightly with a rolling pin to smooth down the pastry. Score lightly around the edge, to create a 3cm (1¼ in) border.

2 Put the apple slices on top of the pastry, within the border. Turn the edge of the pastry halfway over, so that it reaches the edge of the apples, then press down and use your fingers to crimp the edge. Dust heavily with icing sugar.

3 Bake in the oven for 20–25 minutes until the pastry is cooked and the sugar has caramelised. Serve warm, dusted with more icing sugar.

Drunken Pears

Preparation Time 15 minutes • **Cooking Time** 50 minutes • **Serves 4** • **Per Serving** 305 calories, trace fat, 52g carbohydrate, 0g salt • **Vegetarian** • **Gluten Free** • **Dairy Free** • **Easy**

4 Williams or Comice pears
150g (5oz) granulated sugar
300ml (½ pint) red wine
150ml (¼ pint) sloe gin
1 cinnamon stick
zest of 1 orange
6 star anise
Greek yogurt or whipped cream to
    serve (optional)

1 Peel the pears, cut out the calyx at the base of each and leave the stalks intact. Put the sugar, wine, sloe gin and 300ml (½ pint) water into a small pan and heat gently until the sugar dissolves.

2 Bring to the boil and add the cinnamon stick, orange zest and star anise. Add the pears, then cover and poach over a low heat for 30 minutes or until tender.

3 Remove the pears with a slotted spoon, then continue to heat the liquid until it has reduced to about 200ml (7fl oz) or until syrupy. Pour the syrup over the pears. Serve warm or chilled with Greek yogurt or whipped cream, if you like.

★ GET AHEAD
To prepare ahead *Complete the recipe, cool, cover and chill for up to three days.*

Figs in Cinnamon Syrup

Preparation Time 15 minutes • **Cooking Time** 35 minutes, plus cooling and chilling • **Serves 4** • **Per Serving** 336 calories, 2g fat (of which 0g saturates), 68g carbohydrate, 0.2g salt • **Vegetarian** • **Gluten Free** • **Dairy Free** • **Easy**

1 orange
1 lemon
300ml (½ pint) red wine
50g (2oz) golden caster sugar
1 cinnamon stick
450g (1lb) ready-to-eat dried figs
mascarpone cheese or ice cream to serve

1 Pare the zest from the orange and lemon and put into a medium pan. Squeeze the orange and lemon and add their juice, the wine, sugar and cinnamon stick to the pan. Bring very slowly to the boil, stirring occasionally.

2 Add the figs. Simmer very gently for 20 minutes or until plump and soft. Remove the figs, zest and cinnamon with a slotted spoon and transfer to a serving bowl.

3 Bring the liquid to the boil once again and bubble for about 5 minutes or until syrupy. Pour over the figs, then cool, cover and chill.

4 If you like, warm the figs in the syrup for 3–4 minutes, then serve with mascarpone cheese or ice cream.

Hot Spiced Fruit Salad

Preparation Time 10 minutes • **Cooking Time** 1½ hours • **Serves 6** • **Per Serving** 185 calories, 1g fat (of which 0g saturates), 44g carbohydrate, 0.1g salt • **Vegetarian** • **Gluten Free** • **Dairy Free** • **Easy**

3 apples, cored and chopped
3 pears, cored and chopped
12 each ready-to-eat dried apricots
    and figs
juice of 2 large oranges
150ml (¼ pint) apple juice
a pinch of ground cinnamon
1 star anise

1 Preheat the oven to 180°C (160°C fan oven) mark 4. Put the apples and pears into a roasting tin with the apricots and figs, the orange juice, apple juice, ground cinnamon and star anise. Stir, cover with foil and bake in the oven for 1 hour.

2 Remove the foil and bake for a further 30 minutes. Discard the star anise and serve.

★ TRY SOMETHING DIFFERENT
Ready-to-eat prunes or 100g (3½oz) dried cranberries can be substituted for the figs.

Poached Plums with Port

★

Preparation Time 5 minutes • **Cooking Time** 20 minutes • **Serves 4** • **Per Serving** 97 calories, 0g fat, 23g carbohydrate, 0g salt • **Vegetarian** • **Gluten Free** • **Dairy Free** • **Easy**

75g (3oz) golden caster sugar
2 tbsp port
6 large plums, halved and stoned
1 cinnamon stick
vanilla ice cream to serve (optional)

1 Put the sugar into a pan with 500ml (18fl oz) water. Heat gently until the sugar dissolves. Bring to the boil and simmer rapidly for 2 minutes without stirring.

2 Stir in the port. Add the plums to the pan with the cinnamon stick and simmer gently for 5–10 minutes until the fruit is tender but still keeping its shape.

3 Remove the plums and put to one side, discarding the cinnamon. Simmer the syrup until it has reduced by two-thirds. Serve the plums warm or cold, drizzled with syrup and with a scoop of vanilla ice cream alongside, if you like.

Pears with Hot Fudge Sauce

Preparation Time 5 minutes • Cooking Time 15 minutes • Serves 4 • Per Serving 301 calories, 16g fat (of which 10g saturates), 40g carbohydrate, 0.4g salt • **Vegetarian** • **Gluten Free** • **Easy**

75g (3oz) butter
1 tbsp golden syrup
75g (3oz) light muscovado sugar
4 tbsp evaporated milk or single or double cream
4 ripe pears, cored, sliced and chilled

1 Melt the butter, syrup, sugar and evaporated milk or cream together over a very low heat. Stir thoroughly until all the sugar has dissolved, then bring the fudge mixture to the boil without any further stirring.

2 Put each pear in a serving dish and pour the hot fudge sauce over it. Serve immediately.

Chocolate Bread Pudding

★

Preparation Time 20 minutes, plus chilling • **Cooking Time** 55 minutes–1¼ hours • **Serves 6** • **Per Serving** 390 calories, 17g fat (of which 6g saturates), 51g carbohydrate, 0.7g salt • **Vegetarian** • **A Little Effort**

200g (7oz) baguette
100g (3½oz) milk chocolate,
    roughly chopped
500g carton fresh custard
150ml (¼ pint) semi-skimmed milk
1 large egg, beaten
butter to grease
1 tbsp demerara sugar
50g (2oz) walnuts, finely chopped
50g (2oz) plain or milk chocolate, in
    chunks
single cream to serve (optional)

1 Roughly chop the baguette and put it into a large bowl. Put the chopped milk chocolate in a pan with the custard and milk over a low heat. Stir gently until the chocolate has melted. Beat in the egg.

2 Pour the chocolate mixture over the bread, stir well to coat, then cover and chill for at least 4 hours.

3 Preheat the oven to 180°C (160°C fan oven) mark 4. Spoon the soaked bread into a buttered 1.4 litre (2½ pint), 7.5cm (3in) deep, ovenproof dish, then bake for 30–40 minutes.

4 Sprinkle with the sugar, walnuts and chocolate chunks. Put the dish back in the oven for 20–30 minutes until lightly set. Serve the pudding warm, with single cream, if you like.

★ TRY SOMETHING DIFFERENT
Instead of a baguette, use croissants or brioche for a richer pudding.

Panettone Pudding

Preparation Time 20 minutes, plus soaking • **Cooking Time** 35–45 minutes • **Serves 6** • **Per Serving** 581 calories, 29g fat (of which 16g saturates), 73g carbohydrate, 0.9g salt • **Vegetarian** • **Easy**

50g (2oz) butter, at room
   temperature, plus extra to grease
500g (1lb 2oz) panettone (see
   Cook's Tip), cut into slices about
   5mm (¼ in) thick
3 large eggs, beaten
150g (5oz) golden caster sugar
300ml (½ pint) full-fat milk
150ml (¼ pint) double cream
grated zest of 1 orange

1 Butter a 2 litre (3½ pint) ovenproof dish. Lightly butter the panettone slices, then tear them into pieces and arrange in the dish.

2 Mix the eggs with the sugar in a large bowl, then whisk in the milk, cream and orange zest. Pour the mixture over the buttered panettone and leave to soak for 20 minutes. Preheat the oven to 170°C (150°C fan oven) mark 3.

3 Put the dish in a roasting tin and pour in enough hot water to come halfway up the sides. Bake for 35–45 minutes until the pudding is just set in the middle and golden.

★ COOK'S TIP
Panettone is a yeasted fruit cake that is a traditional Christmas treat in Italy and is most widely available around Christmas time. If you can't find it, use brioche or cinnamon and raisin bread.

Rich Chocolate Pots

★

Preparation Time 10 minutes, plus chilling • **Cooking Time** 10 minutes • **Serves 6** • **Per Serving** 895 calories, 66g fat (of which 41g saturates), 66g carbohydrate, 0g salt • **Gluten Free** • **Easy**

300g (11oz) plain chocolate (at least 70% cocoa solids), broken into pieces
300ml (½ pint) double cream
250g (9oz) mascarpone cheese
3 tbsp cognac
1 tbsp vanilla extract
6 tbsp crème fraîche
chocolate curls to decorate (see Cook's Tip)

1 Melt the plain chocolate in a heatproof bowl set over a pan of gently simmering water. Remove the bowl from the heat and add the cream, mascarpone, cognac and vanilla extract. Mix well – the hot chocolate will melt into the cream and mascarpone.

2 Divide the mixture among six 150ml (¼ pint) glasses and chill for 20 minutes. Spoon some crème fraîche on top of each chocolate pot and decorate with the chocolate curls.

★ COOK'S TIP
Chocolate Curls
Melt the chocolate in a heatproof bowl set over a pan of simmering water. Spread it out in a thin layer on a marble slab or clean worksurface. Leave to firm up. Using a sharp blade (such as a pastry scraper, a cook's knife or a very stiff spatula), draw it through the chocolate at a 45° angle. The size of the curls will be determined by the width of the blade.

Peach Brûlée

Preparation Time 10 minutes • **Cooking Time** about 10 minutes • **Serves 4** • **Per Serving** 137 calories, 6g fat (of which 4g saturates), 21g carbohydrate, 0.1g salt • **Vegetarian** • **Gluten Free** • **Easy**

4 ripe peaches, halved and stoned
8 tsp soft cream cheese
8 tsp golden caster sugar

1 Preheat the grill until very hot. Fill each stone cavity in the fruit with 2 tsp cream cheese, then sprinkle each one with 2 tsp caster sugar.

2 Put the fruit halves on a grill pan and cook under the very hot grill until the sugar has browned and caramelised to create a brûlée crust. Serve warm.

★ TRY SOMETHING DIFFERENT
Use nectarines instead of peaches.

Strawberry Brûlée

Preparation Time 15 minutes, plus cooling and chilling • **Cooking Time** 5 minutes • **Serves 4** • **Per Serving** 240 calories, 10g fat (of which 5g saturates), 35g carbohydrate, 0.2g salt • **Vegetarian** • **Gluten Free** • **Easy**

250g (9oz) strawberries, hulled and sliced
2 tsp golden icing sugar
1 vanilla pod
400g (14oz) Greek yogurt
100g (3½oz) golden caster sugar

1 Divide the strawberries among four ramekins and sprinkle with icing sugar.

2 Scrape the seeds from the vanilla pod and stir into the yogurt, then spread the mixture evenly over the strawberries.

3 Preheat the grill to high. Sprinkle the caster sugar evenly over the yogurt until it's well covered.

4 Put the ramekins on a baking sheet or into the grill pan and grill until the sugar turns dark brown and caramelises. Leave for 15 minutes or until the caramel is cool enough to eat, or chill for up to 2 hours before serving.

★ TRY SOMETHING DIFFERENT
Use raspberries or blueberries instead of the strawberries.

Cherry Yogurt Crush

★

Preparation Time 10 minutes, plus chilling • **Serves 4** • **Per Serving** 390 calories, 18g fat (of which 9g saturates), 45g carbohydrate, 0.5g salt • **Vegetarian** • **Easy**

400g can stoned cherries, drained, or 450g (1lb) fresh cherries, stoned
500g (1lb 2oz) Greek yogurt
150g (5oz) ratafia biscuits
4 tbsp cherry brandy (optional)

1 Spoon some cherries into the base of each of four 400ml (14fl oz) serving glasses. Top with a dollop of yogurt, some ratafia biscuits and a drizzle of cherry brandy, if you like. Continue layering up each glass until all the ingredients have been used.

2 Chill for 15 minutes–2 hours before serving.

Quick Lemon Mousse

★

Preparation Time 1–2 minutes • **Serves 4** • **Per Serving** 334 calories, 30g fat (of which 18g saturates), 16g carbohydrate, 0.1g salt • **Vegetarian** • **Gluten Free** • **Easy**

6 tbsp lemon curd
300ml (½ pint) double cream,
  whipped
fresh blueberries to decorate

1 Gently stir the lemon curd through the double cream until combined and decorate with blueberries.

Eton Mess

⋯⋯⋯⋯⋯⋯⋯⋯⋯⋯⋯⋯⋯⋯⋯⋯⋯⋯⋯⋯⋯⋯⋯⋯⋯⋯⋯⋯⋯⋯⋯⋯⋯⋯⋯ ★

Preparation Time 10 minutes • **Serves 6** • **Per Serving** 198 calories, 5g fat (of which 3g saturates), 33g carbohydrate, 0.1g salt • **Vegetarian** • **Gluten Free** • **Easy**

200g (7oz) fromage frais, chilled
200g (7oz) low-fat Greek yogurt, chilled
1 tbsp golden caster sugar
2 tbsp strawberry liqueur
6 meringues, roughly crushed
350g (12oz) strawberries, hulled and halved

1 Put the fromage frais and yogurt into a large bowl and stir to combine.

2 Add the sugar, strawberry liqueur, meringues and strawberries. Mix together gently and divide among six serving dishes.

★ TRY SOMETHING DIFFERENT
Caribbean Crush
Replace the sugar and liqueur with dulce de leche and the strawberries with sliced bananas.

Strawberry Compote

★

Preparation Time 15 minutes, plus overnight chilling • **Cooking Time** 10 minutes • **Serves 4** • **Per Serving** 156 calories, trace fat, 40g carbohydrate, 0g salt • **Vegetarian** • **Gluten Free** • **Dairy Free** • **Easy**

175g (6oz) raspberry conserve
juice of 1 orange
juice of 1 lemon
1 tsp rosewater
350g (12oz) strawberries, hulled
   and thickly sliced
150g (5oz) blueberries

1 Put the raspberry conserve in a pan with the orange and lemon juices. Add 150ml (¼ pint) boiling water. Stir over a low heat to melt the conserve, then leave to cool.

2 Stir in the rosewater and taste – you may want to add a squeeze more lemon juice if it's too sweet. Put the strawberries and blueberries into a serving bowl. Strain over the raspberry conserve mixture. Cover and chill overnight. Remove from the fridge about 30 minutes before serving.

Summer Fruit Compote

Preparation Time 10 minutes • **Cooking Time** 20 minutes, plus cooling and chilling • **Serves 4** • **Per Serving** 122 calories, trace fat, 30g carbohydrate, 0g salt • **Vegetarian** • **Gluten Free** • **Easy**

12 fresh, ripe apricots, halved and stoned
125g (4oz) fresh blueberries
50g (2oz) vanilla sugar
juice of 1 orange
200g (7oz) strawberries, hulled and halved
Greek yogurt to serve

1 Preheat the oven to 180°C (160°C fan oven) mark 4. Put the apricots, blueberries, sugar and orange juice into a large shallow baking dish and bake, uncovered, for about 20 minutes or until just tender.

2 Gently stir in the strawberries. Taste the cooking juices – you may want to add a little extra sugar – then leave to cool. Cover and chill. Serve with a spoonful of Greek yogurt.

⭐ GET AHEAD
To prepare ahead *Make up to a day beforehand. Put into an airtight container and chill.*
To use *Take out of the fridge and allow to reach room temperature (around 30 minutes) before serving.*

Spiced Nectarines

Preparation Time 10 minutes, plus cooling • **Serves 4** • **Per Serving** 95 calories, trace fat, 23g carbohydrate, 0g salt • **Vegetarian** • **Gluten Free** • **Easy**

4 tbsp clear honey
2 star anise
1 tbsp lemon juice
4 ripe nectarines or peaches,
   halved and stoned
cream or vanilla ice cream to serve

1 Put the honey, star anise and lemon juice into a heatproof bowl. Stir in 150ml (¼ pint) boiling water and leave until just warm.

2 Add the nectarines to the warm honey syrup and leave to cool. Serve with cream or vanilla ice cream.

⭐ TRY SOMETHING DIFFERENT
Use a cinnamon stick instead of the star anise.

Baked Apricots with Almonds

Preparation Time 5 minutes • **Cooking Time** 20–25 minutes • **Serves 6** • **Per Serving** 124 calories, 6g fat (of which 2g saturates), 16g carbohydrate, 0.1g salt • **Vegetarian** • **Gluten Free** • **Dairy Free** • **Easy**

12 apricots, halved and stoned
3 tbsp golden caster sugar
2 tbsp amaretto liqueur
25g (1oz) unsalted butter
25g (1oz) flaked almonds
crème fraîche to serve

1 Preheat the oven to 200°C (180°C fan oven) mark 6. Put the apricot halves, cut side up, into an ovenproof dish. Sprinkle with the sugar, drizzle with the liqueur, then dot each apricot half with a little butter. Scatter the flaked almonds over them.

2 Bake in the oven for 20–25 minutes until the apricots are soft and the juices are syrupy. Serve warm, with crème fraîche.

★ TRY SOMETHING DIFFERENT
Use nectarines or peaches instead of apricots.

Spiced Winter Fruit

Preparation Time 20 minutes, plus cooling • **Cooking Time** 20 minutes • **Serves 6** • **Per Serving** 207 calories, trace fat, 45g carbohydrate, 0g salt • **Vegetarian** • **Gluten Free** • **Dairy Free** • **Easy**

50g (2oz) large muscatel raisins or dried blueberries
1 small pineapple, peeled, cored and thinly sliced
1 mango, peeled, stoned and thickly sliced
3 tangerines, peeled and halved horizontally
3 fresh figs, halved

FOR THE SYRUP
150ml (¼ pint) port
150ml (¼ pint) freshly squeezed orange juice
75g (3oz) light muscovado sugar
1 cinnamon stick
6 cardamom pods, lightly crushed
5cm (2in) piece fresh root ginger, peeled and thinly sliced

1 First, make the syrup. Pour the port and orange juice into a small pan, then add the sugar and 300ml (½ pint) cold water. Bring to the boil, stirring all the time. Add the cinnamon stick, cardamom pods and ginger, then bubble gently for 15 minutes.

2 Put all the fruit into a serving bowl. Remove the cinnamon stick and cardamom pods from the syrup – or leave in for a spicier flavour – then pour the syrup over the fruit. Serve warm or cold.

Mango Gratin with Sabayon

Preparation Time 5 minutes, plus optional resting • **Cooking Time** 10 minutes • **Serves 6** • **Per Serving** 249 calories, 5g fat (of which 1g saturates), 45g carbohydrate, 0g salt • **Vegetarian** • **Gluten Free** • **Dairy Free** • **A Little Effort**

3 large ripe mangoes, peeled, stoned and sliced
5 medium egg yolks
6 tbsp golden caster sugar
300ml (½ pint) champagne or sparkling wine
6 tbsp dark muscovado sugar to sprinkle
crisp sweet biscuits to serve

1 Arrange the mangoes in six serving glasses. Whisk the egg yolks and sugar in a large heatproof bowl over a pan of gently simmering water until the mixture is thick and falls in soft ribbon shapes. Add the champagne or sparkling wine and continue to whisk until the mixture is thick and foamy again. Remove from the heat.

2 Spoon the sabayon over the mangoes, sprinkle with the muscovado sugar, then blow-torch the top to caramelise or leave for 10 minutes to go fudgey. Serve with biscuits.

Summer Pudding

★

Preparation Time 10 minutes, plus overnight chilling • **Cooking Time** 10 minutes • **Serves 8** • **Per Serving** 173 calories, 1g fat (of which trace saturates), 38g carbohydrate, 0.4g salt • **Vegetarian** • **Dairy Free** • **Easy**

800g (1¾lb) mixed summer berries, such as 250g (9oz) each redcurrants and blackcurrants and 300g (11oz) raspberries
125g (4oz) golden caster sugar
3 tbsp crème de cassis
9 thick slices of slightly stale white bread, crusts removed
crème fraîche or cream to serve (optional)

1 Put the redcurrants and blackcurrants in a pan. Add the sugar and cassis. Bring to a simmer and cook for 3–5 minutes until the sugar has dissolved. Add the raspberries and cook for 2 minutes. Once the fruit is cooked, taste it – there should be a good balance between tart and sweet.

2 Meanwhile, line a 1 litre (1¾ pint) bowl with clingfilm. Put the base of the bowl on one piece of bread and cut around it. Put the circle of bread in the base of the bowl.

3 Line the inside of the bowl with more slices of bread, slightly overlapping to avoid any gaps. Spoon in the fruit, making sure the juice soaks into the bread. Keep back a few spoonfuls of juice in case the bread is unevenly soaked when you turn out the pudding.

4 Cut the remaining bread to fit the top of the pudding neatly, using a sharp knife to trim any excess bread from around the edges. Wrap in clingfilm, weigh down with a saucer and a tin can, and chill overnight.

5 To serve, unwrap the outer clingfilm, upturn the pudding on to a plate and remove the inner clingfilm. Drizzle over the reserved juice and serve with crème fraîche or cream, if you like.

Vanilla Chilled Risotto

Preparation Time 5 minutes, plus cooling and chilling • **Cooking Time** 40 minutes • **Serves 10** • **Per Serving** 280 calories, 14g fat (of which 9g saturates), 34g carbohydrate, 0.1g salt • **Vegetarian** • **Gluten Free** • **Easy**

900ml (1½ pints) full-fat milk
1 vanilla pod, split lengthways
75g (3oz) risotto rice
40g (1½oz) caster sugar
200ml (7fl oz) double cream
ground cinnamon to sprinkle
Orange Poached Peaches (see
   Cook's Tip) to serve

1 Put the milk and vanilla pod into a large pan and bring slowly to the boil. Stir in the rice, reduce the heat and simmer gently for about 40 minutes, stirring from time to time, or until the rice is soft and most of the liquid has been absorbed. You might need to add a little more milk during the cooking time.

2 Stir in the sugar, remove the vanilla pod and set aside to cool. Once the mixture has cooled, stir in the cream, pour into a large bowl, cover and chill.

3 Just before serving, sprinkle with a little ground cinnamon. Serve with Orange Poached Peaches.

⭐ COOK'S TIP
Orange Poached Peaches
Put 100g (3½oz) caster sugar into a pan with 600ml (1 pint) water and the grated zest and juice of 2 oranges. Bring to the boil and bubble for 5 minutes. Add 10 ripe peaches, bring back to the boil, then cover the pan and simmer for 10–15 minutes until they're almost soft, turning from time to time. Carefully lift out the peaches with a slotted spoon, reserving the liquid. Leave to cool slightly, then remove the skins and put the peaches in a serving dish. Bring the reserved liquid to the boil and bubble for 10 minutes or until syrupy. Strain the syrup over the peaches and allow to cool. Cover and chill.

Rice Pudding

⭐

Preparation Time 5 minutes • **Cooking Time** 1½ hours • **Serves 6** • **Per Serving** 239 calories, 8g fat (of which 5g saturates), 34g carbohydrate, 0.2g salt • **Vegetarian** • **Gluten Free** • **Easy**

butter to grease
125g (4oz) short-grain pudding rice
1.1 litres (2 pints) full-fat milk
50g (2oz) golden caster sugar
1 tsp vanilla extract
grated zest of 1 orange (optional)
freshly grated nutmeg to taste

1 Preheat the oven to 170°C (150°C fan oven) mark 3. Lightly butter a 1.7 litre (3 pint) ovenproof dish. Add the rice, milk, sugar, vanilla extract and orange zest, if using, and stir everything together. Grate the nutmeg over the top of the mixture.

2 Bake the pudding in the middle of the oven for 1½ hours or until the top is golden brown.

Index

A

aduki beans: chicken, bean and spinach curry 105
Alsace chicken 202
apples: honey pork with roast potatoes and apples 135
pheasant casserole with cider and apples 250
pork and apple hotpot 137
quick apple tart 262
apricots: baked apricots with almonds 280
chicken, bean and spinach curry 105
chicken tagine with apricots and almonds 244
Moroccan lamb stew 213
pork and apricot burgers 92
summer fruit compote 278
artichokes: lamb and pasta pot 132
Parma ham and artichoke tagliatelle 140
asparagus: Italian bean stew 173
aubergines: aubergine and chickpea pilau 156
aubergine and lentil curry 163
aubergines in a hot sweet and sour sauce 226
braised aubergines 226
braised lamb shanks 212
chunky one-pot Bolognese 117
curried coconut and vegetable rice 158
leek and broccoli bake 182
Moroccan chickpea stew 171
ratatouille 256
roasted ratatouille 180
roasted summer vegetables 181
Thai curry with prawns and aubergines 221
Turkish lamb stew 129
autumn barley soup 23
autumn vegetable soup 13

B

bacon: beef casserole with black olives 114
mussel and potato stew 60
see also pancetta
baking blind 194
bamboo shoots: egg fu yung 192
lamb and bamboo shoot red curry 214
Szechuan beef 120
barley soup 23
bean sprouts: bean sprouts with peppers and chillies 235
easy veggie pad thai 183
pork and vegetable stir-fry 231
beans: chilli bean cake 169
mushroom and bean hotpot 254
one-pan chicken with tomatoes 84
one-pot spicy beef 118
spicy bean and courgette soup 22
warming winter casserole 208
see also cannellini beans, red kidney beans, etc.

beef: beef and Guinness stew 249
beef casserole with black olives 114
beef goulash 248
beef jambalaya 116
beef with mushrooms and oyster sauce 119
braised beef with mustard and capers 211
braised beef with pancetta and mushrooms 115
marinated beef and vegetable stir-fry 123
Mexican chilli con carne 247
one-pot spicy beef 118
quick beef stroganoff 210
Scotch broth 239
spiced beef and noodle soup 32
Szechuan beef 120
teriyaki beef stir-fry 233
beer: beef and Guinness stew 249
black bean sauce: salmon with 70
squid and vegetables in 222
black-eye beans: black-eye bean chilli 168
Caribbean chicken 103
blueberries: strawberry compote 277
summer fruit compote 278
Bolognese, chunky one-pot 117
borlotti beans: quick winter minestrone 14
spicy sausage and pasta supper 139
bread puddings: chocolate bread pudding 268
panettone pudding 270
savoury pudding 148
summer pudding 283
broccoli: leek and broccoli bake 182
quick chicken stir-fry 230
stir-fried salmon and broccoli 227
stir-fried veg with crispy crumbs 188
turkey and broccoli stir-fry 110
bulgur wheat: salmon and bulgur wheat pilau 44
burgers: chicken tarragon 92
pork and apricot 92
butter beans: chicken with chorizo and beans 245
Spanish-style pork 136
tomato and butter bean stew 172
turkey and bean stew 93

C

cabbage: quick winter minestrone 14
stir-fried prawns with cabbage 77
see also red cabbage
cannellini beans: braised lamb shanks with cannellini beans 126
chicken and bean soup 36
spicy pork and bean stew 138
spring vegetable broth 11
caramel: caramelised onion and goat's cheese tart 194

peach brûlée 272
strawberry brûlée 273
Caribbean chicken 103
cashew nuts, mushrooms with 178
casseroles see stews and casseroles
cheese: caramelised onion and goat's cheese tart 194
courgette and Parmesan frittata 190
pea, mint and ricotta pasta 174
savoury pudding 148
spinach and cheese lasagne 176
tuna melt pizza 52
see also cream cheese; mascarpone
cherry yogurt crush 274
chestnuts: turkey and chestnut soup 37
chicken 80–111
Alsace chicken 202
Caribbean chicken 103
chicken and bean soup 36
chicken and coconut curry 215
chicken and vegetable hotpot 89
chicken, bean and spinach curry 105
chicken cacciatore 201
chicken curry 106
chicken tagine with apricots and almonds 244
chicken tarragon burgers 92
chicken tikka masala 216
chicken with chorizo and beans 245
chicken with fennel and tarragon 203
chicken with green olives and lemons 86
chicken with oyster sauce 108
chicken with peanut sauce 206
chicken with vegetables and noodles 207
classic paella 95
easy chicken casserole 241
easy Thai red chicken curry 217
fiery mango chicken 99
grilled spicy chicken 218
hearty chicken soup with dumplings 35
herb chicken with roasted vegetables 91
hot jungle curry 104
jambalaya 94
lemon chicken 85
Mediterranean chicken 204
Moroccan chicken with chickpeas 98
mulligatawny soup 200
one-pan chicken with tomatoes 84
one-pot chicken 82
oven-baked chicken with garlic potatoes 90
quick chicken stir-fry 230
saffron paella 97
Spanish chicken 242
Spanish chicken parcels 100
spiced chicken pilau 96
spiced one-pot chicken 101

sticky chicken thighs 102
tarragon chicken with fennel 88
Thai chicken broth 34
Thai green curry 109
throw-it-all-together chicken salad 111
chickpeas: aubergine and chickpea pilau 156
chickpea and chilli stir-fry 187
chickpea curry 159
Moroccan chicken with chickpeas 98
Moroccan chickpea stew 171
pasta and chickpea soup with pesto 27
spiced chickpeas with spinach 160
spicy lamb soup 24
Turkish lamb stew 129
veggie curry 161
chillies 19
aubergines in a hot sweet and sour sauce 226
bean sprouts with peppers and chillies 235
black-eye bean chilli 168
chickpea and chilli stir-fry 187
chilli bean cake 169
chilli vegetable and coconut stir-fry 185
fast fish soup 19
Italian braised leg of lamb 131
lentil chilli 167
Mexican chilli con carne 247
prawns and cucumber in a spicy sauce 72
prawns with okra 73
quick crab cakes 67
spiced salad 146
sweet chilli tofu stir-fry 186
Szechuan beef 120
Chinese-style fish 79
chocolate: chocolate bread pudding 268
chocolate curls 271
rich chocolate pots 271
chorizo sausage: chicken with chorizo and beans 245
pan-fried chorizo and potato 145
parsnip soup with chorizo 31
potato and chorizo tortilla 144
saffron paella 97
Spanish chicken parcels 100
chowder, smoked cod and sweetcorn 20
cider: autumn vegetable soup 13
pheasant casserole with cider and apples 250
coconut, creamed: green lentil and coconut soup 28
coconut milk: chicken and coconut curry 215
chicken with peanut sauce 206
chilli vegetable and coconut stir-fry 185
coconut fish pilau 43
curried coconut and vegetable rice 158
easy Thai red chicken curry 217
Thai coconut mussels 58

cod: fish with cherry tomatoes 47
navarin of cod 66
smoked cod and sweetcorn chowder 20
courgettes: courgette and Parmesan frittata 190
courgettes with sesame seeds 179
ratatouille 256
roasted summer vegetables 181
spicy bean and courgette soup 22
stir-fried green vegetables 184
couscous: Moroccan lamb stew 213
pork and roasted vegetable couscous 141
crab cakes, quick 67
cream cheese: peach brûlée 272
cucumber: prawns and cucumber in a spicy sauce 72
curries: aubergine and lentil curry 163
chicken and coconut curry 215
chicken, bean and spinach curry 105
chicken curry 106
chicken tikka masala 216
chickpea curry 159
curried coconut and vegetable rice 158
curried lamb with lentils 252
easy Thai red chicken curry 217
grilled spicy chicken 218
hot jungle curry 104
Kerala fish curry 219
lamb and bamboo shoot red curry 214
lamb, potato and peanut curry 133
Mauritian vegetable curry 164
mulligatawny soup 200
mushroom and bean hotpot 254
one-pot vegetable rice 154
salmon laksa curry 220
spiced one-pot chicken 101
Thai coconut mussels 58
Thai curry with prawns and aubergines 221
Thai green curry 109
Thai green shellfish curry 224
Thai red seafood curry 78
Thai red turkey curry 107
Thai vegetable curry 234
tofu laksa curry 162
tofu noodle curry 225
veggie curry 161
custard: chocolate bread pudding 268

D

drunken pears 263
duck, sweet and sour 229
dumplings 35

E

eggs: cherry tomato and rocket frittata 190
courgette and Parmesan frittata 190

creamy baked eggs 191
egg and pepper pizza 195
egg fu yung 192
piperade 193
potato and chorizo tortilla 144
savoury pudding 148
Eton mess 276

F
fennel: baked tomatoes and fennel 177
chicken with fennel and tarragon 203
tarragon chicken with fennel 88
figs: figs in cinnamon syrup 264
spiced winter fruit 281
fish 41–79
coconut fish pilau 43
fast fish soup 19
fish and vegetable soup 16
Spanish fish stew 61
see also cod, monkfish, etc.
five-minute stir-fry 75
flageolet beans: Italian bean stew 173
frittata: cherry tomato and rocket frittata 190
courgette and Parmesan frittata 190
fruit: fruity rice pudding 258
hot spiced fruit salad 265
spiced winter fruit 281
summer fruit compote 278
summer pudding 283
winter fruit compote 259
see also apples, strawberries, etc.
fudge sauce, pears with 267
full-of-goodness soup 25

G
game and meat 112–51
gammon stew 134
goat's cheese: caramelised onion and goat's cheese tart 194
goulash, beef 248
green beans: pasta with pesto and beans 175
guinea fowl and red cabbage 151
gumbo, seafood 17
gurnard with a summer vegetable broth 48

H
haddock: Chinese-style fish 79
easy fish stew 63
smoked haddock and potato pie 64
ham: Parma ham and artichoke tagliatelle 140
pork, garlic and basil risotto 142
savoury pudding 148
split pea and ham soup 240
haricot beans: spiced bean and vegetable stew 253
harissa, grilled sardines with 54
hazelnut butter, pumpkin risotto with 155
honey pork with roast potatoes and apples 135
hot and sour soup 39
hot jungle curry 104
hotpots: chicken and vegetable 89
luxury lamb and leek 124
mushroom and bean 254
pork and apple 137
see also stews and casseroles

I
Italian bean stew 173
Italian braised leg of lamb 131

J
jambalaya 94
beef jambalaya 116

K
kedgeree: salmon and coriander kedgeree 45
salmon kedgeree 46
Kerala fish curry 219

L
lamb: braised lamb shanks 212
braised lamb shanks with cannellini beans 126
curried lamb with lentils 252
Italian braised leg of lamb 131
lamb and bamboo shoot red curry 214
lamb and pasta pot 132
lamb, potato and peanut curry 133
lamb, prune and almond tagine 130
lamb with orange and mint 125
lamb with red wine and lentils 128
luxury lamb and leek hotpot 124
Moroccan lamb stew 213
spicy lamb soup 24
Turkish lamb stew 129
lasagne, spinach and cheese 176
leeks: leek and broccoli bake 182
luxury lamb and leek hotpot 124
pork chops with mustard sauce 209
lemon: chicken with green olives and lemons 86
lemon chicken 85
quick lemon mousse 275
lentils: aubergine and lentil curry 163
curried lamb with lentils 252
green lentil and coconut soup 28
lamb with red wine and lentils 128
lentil casserole 170
lentil chilli 167
lentils with red pepper 255
one-pot vegetable rice 154
pepper and lentil soup 29
lime: lime and chilli swordfish 49
lime butter 238

M
mackerel, peppered 56
mangetouts: easy Thai red chicken curry 217
stir-fried green vegetables 184
mangoes: fiery mango chicken 99
mango gratin with sabayon 282
spiced winter fruit 281
sweet and sour duck 229
mascarpone: rich chocolate pots 271
Mauritian vegetable curry 164
mayonnaise: mustard mayonnaise 197
watercress mayonnaise 65
meat and game 112–51
Mediterranean chicken 204
meringues: Eton mess 276
Mexican bean soup 238
Mexican chilli con carne 247
milk: rice pudding 285
vanilla chilled risotto 284
minestrone, quick winter 14

miso 26
monkfish: spicy monkfish stew 62
Thai red seafood curry 78
Moroccan chicken with chickpeas 98
Moroccan chickpea stew 171
Moroccan lamb stew 213
moules marinière 57
mousse, quick lemon 275
mulligatawny soup 200
mushrooms: beef casserole with black olives 114
beef with mushrooms and oyster sauce 119
braised beef with pancetta and mushrooms 115
chicken with oyster sauce 108
chicken with vegetables and noodles 207
egg fu yung 192
lentil casserole 170
mushroom and bean hotpot 254
mushroom, spinach and miso soup 26
mushrooms with cashew nuts 178
quick beef stroganoff 210
roast mushrooms with pesto 196
salmon with black bean sauce 70
mussels: classic paella 95
moules marinière 57
mussel and potato stew 60
saffron paella 97
Thai coconut mussels 58
mustard mayonnaise 197

N
navarin of cod 66
nectarines, spiced 279
noodles: chicken with vegetables and noodles 207
easy veggie pad thai 183
marinated beef and vegetable stir-fry 123
pork and chilli noodle soup 38
prawns in yellow bean sauce 71
quick chicken stir-fry 230
quick pad thai 68
salmon laksa curry 220
spiced beef and noodle soup 32
Thai noodles with prawns 74
tofu laksa curry 162
tofu noodle curry 225

O
okra: prawns with okra 73
seafood gumbo 17
olives: beef casserole with black olives 114
chicken cacciatore 201
chicken with green olives and lemons 86
salami and olive tart 143
one-pan chicken with tomatoes 84
one-pot chicken 82
one-pot gammon stew 134
one-pot spicy beef 118
one-pot vegetable rice 154
onions: beef casserole with black olives 114
caramelised onion and goat's cheese tart 194
Italian braised leg of lamb 131
pork chops with mustard sauce 209
roasted ratatouille 180
salmon kedgeree 46

spiced one-pot chicken 101
oranges: braised lamb shanks 212
lamb with orange and mint 125
orange poached peaches 284
oven-baked chicken with garlic potatoes 90
oyster sauce: beef with mushrooms and oyster sauce 119
chicken with oyster sauce 108

P
pad thai: easy veggie pad thai 183
quick pad thai 68
paella: classic paella 95
saffron paella 97
pak choi: full-of-goodness soup 25
prawns in yellow bean sauce 71
salmon with black bean sauce 70
stir-fried prawns with cabbage 77
pancetta, braised beef with mushrooms and 115
panettone pudding 270
Parma ham: Parma ham and artichoke tagliatelle 140
pork, garlic and basil risotto 142
parsnips: chicken and vegetable hotpot 89
parsnip soup with chorizo 31
pasta: chunky one-pot Bolognese 117
lamb and pasta pot 132
Parma ham and artichoke tagliatelle 140
pasta and chickpea soup with pesto 27
pasta with pesto and beans 175
pea, mint and ricotta pasta 174
quick winter minestrone 14
spicy sausage and pasta supper 139
pastry, baking blind 194
peaches: orange poached peaches 284
peach brûlée 272
peanut butter: chicken with peanut sauce 206
lamb, potato and peanut curry 133
pears: drunken pears 263
pears with hot fudge sauce 267
peas: pea, mint and ricotta pasta 174
stir-fried green vegetables 184
see also split peas
peppered mackerel 56
peppered winter stew 121
peppers: bean sprouts with peppers and chillies 235
beef jambalaya 116
chicken with chorizo and beans 245
chicken with vegetables and noodles 207
classic paella 95
egg and pepper pizza 195
Italian braised leg of lamb 131
lamb with orange and mint 125
lentils with red pepper 255
Mediterranean chicken 204
Moroccan chickpea stew 171
pepper and lentil soup 29
piperade 193

ratatouille 256
roasted ratatouille 180
roasted tomato and pepper soup 30
saffron paella 97
Spanish chicken 242
Spanish chicken parcels 100
Spanish fish stew 61
spiced salad 146
spicy sausage and pasta supper 139
stir-fried veg with crispy crumbs 188
Szechuan beef 120
Thai fish in a bag 69
pesto: pasta and chickpea soup with pesto 27
pasta with pesto and beans 175
roast mushrooms with pesto 196
pheasant: pheasant casserole with cider and apples 250
pot-roasted pheasant with red cabbage 149
pilau: aubergine and chickpea pilau 156
coconut fish pilau 43
prawns and vegetable pilau 42
salmon and bulgur wheat pilau 44
spiced chicken pilau 96
pineapple: spiced winter fruit 281
piperade 193
pistou, summer vegetable soup with 12
pizza: egg and pepper pizza 195
tuna melt pizza 52
plums, poached with port 266
pork: honey pork with roast potatoes and apples 135
pork and apple hotpot 137
pork and apricot burgers 92
pork and chilli noodle soup 38
pork and roasted vegetable couscous 141
pork and vegetable stir-fry 231
pork chops with mustard sauce 209
pork, garlic and basil risotto 142
Spanish-style pork 136
spicy pork and bean stew 138
stir-fried pork with Chinese greens 147
warming winter casserole 208
potatoes: baked salmon with Jersey Royals and watercress mayonnaise 65
beef and Guinness stew 249
honey pork with roast potatoes and apples 135
lamb, potato and peanut curry 133
luxury lamb and leek hotpot 124
mashed potatoes 211
mussel and potato stew 60
oven-baked chicken with garlic potatoes 90
pan-fried chorizo and potato 145
pasta with pesto and beans 175
pork and apple hotpot 137
potato and chorizo tortilla 144
roasted summer vegetables 181
saag aloo 166
smoked cod and sweetcorn chowder 20

smoked haddock and potato
  pie 64
spicy monkfish stew 62
poussins, marinated 205
prawns: classic paella 95
  easy fish stew 63
  five-minute stir-fry 75
  jambalaya 94
  prawns and cucumber in a
    spicy sauce 72
  prawns and vegetable pilau
    42
  prawns in yellow bean sauce
    71
  prawns with okra 73
  quick pad thai 68
  saffron paella 97
  stir-fried prawns with
    cabbage 77
  Thai curry with prawns and
    aubergines 221
  Thai green curry 109
  Thai green shellfish curry 224
  Thai noodles with prawns 74
  Thai red seafood curry 78
prunes: lamb, prune and
  almond tagine 130
  rabbit casserole with prunes
    150
pumpkin: pumpkin risotto with
  hazelnut butter 155
  spiced bean and vegetable
    stew 253

R
rabbit casserole with prunes 150
ratatouille 256
  roasted ratatouille 180
red cabbage: braised guinea
  fowl and red cabbage 151
  braised red cabbage 257
  pot-roasted pheasant with red
    cabbage 149
red kidney beans: Mexican bean
  soup 238
  Mexican chilli con carne 247
rice: aubergine and chickpea
  pilau 156
  beef jambalaya 116
  Caribbean chicken 103
  classic paella 95
  coconut fish pilau 43
  curried coconut and
    vegetable rice 158
  easy fish stew 63
  fruity rice pudding 258
  jambalaya 94
  one-pot vegetable rice 154
  pork, garlic and basil risotto
    142
  prawns and vegetable pilau
    42
  pumpkin risotto with hazelnut
    butter 155
  rice pudding 285
  saffron paella 97
  salmon and coriander
    kedgeree 45
  salmon kedgeree 46
  Spanish chicken 242
  spiced chicken pilau 96
  spinach and rice soup 21
  vanilla chilled risotto 284
  warm spiced rice salad 157
risotto: pork, garlic and basil
  risotto 142
  pumpkin risotto with hazelnut
    butter 155
  vanilla chilled risotto 284
rocket: cherry tomato and
  rocket frittata 190

S
saag aloo 166
sabayon, mango gratin with
  282

saffron paella 97
salads: roasted vegetable salad
  with mustard
  mayonnaise 197
  spiced salad 146
  throw-it-all-together chicken
    salad 111
  warm spiced rice salad 157
salami and olive tart 143
salmon: baked salmon with
  Jersey Royals and watercress
  mayonnaise 65
  roasted salmon 50
  salmon and bulgur wheat
    pilau 44
  salmon kedgeree 46
  salmon laksa curry 220
  salmon with black bean sauce
    70
  salmon with a spicy yogurt
    crust 51
  steamed sesame salmon 228
  stir-fried salmon and broccoli
    227
  Thai fish in a bag 69
  see also smoked salmon
salsa 118
sardines: grilled sardines with
  harissa 54
  sardines on toast 55
sausages: chunky one-pot
  Bolognese 117
  spicy sausage and pasta
    supper 139
  see also chorizo
savoury pudding 148
scallops: scallops with ginger 76
  Thai green shellfish curry 224
Scotch broth 239
seafood gumbo 17
shellfish and fish 41–79
  see also mussels, prawns, etc.
smoked cod and sweetcorn
  chowder 20
smoked haddock and potato pie
  64
smoked salmon: salmon and
  coriander kedgeree 45
sole: Kerala fish curry 219
soups 8–39
  autumn barley soup 23
  autumn vegetable soup 13
  chicken and bean soup 36
  fast fish soup 19
  fish and vegetable soup 16
  full-of-goodness soup 25
  green lentil and coconut soup
    28
  hearty chicken soup with
    dumplings 35
  hot and sour soup 39
  Mexican bean soup 238
  mulligatawny soup 200
  mushroom, spinach and miso
    soup 26
  parsnip soup with chorizo 31
  pasta and chickpea soup with
    pesto 27
  pepper and lentil soup 29
  pork and chilli noodle soup
    38
  quick winter minestrone 14
  roasted tomato and pepper
    soup 30
  Scotch broth 239
  seafood gumbo 17
  simple vegetable soup 10
  smoked cod and sweetcorn
    chowder 20
  spiced beef and noodle soup
    32
  spicy bean and courgette
    soup 22
  spicy lamb soup 24
  spinach and rice soup 21
  split pea and ham soup 240

spring vegetable broth 11
summer vegetable soup with
  herb pistou 12
Thai chicken broth 34
turkey and chestnut soup 37
Spanish chicken 242
Spanish chicken parcels 100
Spanish fish stew 61
Spanish-style pork 136
spinach: chicken, bean and
  spinach curry 105
  chicken tikka masala 216
  mushroom, spinach and miso
    soup 26
  saag aloo 166
  spiced chickpeas with spinach
    160
  spinach and cheese lasagne
    176
  spinach and rice soup 21
  split pea and ham soup 240
spring vegetable broth 11
squash: curried coconut and
  vegetable rice 158
  spiced one-pot chicken 101
squid and vegetables in black
  bean sauce 222
stews and casseroles: beef and
  Guinness stew 249
  beef casserole with black
    olives 114
  beef goulash 248
  braised lamb shanks 212
  easy chicken casserole 241
  easy fish stew 63
  Italian bean stew 173
  lentil casserole 170
  Moroccan chickpea stew 171
  Moroccan lamb stew 213
  mussel and potato stew 60
  one-pot gammon stew 134
  peppered winter stew 121
  pheasant casserole with cider
    and apples 250
  rabbit casserole with prunes
    150
  Spanish fish stew 61
  spiced bean and vegetable
    stew 253
  spicy monkfish stew 62
  spicy pork and bean stew 138
  tomato and butter bean stew
    172
  turkey and bean stew 93
  Turkish lamb stew 129
  warming winter casserole 208
  see also curries; hotpots;
    tagines
strawberries: Eton mess 276
  strawberry brûlée 273
  strawberry compote 277
summer fruit compote 278
summer pudding 283
summer vegetable soup with
  herb pistou 12
summer vegetable stir-fry 189
sweet and sour duck 229
sweet chilli tofu stir-fry 186
sweet potatoes: spiced bean
  and vegetable stew 253
  spiced chickpeas with spinach
    160
sweetcorn: easy Thai red
  chicken curry 217
  mussel and potato stew 60
  salmon laksa curry 220
  smoked cod and sweetcorn
    chowder 20
swordfish, lime and chilli 49
Szechuan beef 120

T
tagines: chicken tagine with
  apricots and almonds 244
  lamb, prune and almond
    tagine 130

tagliatelle, Parma ham and
  artichoke 140
tangerines: spiced winter fruit
  281
tarragon chicken with fennel 88
tarts: caramelised onion and
  goat's cheese tart 194
  quick apple tart 262
  salami and olive tart 143
teriyaki beef stir-fry 233
Thai chicken broth 34
Thai coconut mussels 58
Thai curry with prawns and
  aubergines 221
Thai fish in a bag 69
Thai green curry 109
Thai green shellfish curry 224
Thai noodles with prawns 74
Thai red chicken curry 217
Thai red seafood curry 78
Thai red turkey curry 107
Thai vegetable curry 234
throw-it-all-together chicken
  salad 111
tiger prawns see prawns
toast, sardines on 55
tofu: full-of-goodness soup 25
  sweet chilli tofu stir-fry 186
  tofu laksa curry 162
  tofu noodle curry 225
tomatoes: aubergine and lentil
  curry 163
  baked tomatoes and fennel
    177
  beef goulash 248
  black-eye bean chilli 168
  braised lamb shanks 212
  braised lamb shanks with
    cannellini beans 126
  cherry tomato and rocket
    frittata 190
  chicken and bean soup 36
  chicken cacciatore 201
  chunky one-pot Bolognese
    117
  classic paella 95
  creamy baked eggs 191
  curried lamb with lentils 252
  fish with cherry tomatoes 47
  Italian braised leg of lamb
    131
  lamb and pasta pot 132
  leek and broccoli bake 182
  lentil chilli 167
  Mexican chilli con carne 247
  Moroccan lamb stew 213
  mushroom and bean hotpot
    254
  one-pan chicken with
    tomatoes 84
  one-pot spicy beef 118
  piperade 193
  quick winter minestrone 14
  ratatouille 256
  roasted tomato and pepper
    soup 30
  saffron paella 97
  Spanish chicken parcels 100
  spicy monkfish stew 62
  spicy sausage and pasta
    supper 139
  tomato and butter bean stew
    172
  Turkish lamb stew 129
tortilla, potato and chorizo 144
trout, crusted 53
tuna melt pizza 52
turkey: hot and sour soup 39
  Thai red turkey curry 107
  turkey and bean stew 93
  turkey and broccoli stir-fry
    110
  turkey and chestnut soup 37
Turkish lamb stew 129

V
vanilla chilled risotto 284
vegetables: autumn barley soup
  23
  autumn vegetable soup 13
  chilli vegetable and coconut
    stir-fry 185
  fish and vegetable soup 16
  five-minute stir-fry 75
  gurnard with a summer
    vegetable broth 48
  herb chicken with roasted
    vegetables 91
  marinated beef and vegetable
    stir-fry 123
  Mauritian vegetable curry 164
  one-pot gammon stew 134
  one-pot vegetable rice 154
  peppered winter stew 121
  pork and roasted vegetable
    couscous 141
  pork and vegetable stir-fry
    231
  prawns and vegetable pilau
    42
  roasted ratatouille 180
  roasted summer vegetables
    181
  Scotch broth 239
  simple vegetable soup 10
  spring vegetable broth 11
  squid and vegetables in black
    bean sauce 222
  stir-fried green vegetables 184
  stir-fried pork with Chinese
    greens 147
  summer vegetable soup with
    herb pistou 12
  summer vegetable stir-fry 189
  sweet chilli tofu stir-fry 186
  Thai vegetable curry 234
  veggie curry 161
vegetarian recipes 152–97
venison: peppered winter stew
  121

W
warming winter casserole 208
watercress mayonnaise 65
wine: drunken pears 263
  Italian braised leg of lamb
    131
  lamb with red wine and lentils
    128
  mango gratin with sabayon
    282
  peppered winter stew 121
winter fruit compote 259

Y
yellow bean sauce, prawns in 71
yogurt: cherry yogurt crush 274
  Eton mess 276
  grilled spicy chicken 218
  salmon with a spicy yogurt
    crust 51
  strawberry brûlée 273

CONVERSION TABLES

TEMPERATURE

°C	FAN OVEN	GAS MARK	°C	FAN OVEN	GAS MARK
110	90	¼	190	170	5
130	110	½	200	180	6
140	120	1	220	200	7
150	130	2	230	210	8
170	150	3	240	220	9
180	160	4			

LIQUIDS

METRIC	IMPERIAL	METRIC	IMPERIAL
5ml	1 tsp	200ml	7fl oz
15ml	1 tbsp	250ml	9fl oz
25ml	1fl oz	300ml	½ pint
50ml	2fl oz	500ml	18fl oz
100ml	3½ fl oz	600ml	1 pint
125ml	4fl oz	900ml	1½ pints
150ml	5fl oz / ¼ pint	1 litre	1¾ pints
175ml	6fl oz		

MEASURES

METRIC	IMPERIAL	METRIC	IMPERIAL
5mm	¼ in	10cm	4in
1cm	½ in	15cm	6in
2cm	¾ in	18cm	7in
2.5cm	1in	20.5cm	8in
3cm	1¼ in	23cm	9in
4cm	1½ in	25.5cm	10in
5cm	2in	28cm	11in
7.5cm	3in	30.5cm	12in